FOURTH AND FIFTH GENERATION PROGRAMMING LANGUAGES, VOL. I

Other McGraw-Hill Books by the Author

Local Area Networks (1984)
Interactive Message Services (1984)
Management Workstations for Greater Productivity (1986)

Fourth and Fifth Generation Programming Languages, Vol. I:

Integrated Software, Database Languages, and Expert Systems

by Dimitris N. Chorafas

McGraw-Hill Book Company

New York   St. Louis   San Francisco   Auckland
Bogotá   Hamburg   Johannesburg   London   Madrid
Mexico   Montreal   New Delhi   Panama   Paris
São Paulo   Singapore   Sydney   Tokyo   Toronto

Library of Congress Cataloging-in-Publication Data

Chorafas, Dimitris N.
   Fourth and fifth generation programming languages.

   Includes index.
   Contents: v. 1. Integrated software, database
languages, and expert systems.
   1.Programming languages (Electronic computers)
I. Title.
QA76.7.C485   1986   005.13'3   85-16666
ISBN 0-07-010864-1 (v. 1)

1234567890   DOC/DOC   898765

ISBN 0-07-010864-1

The editors for this book were Stephen G. Guty and Galen H. Fleck,
the designer was M.R.P. Design, and the production supervisor
was Thomas G. Kowalczyk. It was set in Century Schoolbook by
McGraw-Hill Information Systems and Technology.

Printed and bound by R. R. Donnelley & Sons Company.

CONTENTS

PREFACE

The choice of a programming language greatly impacts the way in which the application is made, the quality of the resulting software, the maintenance capability and its costs, and, quite importantly, system analyst and programmer productivity. The choice should result from a careful, well-documented study on the advanced software tools that current computer and communications environments can support. The aims should be:

1. To keep up with the best technology can offer
2. To benefit from the cost-effective tools currently available
3. To provide the company with a competitive edge over its competitors

Therefore, fourth-generation languages (4GLs) are a very worthwhile subject within the framework of the strategic objectives established by management. Their implementation is an urgent matter, and decisions are needed to orient the company on future commitments.

This book is primarily written for computer professionals who want to update their skills in terms of *new tools for application development*. In its 16 chapters they will find compelling arguments for developing and implementing computer software in novel, highly productive ways—and to fast timetables.

The book should also appeal to the more advanced computer users. They will find documented evidence that fourth-generation languages have moved computers and communications beyond the mystique stage to a comprehensive level of application. At the same time, fifth-generation languages—more precisely, *expert systems*—have opened up opportunities unparalleled by any previous methods. Both the computer professionals and the end users find it easier to communicate with intelligent machines.

The cutting edge of technology suggests the wisdom of concentrating on fourth- and fifth-generation programming. This has its counterpart in hardware: Today nobody would project a computer with small- or medium-scale integration chips. All effort is being directed not only to large-scale integration but also increasingly to very large-scale integration.

Under no circumstances should the applications programming effort rest on 25-year-old so-called high-level languages. As a lot, they are obsolete, although some of them, notably Cobol, are more obsolete than others. Like obsolete chips, obsolete languages are noncompetitive and result in spoilage of resources. They have far-reaching detrimental effects because they adversely impact on human time, which computers are supposed to assist.

Fourth-generation languages can be classified in five major groups:

1. Programming extensions to the operating system through command interpreters

2. Database management and query

3. New programming languages such as graphics

4. Productivity-oriented tools, through precompilers

5. Spreadsheet systems and integrated software

Fourth-generation languages are not just end user facilities. They can serve both the end users and the computer specialists—each at a different level of sophistication. What is more, they are in full evolution. We can expect a significant 4GL announcement each 6 months or so.

As experience with natural-language programming and expert systems accumulates, the fourth generation will be followed by a fifth. The next generation of languages (5GL) can be expected by the end of this decade and will largely rest on breakthroughs in artificial intelligence.

* * *

As this book was originally designed, I had thought to include a comprehensive approach to Unix, the command interpreter shell, and the facilities supported by the programming language C, in which both Unix and the shell are written. Part of this thought was to cover the use of Ingres as a programming language, including aggregation operations and application by forms.

In terms of sophistication and programming power, the command interpreter of an operating system is followed by the database management system language. The DBMS was originally conceived to manage data on run time—and it has been used that way for over twenty years. But now we have come to realize that, in a data-centered environment, it is also, if not primarily, a programming tool.

Finally I opted out of that approach and chose instead to write a separate volume on Unix, Ingres, and the IBM 4GL. This meant that more space, and greater attention, could be devoted to integrated software, a most fundamental subject for interactive workstations.

* * *

At the level of software development by professionals, 4GLs are found to be powerful system tools. Automation of analysis and programming functions, improved development time, lower cost, and higher software quality result in an innovative system product. That is explained in Chapter 1, which treats information systems as a top knowledge industry. It presents the challenge of remaining a knowledge worker, suggests how to keep on being computer-literate, and offers new perspectives for computer professionals.

To focus attention on the developments which are under way, Chapter 2 presents an overview of *computer technology: today and tomorrow.* Then attention is focused on *efficient program development* and *portability*, the subject of Chapter 3.

Fourth-generation programming is a concept. There are key points to be brought into perspective and images to be created. There is training to be done. Chapter 4 explains why. The easiest 4GL for the nonexpert is the spreadsheet, and slightly more complex is integrated software. Chapter 5 makes this evident and gives examples with Lotus 1-2-3.

Implementation-wise, one of the fastest-growing concepts is commodity software. Chapter 6 examines this issue. It is followed by the fundamental notions concerning interactive graphics (Chapter 7), the manager's own shorthand, decision means, and tool for corrective action.

PC-level operating systems have their own DBMSs for programming purposes. An example is dBase II. It is discussed, along with applications examples, in Chapter 8. Then, in two chapters, emphasis is placed on operating systems: from MS-DOS and CP/M to the competitive OS features embedded in Unix and Pick.

A *natural-level language* is best employed by end users, but, as Chapter 11 explains, we can find much in them in terms of implementation capabilities. They act as the front end and include a wealth of tools for software developers.

Expert systems, knowledgebanks, and the way to use the tip of the 5GL iceberg are the issues to which Chapters 12 and 13 are addressed. They open with an overview of artificial intelligence efforts and close with examples of interaction with expert systems. Chapter 14 expands on this notion and gives practical examples of expert system implementation.

Chapter 15 underscores an issue of growing importance: *software publishing* and the associated quality assurance requirements. The IEEE recommended standards for software developments are among the highlights.

Finally, the last chapter is devoted to case studies. The time has come to draw a very sharp line between the old images which dominated "EDP" for over three decades and the new concepts necessary to design, implement, and exploit information systems in the business world of tomorrow.

Let me close by expressing my thanks to everyone who contributed to making this book successful: from my colleagues for their collaboration, to Steve Ross for his advice, to the organizations I visited in my research for their insight, and to Eva Maria Binder for the drawings, typing, and index.

Valmer and Vitznau   **DIMITRIS N. CHORAFAS**

FOURTH AND FIFTH
GENERATION PROGRAMMING
LANGUAGES, VOL. I

INFORMATION SYSTEMS AS A KNOWLEDGE INDUSTRY

Knowhow, Webster's *Ninth Collegiate* tells us, was first used as a term in 1838. That makes it about 150 years that our civilization has had the concept and has been coping with its implications. *Knowhow disappears when we don't use it—most particularly when we cling to one-dimensional perceptions* that arise from misunderstanding the competitive processes in industry. That's why we must not only acquaint ourselves with but *take the lead in applying the latest developments in our fields,* which now are the advances in computers and communications.

That is totally different from the philosophy that electronic data processing (EDP) professionals, and the second-generation DP/MIS people have followed for 30 or so years:

- You want a report? Submit a request form and we will think about it. Sometime next year, at the earliest.
- You need changes in the tabular presentation of hardcopy output? Forget it.
- You complain about mainframe's tons of paper snowing you under? Our laser printers are very efficient.

Such reactions, to which end users have been steadily subjected, have two origins. The first is that professional data processing people have been slow to adopt the new computer and communications technologies.

In the early to mid-1950s, corporations began to establish data processing departments based on the computer as the means of solving

1

their various data management problems. The implementations, however, created incredible bureaucracies, and all the decisions about who gets what information and when were made by staff hierarchies.

I recall that, in the mid-1950s, Robert Oppenheimer observed that the computer is an engine totally different from an electronic accounting machine—and should be used in novel ways to get maximal worth out of it. It took the user companies, and their computer professionals, three decades to understand what Oppenheimer meant. This was a conceptual failure.

The second origin of EDP reactions was inertia. As their numbers steadily grew (and the software/hardware resources they managed sprawled), computer professionals became burdened with acquired habits. Their judgment has often been warped by their wanting to preserve compatibility with software and hardware of the past.

As a result, data processing (DP) and management information systems (MIS) did not deliver on their promises. Instead of shouting hosannas for increased efficiency, end users muttered nasty remarks about people in computer glasshouses. Large stacks of ply paper gathered dust on desks. Distrust of data processing and its associated technology grew—to everyone's detriment.

Now is the time to change all that. Fourth-generation languages (4GLs) present an opportunity not to be ignored. The 4GLs will be followed by the fifth generation of intelligent systems. This should deeply interest all computer professionals, to whom this book is addressed.

THE CHALLENGE OF REMAINING A KNOWLEDGE WORKER

The two most evident impacts upon society in this century have been made by the *automobile* and the *computer*. Today over 90 percent of the population between the ages of 21 and 65 are auto-literate, but less than 5 percent of that same group are computer-literate. Cars and status no longer correlate; but cars and lifestyles are closely linked. The same thing will be true of computers, with impacts on both information systems professionals and end users.

As managers and other end users grow more knowledgeable about computers and communications, they resent receiving information regulated by someone else's perceptions of their needs. They like to make decisions about the type of information they want and the rate, content, format, and delivery of information into their hands. When they can't, they lose interest.

Today users are better able to identify their real problems because the microcomputer and its easy-to-use languages have arrived in their offices. Originally, the personal computer (PC) made the same promises that MIS made, but it embodied a very important difference: *the user's intimate involvement.* Early microcomputers needed no centralized DP departments, no intermediaries, no bureaucratic structures. The solution was user control of the software, the hardware, and the operation.

Computer-literate people do not have to understand microprocessor design, but they should have an appreciation of basic concepts and tools:

1. Managing their data
2. Systems versus applications software
3. Communications protocols
4. Input/output media
5. Menus, prompts, and help features

In a symposium at which I was a participant in January 1985 in Geneva, Bankers Trust, a leading money-center bank, identified as follows the goals of its office automation, information systems, decision support projects: *"Assure that managers and professionals can spend at least 68 percent of their time on direct, computer-assisted work."* (Figure 1.1)

That is a first-class goal for any of us, but we must plan for it and document it in a valid, factual way. No longer should managers and other professional workers be merely receivers of information products. They should be creators, manipulators, and owners. Whether communicating with databases, mainframes, or workstations, whether processing words, calculating numbers or formulas, or retrieving and handling documents, systems must bring information to management to a degree of efficiency greater than ever before.

At the same time, just as microcomputer users experience a sense of personal accomplishment, so must computer professionals. Here fourth-generation languages can play a leading role. The reason is that the implementation of modern technology is marked by three interrelated trends:

1. Increasingly powerful tools at our disposal
2. Greater time and space separation between planning and execution
3. A steadily faster pace of development

The computer profession has greatly changed. In the mid-1980s there was little resemblance to what had been true 10 or even 5 years before.

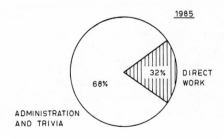

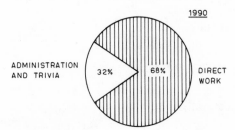

Figure 1.1 Professional time distribution goals of a bank's office automation, information systems, and decision support projects. Note the complete reversal.

This has not yet been widely recognized, but consciousness will increase as time goes by. As it is, when we think of computers, we often tend to conjure up the "hardware" and "software" of the past, forgetting about the complex technology that supports their use and interdependence. Now we should direct such usage to more profitable ends.

The new hardware emphasis will be on microelectronics and multiprocessor architectures. From this, developers hope to obtain at least a thousandfold increase in net computing power.

The orientation also will change. *The new software (and eventually hardware) components will focus on artificial intelligence (AI), particularly in expert systems (Esystems).* They will provide machines with quasi-human, intelligent capabilities. That includes natural-language understanding, vision, speech, and various kinds of automated reasoning.

On top of this technology base, new end-user-oriented applications are being developed. Their success will be in very different guise than originally envisioned: the power of computers and communications as a technological solution to a problem turns out to be only part of the answer.

The real answer is wide diffusion of knowhow. End users no longer accept the proposition that only a few insiders who deal with the day-to-day operation of the machines can be intimately involved with the information process. This has been the dark side of technological solutions. *Now end users want participation.*

This participation is precisely what computer professionals can offer through fourth-generation languages (4GLs). As we will see in the following chapters, 4GLs offer the computer professionals the possibility of having, at the same time, a tool, a mission, and a message. To appreciate that, let's look at the environment.

The typical knowledge worker interacts with diverse systems and workstations, each having its own set of languages, procedures, and databases. The challenge is to:

1. Make office workstations an aggregate of functions while remaining flexible and expandable.
2. Identify the workstation concepts and applications that will be carried over into the next generation of workstations accepted in the office
3. Provide a radically new kind of flexibility and adaptiveness

Requirements analysis and software processes involve design problems and building methods. Computer professionals need a way to assist in the transition between current tools and the tools of the future. At the same time, one of their top challenges is adherence to strict development timetables. The new programming tools at our disposal can be a great help in both directions.

Good answers will be found not in generalizations but in specific choices for well-defined problems. If the first sound advice is *identify your problem*, the second is *choose the appropriate analysis and programming language.*

Figure 1.2 demonstrates a dual movement. One is away from "all professions' language" and toward specialization by type of problem. The other makes itself felt in greater sophistication in programming tools. Both trends are here to stay.

As Niclaus Wirth remarked in his Turing Award lecture, the difficulty of resolving many demands with a single language had emerged, and the goal itself had become questionable. Also, the size of the compiler had grown beyond the limits within which one could rest comfortably with the feeling of having a grasp, a mental understanding, of the whole program. Systems programming required an efficient compiler generating efficient code that operated without a fixed, hidden, and large so-called run-time package.

Fourth-generation languages are the means of transition in both the above-mentioned directions. In the majority, they are defined with clarity and their syntax is specified in a rigorous formalism. Such clear

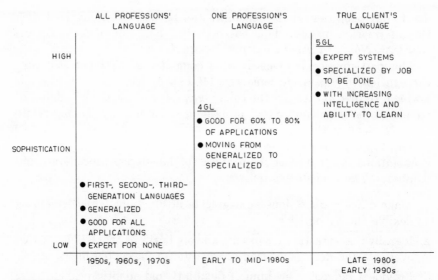

Figure 1.2   Movement away from all-professions' languages toward language specialization by type of problem, greater sophistication, and improved productivity in programming tools.

specification is a necessary (though not sufficient) condition for a reliable and effective implementation.

Keeping up with the latest developments characterizing the professional aspects of computers and communications is part and parcel of the challenge of remaining a knowledge worker. *The wave of change to which computer specialists must now adapt should be seen not as a problem, but as an opportunity.*

NEW PERSPECTIVES FOR COMPUTER PROFESSIONALS

When we speak of information systems as a knowledge industry, one of our key obligations is to education. There is a natural and growing interdependence between lifelong learning and professional results. Even the foundation on which the training of computer and communications scientists rests must be restructured. Back in the 1960s, thousands of computer specialists were working in industry, but they had been educated as mathematicians, physicists, and engineers. They learned computer science on their jobs—in effect, by apprenticeship.

Only in 1964 was the first advanced degree in computer science awarded. The roots should be looked for nearly two decades ago—a fact not appreciated because of lack of knowhow. In the late 1960s and early

1970s, the industry became highly dependent on microelectronics, yet no degrees were granted in large-scale integrated electronics until the late 1970s.

The same situation is found in our dependence on new programming technologies. As we push the limits, we find ourselves using software and logical tools in ways never before attempted—and for which our specialists are not necessarily prepared.

Again professional opportunity knocks at the door. The time is past when most end user personal computing in large corporations was performed on desktop personal computers: first-generation systems such as Apple II, Commodore PET, Tandy TRS-80, or even IBM PCs and other 16-bit personal computers.

That early thrust was partly the result of applications packages, notably financial planning spreadsheets, being more widely available for personal computers. Partly also it was the users' response to the astonishing insensitivity of central computer operations to changing needs.

But the first-generation applications packages for the Apple II and other 8-bit PCs deal with only one application each: spreadsheet, word processing, graphics, and database. Different vendors' packages have dominated different applications:

• VisiCalc for spreadsheets

• WordStar for word processing

• dBase II for database management

Though these packages are clever, their usage is not free of problems. A major problem is that editing conventions and data formats are not always compatible. This confuses users and forces them into needless conversion housekeeping functions.

Then there was proliferation: Sorcim SuperCalc, SuperWriter, Super-File, MicroPro WordStar, CalcStar, VisiOn, MS-Win, Concurrent DOS, Topview, Lotus 1-2-3, Symphony, MDBS Knowledge Manager, and Ashton-Tate's Framework. Users would have welcomed the computer professionals' return, had the latter seized the opportunity.

A new professional opportunity now comes into view. The computer and communications industry is entering a second age, that in which the computer serves as a communicator. System designers must be able to link as many computers and databases (which hold large amounts of information) as possible. Such databases and workstations should be accessible to everyone working on the network.

This highlights the growing need for PC-to-mainframe links and compatibility. End user personal computing cannot be entirely independent of the corporate mainframe and its databases. Technical solutions are necessary for networking the information center mainframes with end users' personal computers.

Computer and communications specialists must analyze the issues and review the implications of recent system software developments. The latter include a growing number of mainframe and PC packages that enable workstation users to:

- Extract data from mainframe databases
- Download into the PC's storage for local personal computing

There are, as well, portable operating systems across different processor architectures and systems sizes (UNIX, Pick, VM/CMS) to be evaluated. Decisions have to be made, and implementations will follow.

System integration requirements must also be brought into perspective. Should individual managers' PCs be connected directly to the host mainframe computer by individual point-to-point communication lines or indirectly via a department file and communications server? What type of local area network should there be? Which method:

- Minimizes communications line costs?
- Provides better backing storage?
- Makes it easier to delegate to the user community the task of extracting data from the mainframe-held corporate database?

Computer specialists must be able to assure a detailed analysis of these issues, evaluate developments in local area network technology, and assess the role of fully distributed systems. They must definitely establish a PC strategy rather than just drift along. The microcomputer technology is here and spreading. It is in the professionals' own interest to:

- Encourage a fast implementation of micros to automate the workplace
- Protect access to the database but make it easy for all authorized users
- Import and export files on a dynamic basis
- Avoid duplicating central DP functions unless there is a specific reason to do so

By keeping the components small and making them intelligent, we place ourselves in a strong position. We can shape, sharpen and restructure the system as requirements and loads evolve.

The emphasis on the micro does not mean that the mainframes are out. *Their role is changing*, but the demand for them grows. IBM says that the power invested in mainframe installations will increase by an impressive 80 to 120 percent per year *because of the PC*. For every million instructions per second (MIPS) installed under the managerial, professional, and clerical desks, 0.33 to 0.50 MIPS in central and regional resources will be needed.

REVERSE ENGINEERING

Technology will continue to move ahead at an accelerated pace while creating new applications and opportunities. Yet also looming ahead are problems that threaten our growth. Those obstacles are not technological, but human. The key issue is adaptation. If these problems are not adequately addressed, they could block our continued progress.

What we need in the new information science is a process of *reverse engineering* applied from the technological peak which we have reached toward the applications. Here again the services which can be offered by fourth-and fifth-generation languages will be instrumental in bridging the gap between technological advances and the need to revamp the knowhow of professionals.

Let's look at the process. By examining the spiderweb of circuit lines on a semiconductor, designers at competitive shops can discover and replicate the ideas that may have taken the original company years and millions of dollars to develop. Reverse engineering is a common practice among semiconductor makers.

In a parallel operation applied to systems development principles, we have to examine the user-perceived quality of interactive systems. The top five key problems are:

1. Adequate usability
2. User control
3. Self-descriptiveness
4. Ease of learning
5. Fault tolerance

Each and every one of these problems has a direct correspondence with user expectations. Adequate usability implies independent task preparation, the ability to use changeable default values, adjustable output-to-user performance, and a dialog focused on the application area.

User control involves manipulation of the progress of dialog (including its speed), user-definable ways to exchange information, and system learning from the past and the actual point in such dialog. It also means reversible actions and user confirmation of special critical steps. *A dialog is user-controllable* if the user is able to really control this dialog.

Self-descriptiveness involves adequate clarification of the capacity of the software and hardware tools we put at the user's disposal—as well as of the assumptions of their usage. At the user's request, the purpose and method must be readily explained during the dialog. The explanation must be geared to the user and include both the dialog situation and its context.

Ease of learning involves the capability for stepwise explanation during dialog performance. If technical terms are present, they should be tuned to the knowledge of the user:

• Small examples for the beginners

• Help for more complex recognition by experienced communicators

In both cases, a dialog is easy to follow if the user is so supported that he or she can gain knowledge about the application and perform the task in a self-sufficient manner.

Fault tolerance has several aspects. Basically, it calls for reliability and availability. From the operations standpoint, it requires information about correction procedures, the ability to find all detectable errors, and the provision of tools for correction. Only comprehensive, relevant, and constructive error messages can be admissible. Fault tolerance is the capacity of a system to process user's input in such a way that, although wrong input may have gone into the system, the desired result of the task can still be achieved. Otherwise, the user will be provided with comprehensive information about the origin of the error so corrective steps can be taken.

These are the demanding tasks to which the new masters of the computer and communications profession should address themselves. Cobol programming will be only for the underlings. Systems specialists will apply their skills to *design strategy*:

• *Configuring*, that is, adapting a system according to given parameters

• *Tailoring* software and hardware to user requirements and application needs

• Providing for *intelligent dialog* and its description, including the flow and steps of interaction

• Assuring *dialog implementation*, including monitoring and evaluation

Among the goals in the design strategy are monitoring, registering, measuring, analyzing, and justifying both user and system behavior. Part of the challenge is the establishment of criteria for system improvement.

Whereas the application programmer can concentrate on the implementation of the specific task, the author of the interactive dialog must have a tool to program the man-machine interface.* The proper evaluation of an interactive dialog should permit the adaptation of the system to different user demands. This adaptation too must be user-implemented.

Design strategy should also include great attention to response time. Managers and professionals should not sit idly in front of the video: 1 sec response time is optimal; 2 sec is acceptable. In terms of global implementation, flexibility is at a premium. Each end user will discover in his or her own way how the personal computer is going to work. Just as the brain in each person is unique, so are the capabilities which it supports.

These are fairly new notions in information science. Until the availability of personal computers, which started with the computer kit in 1975, even distributed information systems were a centralized operation that required complex interfacing between the man and the machine. Slowly we came to realize that the real value of the personal computer and of user-friendly languages is *not* that of number crunching or doing the chores of small business systems at lower cost. It is that of giving *able assistance to people in doing their work better and faster. This is just as true of end users as of computer professionals.*

FORWARD STRIDES ON THE HARDWARE SIDE OF TECHNOLOGY

A brief survey of technology, current and anticipated, is worthy of attention. Progress has been so fast that there seems to have been a never-ending series of breakthroughs coming at a rapid rate. Moreover, this progress has come in a very cost-effective manner and has brought computing to the desks of managers and professionals in banking, industry, government, and academia.

An ever-improving price/performance ratio continues to support the activity. For about the price of a mid-1980s personal computer, before the end of the decade we may buy a 32-bit workstation operating at 5 MIPS with up to 8 Mbytes (megabytes) of central memory and 200 Mbytes of disk storage. The eight-chip VAX now under development is

---

*The term "man-machine" was coined by Norbert Weiner, an American mathematician who did pioneering work in communication between human beings and machines. In defiance of the view that "man" is sexist, I have chosen to use it.

believed to have all the power and functionality of a full VAX 11/780. The true significance is that, perhaps by as early as 1986, Digital Equipment Corporation (DEC) can reduce its VAX 780:

- From 3200 integrated circuits to eight very large scale integration (VLSI) chips
- From 4000 in^2 of board space to 18 in^2
- From 1000 W of power consumption to 20 W

According to some estimates, the potential cost reduction from today's VAX 780 processor could be as much as 80 to 90 percent through a drastic reduction of the processor board count from a current total of almost 30 boards. In addition, the eight-chip set would allow the manufacturer to package full 780 performance into a desk bottom system.

Yet in spite of this explosion of distributed personal resources—or, more precisely, because of it—the centralized system, or glasshouse, will continue to grow with multiple systems per center and multiple centers per company. Networks will tie the various levels of computing together.

There is today a pressing need for an engineering philosophy in information systems design. As shown by Figure 1.3, it involves three layers of reference: architecture, technology, and products in that order. Each layer is served by and promotes software and hardware. And, in its own way, each layer contributes to the MIPS shortage.

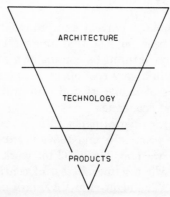

Figure 1.3 Implementing an engineering philosophy in information systems design. At the top is the architecture; at the bottom, the products.

For the first time since the mid-1970s there is talk of a MIPS shortage which promises the revival the mainframe business. Ironically, this develops out of the fast-spreading PC—not the lack of it—as well as from office automation (OA). The workstation (WS) and local area network (LAN) implementations act like *MIPS sponges* when it comes to:

• Central database access
• Data communications switching facilities

As a result, the manufacturers who will be best able to profit from the resurgence in demand for mainframes will be those that have known how to master the booming PC market. Within the 1985 to 1988 time frame, PCs, LANs, and OA may increase the demand for mainframes by 50 percent over a 3-year period. The coming large-scale systems will have 100- to 400-MIPS uniprocessors, a hierarchy of storage sizes and speeds, and transaction rates of 10,000 per second versus the 50 to 300 of the mid-1980s. There will be integration of data, text, image, and voice. Private branch exchanges (PBXs) will have data processing functions built in, and data systems will feature voice capability.

A recent study supports the estimate that text and data storage capacity installed on IBM mainframes in the United States is growing at a rate of 60 percent each year. The end of 1985 saw a disk capacity for more than 100 million Mbytes—80 times that on the shelves of the Library of Congress.

Japan's superspeed goal is 10 billion operations per second; in contrast, an IBM PC can execute about 200,000. The difference is nearly 4 orders of magnitude. The winners in this race to build the next generation of computers will have a huge technological and commercial advantage. The new computers will be used for microelectronics design to build even smarter and more powerful machines.

The uses of the early supercomputers in America will most likely be along current lines: defense (roughly 40 percent of installed units), oil companies (12 percent), universities (10 percent), nuclear research (8 percent), space research (8 percent), meteorology (8 percent), the computer companies themselves (8 percent), and others (6 percent). Most important, the applications of the new generation, the supercomputers, will be largely characterized by artificial intelligence and expert systems software. The aim of fifth-generation projects is to design and produce computer hardware and software for *knowledge engineering* in a wide range of applications:

- Expert systems
- Natural-language understanding by machines
- Robotics

For those applications we need more than dramatic improvement in computing capabilities; we also need major innovations in existing technology that will enable the new generation of computers to:

1. Support very large *knowledgebanks*
2. Allow very fast associative retrievals
3. Perform logical inference operations as fast as current computers perform arithmetic operations
4. Utilize parallelism in program speed
5. Develop man-machine interfaces that permit significant use of natural speech and images

Developments now underway aim to demonstrate that machines can exhibit artificial intelligence: they can think and reason somewhat like a human and understand information conveyed by sight, motion, and speech. By the mid-1990s, both the Americans and the Japanese aim to develop knowledgebase capacity that will be able to handle tens of thousands of inference rules and 100 million objects. Although not yet realized in hardware, such machine architectures are generally viewed as comprising an essential feature of both the fifth-generation computer and the AI engine.

There will be computer conferencing and teleconferencing between enterprises, file sharing among nonsimilar workstations, software that integrates systems across the network, and text and data portability. Artificial intelligence tools and techniques will be widely available to help generate new applications and thereby improve the productivity of programmers and users.

All these systems will be connected by networks involving centralized machines, distributed systems, and workstations. The key to all this growth will be software. From the user's viewpoint:

- Hardware is the *intellectually passive* component of computers and communications systems.
- Software is the *intellectually active* part.

Hardware is the tangible vehicle for the intangible software: from operating systems to database management, communications protocols, and applications routines. Technology will continue to create tremendous opportunities in both hardware and software for the industry and its customers.

BETTING ON COMPUTER LITERACY

While technology moves ahead in a breathtaking pace, the difficulty that remains lies in human interaction with the machines at our disposal. In this connection, much depends on motivation, and much also depends on proper understanding of the tools we have available. Just about anything in human experience can add to the inventory of knowledge—if we properly plan for it. Computer literacy is very important, and this is just as true of end users as of computer professionals.

We are talking, of course, of two different computer literacy thresholds. The end user should be working extensively with the easy-to-implement 4GLs: spreadsheets, graphics packages, electronic mail devices, calendaring services, word processing, and integrated software. By knowing how to use those tools, the end user will, by mid-1980s standards, be computer-literate. But only for a while. By the end of the decade computer literacy on the end user side will be judged by ability to interact with expert systems in an intelligent, purposeful manner.

For a computer professional, the literacy criteria are quite different—and much tougher. Rightly so. The specialist must know more things and know them better than the end user and should steadily upgrade those skills. Specifically, the computer professional who keeps on working with obsolete, ossified languages such as Cobol and Fortran is illiterate. It's a pity that degrees and honors cannot be withdrawn from the computer specialists in the way accreditation is from schools and universities.

The computer specialist who fails to use the best, most efficient tools that computer science makes available is falling short of an ethical standard. Advances in science and technology have brought new opportunities, but also new responsibilities, to the computer profession. Advances in science and technology compel us to take a new look at such old problems as quality, privacy, security, fraud—and also productivity. On ethical issues, computer professionals must perform a service to society by enhancing efficiency in the use of resources.

Such is the case also with professional productivity. In a limited sense, *programmer productivity* is traditionally defined as the number of source lines designed, coded, tested, and documented per unit of time, typically an hour, a day, or a month. In a broader sense, however, gaining a competitive edge and improving *mental productivity* are two highly related issues. They involve, among other things, quality of results. But we also need to quantify. The algorithm is:

$$\text{General productivity} = \frac{\text{revenue}}{\text{expense}}$$

Saving on expense will be the wrong policy if it results in the employment of a lower level of skill. The revenue also will be much lower, and the ratio will be to our disadvantage.

Who pays peanuts attracts only monkeys; but although it is one of the prerequisites, good pay is not a sufficient condition for high productivity. Motivation, hard work, imagination, and an open mind also are prerequisites, and most particularly is that true of *lifelong learning*.

At both the end user level and the computer and communications professional level we must put high technology to work. Figure 1.4 reflects the results obtained by a leading computer manufacturer in just that way. Over many years, revenues trailed employment. When high technology was applied in the right way to the internal operations, the employment curve was bent downward.

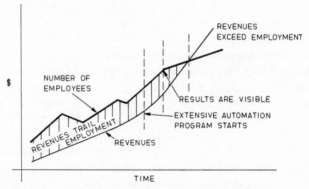

Figure 1.4 Positive effect on the revenues-employment relationship of putting high technology to work.

To better appreciate how and why fourth-generation languages help professionals in that direction, let's turn to the strictly technical aspects. Classically, productivity is a measure of output primarily based on physical units: product in relation to an input factor such as labor-hours. But we all know that, to be meaningful, a measure of productivity must be suited to the problem and the production system at hand. We also appreciate that there are different views of productivity measurements:

- Economists stress the ability of a production system to deliver goods and services for consumption.
- Business managers usually compare the input/output relations of similar departments or businesses.
- In manufacturing, we compare output to worker-hour input.

By those means we attempt to gauge how changes in production methods affect output. The trouble is that there is no universally valid measure of input. During the past 100 years, labor was a useful thing to measure because it was such a large part of the cost of most products. With automation, that is no longer true. If productivity is tied closely to labor, we will have to look at the worker within a broad context. We should not consider technical factors alone; many other forces also are at work.

Work backlog is an example of how fourth-generation languages can be a nice solution. A backlog of work is symptomatic of our society's radical shift toward an information economy with increasingly greater demands posed in the design phase. This problem is especially acute in endeavors that lack an enlightened, coherent, far-sighted information policy. An increase in the complexity of any system—and software development is just one good example—causes productivity problems. These problems cannot be solved unless the development team has become proficient with new design tools.

In other terms, an organization's productivity cannot always be measured simply in terms of labor per hour. We must also account for factors ranging from managerial effectiveness to user satisfaction and derived from the quality of knowledge possessed by the system developer. Productivity objectives for system development should stress the new ten commandments:

1. Reduced costs
2. Faster implementation
3. Tight timetable
4. Fewer worker-hours
5. Interactive approaches
6. System quality
7. Integration characteristics
8. User control
9. Very easy maintenance
10. Overall flexibility

The possibility of effectuating those commandments will become more apparent when 4GL tools are applied more widely. The best proof will be the completion of spearhead projects. With successful implementation under control, the firm will have gained valuable experience in promoting change. Not only will a significant amount of education have occurred but the application itself will be the best demonstrator of feasibility.

It is also worth noting that increasing an intellectual worker's productivity is not merely a matter of providing a better tool. We also have to be willing to improve all aspects of the job, and time is pressing.

In 30 years the computer industry grew to about $250 billion. By the early 1990s, its sales will have exceeded $1 trillion. The reason for that explosive growth is simple supply and demand. People create the demand with their ever-growing list of problems, which are everywhere. The information industry can help supply solutions to the problems if its professionals are properly trained. *Our ability to deliver those solutions should be growing by better than 50 percent annually, or more than twice as fast as computing capacity is growing.*

2

COMPUTER TECHNOLOGY:
TODAY AND TOMORROW

In the nineteenth century, the high cost of engines made it uneconomical to produce individual transportation. Instead, people shared trains and coaches. In the mid-twentieth century, the same kind of thing happened with mainframe computers.

When the means of transportation were rare and the services were mass-oriented, industry used specialized personnel: railroad conductors, coachmen, and drivers. When mass production made the internal-combustion engine readily available, car ownership became increasingly common and each of us became a driver.

Something similar is now happening in the computer industry. In the mass-oriented mainframe environment we needed specialized personnel to program and operate the machines. In an age of personal computing everyone of us has to become programmer and operator of a machine. This is a purpose that fourth-generation languages (4GLs) aim to serve. They open the hitherto exclusive system analysis and programming environment to every user.

Therefore, the early offerings of 4GL were thought to be only for the end user. In reality, they are much more than that. But is there a realistic appraisal of 4GLs? What is the range of the offerings? What may be coming next by way of evolution? Figure 2.1 gives the answer diagrammatically.

Among the two dozen or so *spreadsheet* products we can distinguish Multiplan, SuperCalc 2, and VisiCalc IV. VisiCalc was the original version which opened the broad perspectives of *user-driven* approaches.

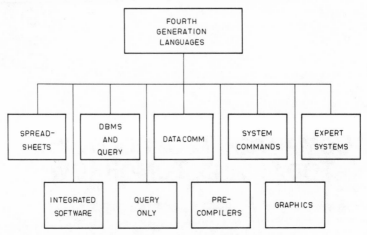

Figure 2.1   Range and coverage of fourth-generation languages.

Spreadsheets are commodity products intended to be useful in refining, examining, analyzing, and presenting information. The goal is to assist the decision maker through well-rounded, friendly, and modular support packages which can be obtained off the shelf at very reasonable prices.

Value-added spreadsheet offerings have developed into *integrated software* (Isoft). Examples are Lotus 1-2-3 and Symphony (also from Lotus Development), SuperCalc 3, Intuit, and Decision Manager. As with any other product, there are generations. Symphony (1984) is the second generation of Lotus 1-2-3 (1983).

DBMS and query fourth-generation programming products include Ingres, Oracle, Informix, DB 2, SQL, Mapper, Natural, ADS, and Mantis on the supermicro-to-mainframe level. PFS: File, MDBS, and dBase II are among the personal filing system offerings that appeal to the PC user. Examples of *query only* languages are ADRS/ADI and SAS. Examples of *data communications* languages are PLPS (with videotex), Idel, Visianswer—and also NIL, a new networking-oriented language by IBM.

Precompilers come under different names and are intended for different types of machines: ADF, Focus, and Ramis II for mainframes, for example. IBM's Application System (AS) is a first-class product based on a relational DBMS. It works with both mainframes and PCs. Again by IBM, The Information Facility (TIF) runs under MVS/TSO and VM/CMS but also on the PC XT/370. There is a PROFS-TIF integration perspective. Some of the best *system commands* are provided by the shell of Unix, but other approaches are now under development. For *graphics* we have CAD/CAM tools and also supports embedded in integrated software.

Programming can be done through properly tuned menu selection capability. This can be presented to the end user in plain English or through icons. In both cases (but most particularly in the former) we speak of natural-language programming, which stands halfway between fourth- and fifth-generation languages (5GLs). To decide which way it should be classified, we should know how much artificial intelligence is invested in its construction. The best example of artificial intelligence in action is expert systems (Esystems). The range of applications in this field is already impressive, particularly in medicine and engineering. Among the expert systems languages are EMycin and Prolog.

For each one of these 4GLs and 5GLs there is a niche in the programming environment of today and tomorrow. Some appeal to simpler problems and smaller machines; others appeal to more complex problems and bigger machines. What ties them together is the new outlook necessary for their usage.

FOURTH-GENERATION LANGUAGES
AND END USER COMPUTING

In the coming years, *user-driven computing* will become one of the major implementation fields of office automation. It is expected that it will reach over 65 percent of the total million instructions per second (MIPS) available and that user-oriented databases will become an integral part of the working environment.

But 4GLs require changes in the conventional software development procedures, which are largely based on the characteristics of third-generation languages such as Cobol and Fortran.* Without radically new images, the use of 4GLs will produce only marginal payoff, if any at all. This is a different way of looking at software (SW).

We should look at 4GLs not as a problem but as an opportunity. We should also remember that there are plenty of examples to demonstrate that *avoiding problems by avoiding change* leads logically to an even more absurd conclusion: *avoiding the solution of problems by avoiding the use of high technology.*

With the old technology, the cost is there but the results are coming far less frequently. Computer power must support the human elements rather than bureaucracy and organizational red tape. Project teams must be agile, lean, and small, and new tools should be used as soon as they become available.

---

*Cobol, Fortran, and so on, were called high-level languages in the 1950s and 1960s. Now they are referred to as third-generation languages.

In information systems as in any other field, to survive in a tough, competitive market, we must establish goals and objectives. We must study *workflow*, simplify and consolidate, establish *productivity ratios*, and identify *priority areas*, which can be rationalized through computers and communications.

Priorities are situational. They should be defined by management after a factual, documented study. But in the general case the chances are that they look like this:

1. Integrated word and data processing (WP/DP)

A system is integrated if its text and database are integrated. Company-wide integration also means communicating processors.

In the coming years, communicating workstations will comprise the vast majority of computer installations. Figure 2.2 dramatizes this point by projecting 37 million installed workstations by 1989—an IBM estimate.

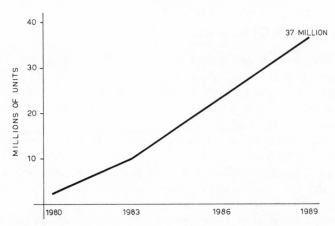

Figure 2.2 Current and projected communicating workstations in the United States.

2. New approaches to text and data capture and to reporting

Text and data collection should always start at the point of origin. Reporting should be done directly at the point of destination.

3. Electronic mail (Email) and computer conferencing

Email is the first function really able to help in communications among managers and professionals. It affects all the principal information workers in the enterprise.

Computer conferencing is still more modern and slightly more complex. The need for it is evidenced by the fact that most people want to communicate with computers rather than compute with them.

4. Graphics and color capability

If spreadsheets are the first and foremost of the executive productivity tools at the personal computer level, graphics and color enhance both exception reporting and decision support systems. Communicating workstations also offer their users such value-added services as calendaring, micro-to-mainframe links, and access to public databases.

In all these areas, basic enabling, dialog management, and technology integration are the paving stones of productivity. Not only do we need to properly identify the best sectors for *full automation*; we must also set up and implement *quality assurance* measures.

We need a *systems architecture* which provides a stable basis for planning, gives a common direction to distributed developments, and makes it possible to integrate software and hardware from many manufacturers. This architecture should assure that technology will be made to work the way people work.

Management must also be keen to establish *the right direction.* Because the centralized information systems have become inflexible and too complex, the classical data processing (DP) people have both their images and their time devoted to maintaining the systems. They do not address themselves properly to the vital activities for the 1980s:

1. Integrating HW and SW components
2. Automating the workplace
3. Providing efficient communications
4. Assuring database interactivity
5. Reducing labor costs and paper loads

The argument is not that of choosing between PCs and mainframes. That is a totally distorted concept; the critical question is misplaced. The point of departure should be *both PCs and mainframes.* Then the critical question becomes: How can we integrate them? Trying to do everything on a mainframe is irrational: the smaller the problem, the larger the overhead. More than 90 percent of the effort goes into the environmental connections and less than 10 percent into the problem itself.

Only very large projects should be put on mainframes. But should there be very large projects? Fourth-generation languages give us the means of avoiding them. Projects become manageable. In 1985 I contributed to a commercial paper collection and automatic dispatching project to which other banks had already devoted 10 worker-years of effort by the classical means: Cobol and structured programming. By using Ingres on the supermicro, which was chosen as the automatic dispatching engine, and Basic for the PC interfacing to the banker as a personal workstation, this project was completed in 2 worker-months.

In that project, two specialists worked together. Prototyping (through Ingres) took 1 week. Subsequently, only one specialist was involved. Database design and programming proper took 3 weeks, and reprogramming to improve response time 1 week more. Another 4 weeks went for the programs in Basic on the PC.

Processing should no longer be done on mainframes. The mainframes should be reserved for two activities that neither the PC nor the supermicro is suited for. The first is storing and managing the very large text and data warehouses we will need in the future. The second is acting as giant communications switches for the intelligent workstations to be installed at every desk and the local area networks (LANs) that will interconnect them. Each type of engine in computers and communications will need a programming language level corresponding to its capabilities. That is why I said in the introduction that 4GLs are much more than user-oriented tools.

Three trends that have become evident in the data processing profession are due to the new software technology:

1. Increasing knowledge of the application and the ability to design complete systems
2. DP and MIS managers becoming more closely integrated into the overall senior management teams of their organizations and ceasing to be technical outsiders
3. Reducing cost of application development by at least one order of magnitude

This cost reduction does not apply only to new developments: With such a drastic productivity improvement, it becomes economical to replace existing HLL application programs (Cobol, Fortran, PL/1, etc.) and thereby improve procedures and directly involve the end user during the development phase. In that way, application programs are more likely to meet user requirements. Users will be able to control their application software and also contribute their knowledge of what needs to be done.

SOFTWARE INVESTMENTS

Personal productivity applications give us the most critical aspect of a personal information system; they provide users with a friendly, uniform, and easy-to-implement environment. The end user can enter or access information, update it, analyze it through words, numbers or graphics, and communicate the results to another intelligent workstation (WS) and/or mainframe.

Whether the 4GL software tools which we choose are loosely coupled, that is, work together but often utilize different formats and commands, or are tightly coupled in an integrated computer and communications system, there are prerequisites. They include new concepts, common databasing and data communications facilities, standards, and protocols.

The tools to be chosen must together provide the means of building professional productivity. At the same time, we must care about transition from the old system to the new, and we must also consider what to do with the usually very large library of mainframe-oriented programs.

In short, *how should we handle aged applications*? There are three ways to do so:

1. One is to rewrite them on microcomputers, through professionals.

This is a most serious approach, since much of the DP activity is personal or local anyway, and it can be best executed at the workplace.

Rewriting should not be done blindly. The application must first be revamped and redimensioned and then programmed in a fourth-generation language—preferably a database-oriented system.

There is a cost figure attached to that statement. For every dollar spent on hardware we must invest $2 or $3 not only on software but also on training, organizational costs, job redesign, and quality evaluations.

2. The second approach is to let the end user take care of the rewriting on a WS.

This WS will typically be a PC with spreadsheet or integrated software. It will involve graphics, and it will fit the requirements of the user's specific job.

The second solution is the sound one, not only because of the 4GL tools at our disposal but also because of the crushing size of the job. Programming some 37 million WSs by 1989, as Figure 2.3 suggests, is no trivial operation. Interestingly enough, the second largest population of users comprises the very small companies which can ill-afford a

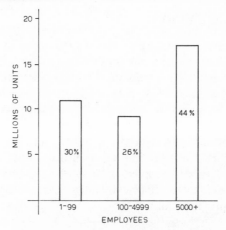

Figure 2.3 A 1989 projection of professional workstations, by size of firm. The percents are of total PC usage in business and industry.

professional DP staff. Among these users we should also expect some of the most exciting implementations of 4GLs over the coming 5 years.

3. Furthermore, a new generation of PCs now being brought to the market offers mainframe program portability.

A good example is IBM's PC 370. It is well, however, to remember that aging 370 mainframe applications must be of a size that can fit on a microcomputer. To be compatible with IBM, competitors in personal computer gear will have to support MS-DOS, VM, and Unix. Or, at least, they will have to provide upgrading capabilities in their distributed information systems environment.

That being said, there is no doubt that we confront a market waiting to be controlled. Over the first 30 years of computer usage (1953–1983) an estimated $400 billion was spent worldwide in developing computer applications and supporting files. Today, an estimated 500,000 programmers are working to maintain, enhance, or replace that investment. Including salaries, benefits, and overhead, half a million programmers represent $30 billion annually. Alternatively, the sum could support 6 billion PCs with software and applications programming.

A different way to look at those billions of dollars of software investment is that computer users have collectively been trapped into a software development effort which may become useless. Each of many user organizations has put hundreds of worker-years on a proprietary HW/SW system—and for all practical purposes has been locked in.

Such statistics cannot escape the attention of management. *Something has to change in a big way.* We must take into account the fact that there is a tremendous *backlog* in computer applications. Many DP executives do not appreciate the seriousness of the backlog problem. The typical case is that of a 3- to 5-year backlog of applications to be developed. This is sometimes superficially interpreted as providing job security, but in reality it is a destabilizing factor in every executive position.

Fourth-generation languages have been demonstrated to provide a productivity increase ranging from 600 to 6000 percent. This far exceeds what we ever had during the first three decades of computer usage. In the 1970s, structured programming, report generators, and query languages were introduced to boost programmer productivity. Despite those aids, programmers were still unable to respond to end user requests. The productivity improvements were rather marginal.

Fourth-generation languages can also contribute a greater efficiency in machine usage. Because fewer statements are required structured query language (SQL), for instance, has been estimated to be 5 to 20 times faster than Cobol at IBM sites. In addition, it does not require the technical virtuosity on the part of the programmer that the old language does.

The challenges to the professional programmers and their managers do not end there. During the last of the 1980s the professional programmers' work force will, in effect, be augmented by an estimated 20 million business professionals. Their contributions will far exceed what the professional DP people have been able to provide—even if both populations use the same programming tools.

A recent experience in the banking environment is instructive. The participants in a Unix/C/Ingres course were two-thirds DP professionals and one-third end users. One young man among the latter came from the bank's foreign operations department. After the course was over, it took this end user 4 weeks to program an export insurance application in Ingres and C. Half of that time was invested in gaining practical experience on how to use the languages. The application had been on the DP backlog list for 3 years. The user did it on his own.

Examples of such software development are now emerging daily. They demonstrate the ability of end users to move easily among formerly exclusive DP areas into which only the high priests of the profession formerly had the right to enter.

There is another important 4GL contribution; it is the new freedom to be found in *applications programming (AP) portability.* The twofold emergence of portable operating systems and two-level compilers insulates applications programs from hardware details and makes it feasible to move without major problems from one piece of hardware to another. That changes the basis on which business decisions will be made in the future.

Technology changes, and so does the basis for making decisions. In procurement, management should act:

- More from the software interface
- Much less from the hardware

Fourth-generation languages and generic processors make hardware inconsequential to the user. This is the sense of an open vendor policy. There are three steps to SW/HW freedom.

1. Commodity operating systems (OS) such as C/PM for 8-bit, MS-DOS for 16-bit, and Unix for 32-bit micros
2. Two-level compilers (front end and back end)
3. Generic processors (simultaneously running commodity OSs and compilers)

Acceptable standards must also be established in three other key areas:

4. Graphics
5. DBMS
6. End-to-end communications

In the latter area there is the Open System Interconnection of the International Standards Organization (ISO/OSI), the CCITT recommendations, and the de facto standards brought about by IBM. Examples include protocols such as 2780/3780, 3270, SDLC, network architectures like SNA, and the Document Interchange Architecture/Document Content Architecture (DIA/DCA) for the application layer of ISO/OSI.

INFORMATION TECHNOLOGY AS A COMPETITIVE WEAPON

Information technology is viewed in many industries and industrial sectors as a competitive weapon. It is an integral part of a strategic plan. *Management must decide what it is to be.* There is no purely information systems strategy, nor is there a purely financial strategy.

Either strategy is global or there is no strategy. Strategy is based on clear vision and unambiguous management choices. When management cannot make up its mind on goals, products, systems, competitive position, and a concrete plan, there can be no success.

In many cases, technology per se enabled newcomers to get an impressive market share. Technology may not be the most important reason for radical changes in banking, business, and industry, *but it is a competitive weapon.*

In Toshiba's *decision room,* paneled walls slide open to reveal huge screens that fill with multicolored charts when voice commands are given to workstations. The 40-story headquarters is a technopolis that is setting the pace for other companies ready to replace their antiquated office buildings with high-technology facilities. The aim is to consolidate corporate operations within a single center and install sophisticated electronics systems to speed the flow of information. Computer and communications systems not only eliminate tedious paperwork but also cut down on travel time and expense.

The new facilities are catapulting corporations into an age in which the collection, processing, storage, and distribution of information can be as critical to profits as robotics are in manufacturing. *Information has become the fourth largest resource, after people, material, and money.*

To cope with the increasing pace and importance of information technology, responsible executives must anticipate and respond in a rapid, accurate manner to competitive initiatives and identify new opportunities in the process. This is the sense of strategic planning.

The progression of data processing from batch, closed-shop operations to online interactive implementations with intelligent workstations at the user's desk has radically changed our design images. It has not only tremendously increased user visibility but also altered the ways to program the machines. *This is the primary reason for 4GLs.*

At the same time, technological development has led to large-scale computer and communications systems. *Big systems are not little systems that have outgrown their original size*; they are totally different in terms of:

- Design
- Implementation
- Verification
- Maintenance

To achieve integration of technology, we must have communication between man and information the way it used to be: Both software and hardware must be fully transparent to the user.

The cutting edge of technology has also accelerated life cycles. *Today we should not project new systems with more than 5-year life cycles.*

That puts emphasis on cost cutting from the start. The pillars of the new environment are:

- 4GLs
- PCs
- Communications links

Five-year life cycles also underscore the need to foresee a replacement for a system which may only be in its early design stages. We should not enter a tunnel until the exit is clear. The point is that falling behind in innovation and modernization will seriously reduce our competitiveness. Even the most automated firm today, because of the great strides of computer and communications technology, risks having too many labor-intensive tasks in 5 years.

At the same time, *5-year life cycles in information systems investment imply*:

1. Very fast, high-productivity software development
2. Development time of less than 4 months, but surely less than half a year
3. Low-cost components (SW, HW) and an open vendor policy
4. Support for *new* functions, previously offered manually or not at all
5. Functions already computer-based, to be restructured, modernized, personalized, and integrated

To repeat the advice given above: *Don't design a new system unless you have a notion of the next one.* At the same time, make a business opportunity report to focus on the benefit your firm may derive from the new system. Business, industrial, and financial institutions—from basics to sophisticated services—are emphasizing productivity as a means of increasing profitability. Improving productivity has become imperative.

There are many opportunities for improving personal productivity, but the goals are changing. Until recently, improving office productivity focused primarily on secretarial and clerical workers. Now, attention has turned to the productivity and performance of managers and knowledge workers.

Information is both the input and the output of knowledge workers. As the business world becomes more complex, it generates and uses more information. This:

- Causes office bottlenecks
- Diverts management from important actions
- Hampers productivity

One of the knowledge worker's most powerful tools is effective control over the proliferation of paper-based information. Interactive solutions, personal workstations, microfiles (personal files), and corporate-wide communications find much of their justification in this effective information control. For productivity gains, the three most important dimensions are completeness, power, and simplicity. Simplicity comprises both ease of learning and ease of use, and it in turn is heavily affected by integration.

Integration means ease of moving among the various functions of a product offering and making different components appear similar to the user—typically because they actually use identical subroutines and common files. For integrity, security, and cost reasons, however, the appropriate tools have to be carefully tailored to the user's requirements. They must also be embedded into a total information management concept.

A corporate information systems plan should answer in a factual and documented manner six questions:

1. Where are we now?

This calls for an assessment of current resources, strengths, and weaknesses.

2. Why change?

To exploit new opportunities, we should identify business perspectives, market evolution, and technological development. To survive, we should position our own company with the forces of the future.

3. What can be done?

Strategic aftermaths, obstacles, risks, opportunities, fundings, and cost-benefit are part of the answer to be given to this question.

4. What could we do?

We must make basic choices, evaluate components, analyze policy decisions, proceed with system integration, and elaborate possible implementation strategies.

5. How do we get there?

To answer this question we must consider client relations, product evolution, resource allocation, business system development, information system (IS) project management, priorities, and training.

6. Did we get there?

That's the feedback. We need it to be able to focus on the proper corrective action. To obtain it, we must have metrics, measurement, and appraisal.

Above all, we must be *managing information as a product.* In most financial and industrial organizations, information is not managed. It is available in overabundance or not at all. It is seldom timely and complete. And it is provided at a cost that cannot be determined.

Quite often, today's approach to information management is based on yesterday's concepts and technologies. The image of what can be done with present-day media dates back three or four decades. Yet *every 6 months something very significant happens and changes the way we look at the workplace. As well as we can currently project, this will continue to be true in some measure well into the 1990s.*

TECHNOLOGY TRANSFER

New approaches to software development are almost invariably computer-based in an effort to automate work which for three decades was basically manual. Yet even if the new tools have proved to be very effective, organizations resist them rather than embrace them.

There are many reasons for the reluctance to put computer-based software technology into practice. One is the lack of perception about the penalties: from obsolescence to lower product quality and higher labor costs. Nor is the return on investment in software tools well understood. Even among businesses known to be sharp in cost cutting, there is ignorance about accounting practices for software assets. There is also reluctance to engage in continued education, training, and information distribution to keep programmers aware of new technologies.

To level the balances, a comparative evaluation of competing technologies must be performed. This is not possible without nearly full-scale experiments in a realistic environment. Then, once the choice is identified, the actual introduction into practice must be organized, the personnel trained, and the programs which were constructed in the old ways adapted to the new technology. This underscores the importance of technology transfer. It always takes place between two organizations: one is the source and the other is the recipient. The secret of successful transfer is to find the best match of pairs.

Technology transfer is a process, and we must understand its phases. The most basic phase is to be the potential recipient of a technology that is abreast of what is going on in the field and combine education with consultation. This means that the educational material must be customized to fit the problem at hand.

The objective must be not only to train but also to change behavior. It is not possible to force-feed new technology to an unwilling or unprepared organization. The source must have a solution and the recipient must have a perceived problem. The target organization must be able and willing to formalize its problems and call them to the attention of the source.

Without preparation, technology will not be readily received. The main reason is inertia: An organization is designed for equilibrium, a steady state, and any attempt to perturb it is resisted. Ironically, the better designed and organized the development process is, the greater is the difficulty of changing it. Smooth change means preparation of the personnel and of the development process itself.

Change should be tool-centered. The transfer of tools pays off better than that of methods.

- Methods can be misinterpreted.
- Methods enforcement in a large organization is almost impossible.
- Training on new tools is relatively efficient.
- Tools can be permanent because they are combined with hands-on experience.
- The impact of tools on quality is more consistent and predictable, since different persons modify methods to their own taste.
- If tools were not available, new methods would not hold.

The most convincing sales pitch is the solid demonstration of the benefits which the changes would bring about. The evaluation concludes the transfer process. One stumbling block is the lack of standard ways in which performance can be evaluated; another is that many organizations are not quite clear how to start and where to go.

A specific information technology mission should be to analyze issues which are of medium to long term (2 to 5 years) and have strategic importance to the organization. Software development has become such an issue, and it will be an even greater issue in the future. A critical question to ask is what support technologies are necessary: telecommunications networks, PCs, software, databases, end user facilities. The next question is how *our firm* organizes to capitalize upon a technical resource capacity and the opportunities that present themselves.

The costs and value associated with technology transfer should be objectively evaluated and the implementation plans established thereafter. Control action should include management authorization, design reviews, budgets, timetables, and quality assurance.

These are tactical subjects with a major impact on the value-added structure of the business. The strategic issue is technology transfer itself, and it calls for interdisciplinary analyses. They require corporate rather than departmental focus for their successful resolution.

A critical role in this strategic issue is establishing information technology policies and directives which untie the prevailing knots. The most important is ensuring that human and technical resources are available to implement the new policies and directives.

Obtaining corporate-wide commitment to the policies and directives and monitoring results of the activities related to implementation are milestones. Advanced technology requires much better monitoring and tighter control than the implementation of mature—and therefore obsolete—tools and means.

3

LANGUAGES FOR EFFICIENT PROGRAM DEVELOPMENT AND PORTABILITY

Like any other computer subject, programming languages have undergone significant development, which is expressed in generations. Unlike other subjects, however, most of this development was concentrated in the first decade of the computer era. Though we talk today of the fourth-generation languages (4GLs), we often fail to realize that the other three generations are of the 1950s, as we will see in the first section. This has had its impact on program sophistication and on programming costs.

Developments in programming languages are necessary to save time in instructing the machine in the functions it is to perform. This is equally true of building and maintaining databases accessible to the computer's language. In principle, machines should not be programmed the way we used to program them in the 1950s and Cobol programs them today. Packages have been a good solution since the mid-1970s. Now a better answer is given through 4GLs.

Fourth-generation programming languages permit significant productivity gains if an integrated effort is made with the right initiative. Improvements in software productivity can have a large payoff provided there is sustained action and commitment. In the longer run the biggest productivity gains will come from a more fundamental understanding of man-machine communication. We still have an incomplete comprehension of this issue, but available statistics indicate that, with

4GL, programmer productivity can improve anywhere between 600 and 6000 percent.

That is valid for all types of computers, although its impact will be felt mainly at workstations. Yet tools alone may be of limited value if other factors do not contribute to the productivity goal, which has four components:

1. Motivation

2. Effective learning of the new methodology

3. Computer-based tools

4. Workstation (WS) support at each programmer's desk

It is relatively easy for programmers to know how to use the new programming tools—if they want to. By using the features of 4GLs, developers can produce thousands of lines of code in a short time. Better development tools also improve motivation. The object of a 4GL is to provide a fast, versatile, and intelligently organized programming system able to save programmer time, eliminate the need for low-level coding, provide testing facilities, assure the program documentation, and update this documentation with program upkeep.

This observation is much more important than it may appear to be at first sight. *The language we use conditions our mind.* That is just as true of a programming language as it is of a natural language.

THREE GENERATIONS OF PROGRAMMING EFFORT

The evolution of communications between man and computer has taken two distinct paths:

1. Data

2. Programs

Programs are needed to handle data and tell the machine how to collect data and clear, store, retrieve, compute, and present information. The first 30 years of computers were characterized by a steady, tedious programming effort. Slowly, however, programmers have begun to get away from the physical machine. They have moved toward an abstract machine that comes closer to human needs and our manner of thinking.

That has led to the introduction of abstractions for data and programs, including operations and control aspects. As a matter of fact:

- First came operation abstraction through the introduction of procedural approaches.
- Control abstraction became a reality through the use of high-level language (HLL) control constructs.
- Then data abstraction developed and was helped by the use of abstract data structures.

By invoking operations on an abstract machine, the programmer became free to introduce commands as required by the applications, rather than be limited to the machine-level instructions the machine can readily understand. Though the original goal of symbolic (assembler) programming was a different one, this freedom came with the next logical step: through compilers and macrooperations.

Computer commands aim at two distinct but related areas:

- Program flow
- Data control

Abstraction in control procedures relative to program flow permits the programmer to define a sequence of operations in the sense of a virtual machine, rather than control every step of the physical engine. Data control determines data objects, their types, their names, and the goal of those names.

Data abstraction permits us to view only the nature of data objects rather than their representation. This possibility is introduced through abstract data types.

- A data type is both a class of data objects and a set of functions applicable to the objects.
- Such a data type is abstract if its class properties are defined solely by the effect the execution of functions has on the objects.

In an abstract data type, the behavior of the functions of the type is the only visible aspect. The internal structure and representation of the objects are hidden from the programmer. Data encapsulation and the use of database management systems see to it that the functions of a given data type are the only operations to which the data may be subjected.

The evolution of programming languages has generally followed this path toward a greater abstraction of program flow and data control. Evidently the goals we see today are not those of the 1950s. That is why it is so important to look at historical developments in order to gain perspective.

Languages vary in the way they address the needed programming job: from low level (which means machine code orientation) to very high level. As stated, the latter are also known as fourth generation. But what is a programming language generation?

1. **The first generation of programming effort was centered on machine level languages (ML). These are often called low level.**

Machine level languages came along with the very early commercially available computers (1953) and died rather slowly as a language for applications programmers. Through the 1950s and 1960s, "real programmers" distinguished themselves by their ability to manipulate a bit-level code.

But ML was no answer to the increasing programming requirements and the broadening population of programmers:

2. **The second generation of programming languages was symbolic-code-based and used an assembly routine to convert into ML. Symbolic (assembler type) are intermediate-level languages.**

Originally, the symbolic code was seen as an interface friendly to the programmer. In fact, the very first effort was more advanced than that. Developed in 1954 by Dr. Hopper, *Flowmatic* tackled the programming problem at the flowcharting level, but the profession for some reason did not stick to it. One of the earlier, and for its time one of the best, examples of symbolic coding was SŌAP, the symbolic optimal assembly program for the IBM 650. Other examples are SAP and SCAT.

Though the need for a quality software architecture was not felt at that time, the foundations had been laid for what later became the central problem of modern software engineering: the production of software that is easy to write, comprehensible, reliable, and maintainable. Three significant developments took place in those years:

• One was the use of subroutines which gained amplitude and led to compilers.

• The second effort was toward a universal computer language (UNCOL), which failed.

• The third was the division between compiling and interpreting.

In a nutshell, interpreters permit errors to be immediately detected and corrected, make debugging feasible, and require no extra overhead for optimization. Compilers offer the advantages that they:

- Execute faster
- Require less memory for the program
- Recompile easily

The best examples of interpreting are IT (internal translator) by Alan Perlis, and PRINT, a scientific interpreter for the IBM 705. Based on the IT concepts, Jim Backus designed Fortran/Fortransit. These developments led to:

3. **The third generation of programming languages.** These have been procedure-oriented and largely divided between business and scientific. At the same time, they have been called high level languages (HLL).

Fortran (1957) and subsequently Algol (1959) by Bauer, Samuelson, et al., are examples of scientific programming languages. Cobol (1958) by Codasyl is a commercial business-oriented language. Taken together with what happened in the 1960s, they represent the third generation.

The 20 years following 1959 saw nothing as exciting in pace of development as in the 1953 to 1958 period. IBM designed PL/1 in 1967 as an improved version of Cobol and Fortran, but it was not sufficiently improved to become a new standard. Major computer users, such as Boeing and GM, offered to cooperate with IBM on a 3-year experimental period to polish PL/1, but the mainframer refused.

Yet there were at the time significant programming ideas which, if put together, might have created the fourth generation. There were LISP (the first concrete list processing effort), APL, SNOBOL, and SIMULA (for the simulation techniques which were becoming popular). There was also felt the beginning of a need for *software engineering* aimed toward:

- Better software design methods
- Improved specification tools
- More sophisticated programming languages
- Computer-based approaches

However, breakthroughs in software engineering had to wait for some dramatic progress in hardware.

Third-generation languages had kids—something like a half-generation development. Algol died out, but its basic ideas were used in Pascal (1968). LOGO is a LISP descendant. C integrated the best available in systems programming around 1970.

TOWARD A FOURTH GENERATION

The 1970s were not as sterile as they may appear to have been at first glance. Their main contribution was program modularization through hierarchies of abstract data types (Figure 3.1).

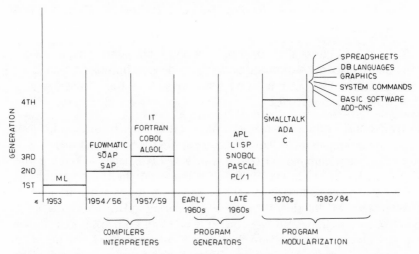

Figure 3.1 Programming developments from the 1950s to the 1980s.

Research on programming languages indicates that the functional behavior which defines an abstract data type may be specified in terms of abstract programs in which functions of simpler virtual data types are applied to objects that serve as representations of the objects in a type to be specified. This approach is known as *abstract model specification*. Should the behavior of program modules be described by abstract data types, then the stated approach corresponds to the principle of hierarchical decomposition of program complexity.

An example of an object-oriented language is *SmallTalk* by Xerox. The objects are data or procedures. "An object gets a message" is equal to "A function is applied to an object." "An object sends a message to another object" means "A procedure calls another procedure." "An object sends a message back" corresponds to "A procedure yields a value."

Among the criteria to be used in evaluating how well a given language fits the programming needs, we distinguish:

1. Computing characteristics
   - Ease with which programs are written

- Language simplicity for learning purposes
- Ability to answer specific requirements in program writing
- Readability of the code
- Concise program presentation
- Computer-based documentation

2. Databasing aspects
   - Handling of data structures
   - Abstract data type orientation
   - File management
   - Input and output manipulation
   - Open perspective to data communication
   - Control structure characteristics

3. General issues
   - End code efficiency
   - Testability
   - Online debugging tools
   - Ability to decompose
   - Observance of standards
   - Availability of packages
   - Ability to compile from mainframes to micros
   - Trained programmer availability

Many of these criteria complement one another; just as many, however, are contradictory. The "perfect language" has not yet been created, and linguistic architectural efforts often work contrary to a solution mainly because of the complexity of executive environment. User interfaces, shared resources, and distributed systems further complicate the task.

In fact, one of the problems with programming languages is separating the specifications, design, and implementation from each other. Another key issue is the development of language(s) valid for families of computer systems. Design trends today include the development of languages that can be formalized incrementally, an applications orientation which allows user participation, and logic-intensive characteristics. These are fundamental for system building, artificial intelligence, and robotics.

Some of the key issues in language design are how to verify the formal specifications in order to satisfy original requirements and how to show that the nonfunctional requirements are satisfied. Such nonfunctional attributes may be:

• **Quantifiable.** Examples are 16 decimal digits of significance and a mean time between failures (MTBF) of x years over a mission time of n years.

• **Nonquantifiable.** Among such attributes are language flexibility, understandability, easiness, and general utility.

These are the perspectives from which should be seen the fourth-generation programming languages that, in the early 1980s, moved from a vague concept to reality. Such languages involve not only one system but many types of systems:

1. Spreadsheet approaches
2. Database (DBMS) and query
3. Productivity-oriented languages
4. Add-ons to the existing basic software

These are very high level languages (VHLL). The first class is cut to the size of the end user, and it is a very friendly facility. VisiCalc, Multiplan, and Lotus 1-2-3 are examples.

Something similar can be said of the second class, except that it is more difficult than the first and should also appeal to the professional programmers. Quad, dBase II, and DB 2 are but a few examples. By using a spreadsheet on a PC, two experts did a given job in $1\frac{1}{2}$ days, including analysis and programming. Confronted with an evaluation of how many days it might take to do the same job in Cobol, other systems experts guesstimated anywhere from 6 to 48 worker-months, which is some two orders of magnitude more than what was required with the spreadsheet.

If something more than a spreadsheet is necessary, it should be written in a database language such as dBase II. The workstation can nicely have:

• One floppy for word processing (WP)
• One floppy for the dBase software

FOCUS is a good example of class 3, the productivity-oriented language. The object is to do what is simple at a fast programming pace. But what is "simple"? Figure 3.2 gives the answer: The dividing line between simple and complex is where our knowledge stands at the moment. For the complex side we need more detailed, less power-consuming tools, and

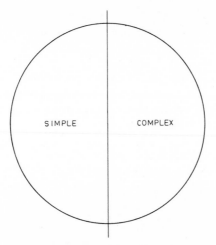

Figure 3.2 The universe of possible solutions can be simple or complex. The dividing line is where our knowledge stands at the moment.

they can be found in class 4, add-ons to the existing basic software. An example is IBM's ADF working with IMS/DC for online transactions.

A common characteristic of the new generation of languages is the emphasis which has been placed on the intensity of testing. Testing can be reduced through:

- Formal derivation from requirements
- Prototyping and reuse of previously tested parts
- The employment of a valid style of programming
- Test case generation

All new programming languages address these issues and stress the importance of inspections, walkthroughs, and design reviews—as well as the need for generating correct outputs for test cases. The years to come will undoubtedly see more programming tools and more features. The important thing to notice is that we are at present at a turning point: Once computers and communications get moving, they move fast.

CHOOSING A PORTABLE LANGUAGE

Like good ideas, good programming languages are elegant in their simplicity. Simplicity should be expressed in two senses:

1. The interfacing toward the end user
2. The design characteristics of the language itself

The simplest programming product to be used is the package. One good criterion for the selection of a software package is to determine if the package is taught at a university; another is the size of the population employing it. Not all applications will be covered by packages and the choice of a language is therefore necessary. We have spoken of simplicity. Elegant language design sees to it that the newer language generations help simplify issues which were formerly complex.

Fourth-generation programming languages also present two other characteristics which constitute key references for the future:

3. Being flexible and open-ended, 4GLs make it possible to keep up with technological evolution.

This is very important. Current projections are that, by 1992, we will most likely have doubled the technological base developed during the preceding 20 years. Still more important, that pace of technological advance will be duplicated once again during the following 3 years, so that, by the mid-1990s, companies at the peak of technology may have 4 times as much science-based support as they had in the mid-1980s.

The accelerated progress of computers and communications will necessitate a fast-growing number of programs, and we have to use the latest tools in order to meet those demands. We also have to provide able solutions regarding:

4. The need for program portability

Just because of the fast pace of change, program portability is one of the key topics of interest. Portability means the avoidance of throwaway software and is, above all, a philosophy of using available resources.

Policies and procedures governing program development are necessary to achieve portability, but technical issues must also be observed. Some features are outstanding. If the *system calls* are the same, *then* programs are transportable provided that:

1. The language being used is not expressed in different dialects

2. The compiler being used is homogeneous

3. The OS is the same (for instance Unix)

4. The microprocessor is the same (for example, Motorola 68000 or Intel 80186)

An example of portability at the systems level can be provided through stand-alone and networking PCs. *If* the local area network (LAN) calls are observed and the available procedural rules (file, server, piping, mailboxes) are honored, the programs have a good chance of being portable.

Figure 3.3 is addressed to the lower three layers: compiler, OS, and microprocessor. The same Pascal programs processed through two different compilers in two different SW/HW engines will produce versions A and B, which are not transportable.

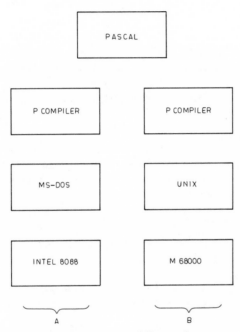

Figure 3.3 Program portability at the system level. Languages using different compilers are not transportable.

Let's note that the language itself may have differences: at the design level (different dialects) or because of the compiler. We must therefore look in the most careful way at the language we choose, and the more structured it is the better.

- Cobol is an obsolete, highly unstructured language. There are over 250 dialects of it, and Cobol ANSI itself has many versions.
- Pascal is a structured language, but there are no unique specifications for it—though CCITT has defined one set.

- C also is a structured language, although many organizations adopting it tend to define further structured subsets answering their specific requirements.

There is a CCITT-approved higher-level language with a database structure. It is essentially Pascal-based. Some companies, for instance GTE, have worked out versions of Pascal with external references. One of the developments is a proprietary compiler which runs on a 3033 mainframe and compiles for Intel 8086–based machines.

Codasyl redesigned Pascal as an internal development language because of its structured characteristics. Another post-Pascal effort is Modula. It has been done by Dr. N. Wirth to clean up unfinished ideas in Pascal, including screening facilities and increased structural characteristics. Another development is concurrent Pascal, created at the University of California, Berkeley, by a Scandinavian designer. It is primarily intended to implement OS, DBMS, and communications—down to the driver level.*

ADA is still another follow-up on Pascal. Its object is to ease realtime programming (Strawman, Ironman, Steelman projects). C also addresses some of the same issues. In other words, work similar to that done with the Pascal dialects can be done with C. Indeed, the latter has several advantages over Pascal, not the least of them being that Pascal experience has been used in its design. Let's recall that the original work on C had as a goal the provision of a programmer's workbench (PWB) valid for all makes of equipment. The shell concept in Unix is an attempt to implement the PWB with edit and other capabilities for later compilation.

Since Unix is written in C language, programs in C integrate in the best possible way with the OS. This is quite valuable in operations such as:

- Adding and deleting files
- Creating a catalog tree structure

At the same time it supports portability much better than other languages because it was designed from the beginning for portability. Many people in the industry say, "If you wish to be close to the OS, then program in C." Several software houses are moving to the C language, and others are adding bit-slice language processors to make their machines run faster.

Whatever the programming language choice may be, failure to use one standard for the chosen programming language—and one type of

---

*A driver is software that drives hardware.

compiler—throughout the organization leaves the DP department with two options:

- Intervene and change, say, the 2 to 5 percent of code incurring practically 30 percent or more of the original cost.
- Define the interfaces very carefully and pay the penalties for language translation at run time

Interfacing can best be explained by way of solutions to be provided for two different OSs. Their usage might be mandatory because of hardware characteristics, one of the most important being bits per word (BPW) supported by the microprocessor.

The leading market trend can be neatly reduced to three statements:

1. CP/M as the preferred OS for 8 BPW
2. MS-DOS for 16 BPW (single user)
3. Unix for multiple-user 16 BPW and most particularly for 32 BPW

(The Unix issue is the more important, given the microUnix development for smaller PCs, and the steadily advancing technology. We can expect a low-cost PC with Unix in the next couple of years, and recent AT&T announcements point in that direction.)

Furthermore, job requirements may imply certain choices. Engineering WSs will be largely Unix-based. Another interesting question is: What about the now-developing 64 BPW; will it be Unix or MVS? Will users be willing to accept *multiple personality* microcomputers which can run Unix and MVX with equal ease, as today we can run CP/M and MS-DOS?

A 64-BPW micro will support lots of parallel processing. The Unix released by the University of California, Berkeley (not by Bell Labs) *might* be compared with MVS. Still, we would need to see a couple of years of experience with 64-BPW machines before having an opinion.

Let's, however, assume that, for reasons beyond our control, we need to use two different OSs and two different equipments and still would like to have transportable programs. What policy could we adopt? There are two alternatives:

1. Find a common way to access the two OSs prior to programming.
2. Write the needed transit routines interfacing the operating systems Unix and MS-DOS (Figure 3.4).

Like all interfaces, solution 2 is costly. It is, therefore, preferable to plan ahead and define the needed functions (solution 1). Another nonelegant possibility is to:

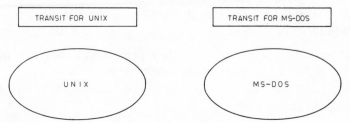

Figure 3.4   One way to have portable programs, in this case Pascal to Pascal.

3. Run an emulator on one of the two OSs.

This is technically possible: It can work at runtime but at a cost which can be as high as a factor of 10 in terms of efficiency. In program portability, as in all other implementations, planning ahead is the best solution.

PC Compatibility: Real or Fanciful?

The best advice to be given in regard to program portability is to stay close to industry standard. The real test is how well the language sells itself to the user population. Program portability is an issue closely linked to machine compatibility. The latter is a prerequisite to the former, and it involves nine major issues the most critical of which are the microprocessor, the operating system, and the programming language.

1. The microprocessor

The type of microprocessor chosen is fundamental to assuring work-alike features. Today, this is made easier by *commodity microprocessors*; but although such compatibility is most important, it is not enough.

The heart of a micro is the processor chip. The large majority of today's PCs are built around a small number of *commodity microprocessors*: Intel's 8088, 8086, 80186, and 80286 and Motorola's 68000, 68010, and 68020. The NSC 32000 series is a challenger, and for 8-bit engines the star was Zilog's Z-80. The current movement from 16-bit to 32-bit processors will spawn a new crop of high-power PCs, a trend to be followed by the eventual transition to 64-bit engines.

2. The use of read-only memory (ROM)

Applications which call on functions stored in ROM are not portable. This may have several aspects, including basic I/O subsystems (BIOS), as with the IBM PC, and microcode routines. The BIOS varies from machine to machine because everybody's hardware is different, but horizontal software is written with the layered solution in mind (Figure 3.5).

Programs can always be written to bypass some of the ROM functions, but they are not quite the same. Sometimes even an approximation may be impossible. An example is Fax by Microsoft, which will not run on anything but the IBM PC. (However, the Phoenix solution has shown its ability to bypass proprietary BIOS characteristics without patent infringements.)

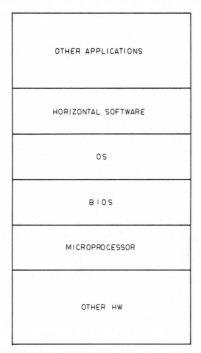

Figure 3.5 A layered solution: from microprocessors to applications based on horizontal software.

Quite similarly, if one computer manufacturer uses a character generator and another does not have the same character code and CRT interface, it will not be possible to present graphics on the screen.

3. The CRT interface

In the case of the IBM PC work-alikes, mainly Compaq, Columbia, and Corona, assure a close-enough CRT interface. The Hewlett-Packard,

Texas Instruments, and NCR DM V are not compatible. Such interfacing is so close to straight copying that big companies can't do it—or will be in legal trouble if they do. Compaq is an exception. Its basic input/output system (BIOS) works in a different way, and the Phoenix system has a high level of compatibility.

4. The keyboard

Keyboard functionality can be emulated through software; but if the results are not the same, the keyboard can cause lots of headaches. Manufacturers try to protect their products through self-imposed constraints. For instance, the IBM PC has only 10 function keys. An application can't be run on a machine with fewer keys unless it runs clumsily with double keys—control A, key B—and that is not user-friendly.

5. The I/O bus

Again taking the IBM PC as an example, it has four bus connectors with specific standards. Compaq has the same arrangement; the others do not have it. Not only are there different approaches to bus design but they, being mainly hardware features, can be properly protected by patents. That makes compatibility so much more difficult.

6. Other hardware characteristics

Programming code is not automatically machine-independent. The most common notions of bits per word (BPW) and properties of floating point may even be less of a problem than, say,

• Sign extension (converting a negative character into a negative integer)
• The order in which bytes are placed in a word
• The number of register variables that can be handled
• The handling of fields, words, and characters

Some of these may be invisible to isolated programs but make a difference in a job stream and account for incompatibility between machines.

7. OS and generic interface compatibility

As with the microprocessor, the *commodity OS* makes it feasible to adopt a look-alike stance. How nearly the machine will also be a work-alike depends on the other features we have outlined. ROM is, of course, a specific reference point, and we return to the BIOS example—which varies from one machine to another. Therefore, a commodity OS, though a prerequisite, may not be a sufficient condition.

8. Data file compatibility

In the simplest form this means that the machine must be able to read from and write on a floppy. Both coding and tracks per inch may handicap this capability.

The read/write issue is further complicated by the fact that there is no standard for $5\,^1/_4$ in or less in diameter—though IBM is becoming the virtual standard. Hence, 48 tracks per inch is a good way to data file compatibility.

9. Programming language

Language is the oldest approach in the search for portable programming, but it would be too much to say that it has been successful. Even languages normalized by international standards bodies are far from being portable.

Quite evidently, the language issue does not end with the macroscopic view of the programming language itself. The dialect is very important, as are the compilers and interpreters for a given piece of equipment. Another way to make that statement is to stress the importance of selecting machines which can support the language in which one has decided to do programming. It is wise to benchmark the available compiler(s) as to their ability to handle, as is, the lines of code which have been developed.

In conclusion, we see that program compatibility and portability are more complex issues that depend on more facts than might originally have been thought. Issues 1, 6, and 8 are commodity options, but the others can be proprietary. Any equipment which is exactly the same as another in these respects will be a copy.

4

FOURTH-GENERATION
PROGRAMMING

Software development is as much an art as a science, and a computer program is a marketable asset such as other product designs rarely are. On these few words rests *the whole concept of fourth-generation programming.*

If software is a marketable commodity (which it is), we should be keen to industrialize its production by calling into the process not only computer power but also whatever is necessary for the optimization of the effort. Most of all, this means valid, properly documented policies and procedures.

In a meeting with the Microelectronics and Computer Technology Corporation of Austin, Texas, I was given the following statistics which should be written in block letters in every MIS/DP manager's desk:

> About 80 percent of programs in a computer facility use 2 percent of the machine cycles, but their existence is critical.

This is the population for fourth-generation languages (4GL). Programming productivity is the issue in this class, not the consumption of more or less computer power.

> About 2 percent of the programs use 50 percent of the machine cycles.

They should be programmed in C (in a Unix environment) or any other similar language; Pascal and Basic being examples. Not the fat and creaky Cobol, nor Fortran either. I will return to this argument.

The remaining 18 percent use 48 percent of the machine cycles.

These existing and projected programs should be sorted out carefully as to the language to use. Chances are that, after a study, it will be advisable to do half of them in 4GL and the balance in C or a similar programming language. But there should be a factual study. Roughly, this will tend to divide the population of the computer programs to be done along a 90-10 percent rule. The 90 percent of the programming effort should be done through 4GL for high productivity in software development. This may require more machine cycles. And then what?

First, the most expensive commodity today is labor. That's where our savings should be. Hardware costs are steadily dropping—and at an impressive yearly rate. Furthermore, as we will see in this chapter, 4GLs permit *prototyping*. In turn, this may save computer power because it makes feasible the detection and correction of the software's weak spots in the early development stage. Prototyping is a cornerstone of fourth-generation programming.

Second, over 75 percent of the computer power to be installed by the end of this decade will be under the "hood of your desks." Some estimates are that it will be 90 percent in the early 1990s. Such statistics closely resemble the installed power-production capability. In a 1961 symposium it was suggested that 90 percent of all installed power in the United States was under the hood of our cars. Personal computing and personal transport have a statistic in common, albeit with time phasing.

The Choice of a Programming Language

When we talk of programming languages, our first, second, and third choices should go to efficiency in software development, short timetables, and quality assurance. This means that, now and in the future, only very high level structures deserve management's attention.

Higher-order software needs an overstructure, a main structure, and an understructure. Depending on the advance of technology, these three layers will be served both by software and by hardware. Provided we have clear ideas about what we wish to achieve, supporting this functionality poses no problems. Very large scale integration (VLSI) promises up to

500,000 components for a few dollars. The basic building blocks will no longer be gates or multipliers, but units capable of speech synthesis, probabilistic reasoning, and so on.

With time and experience, off-the-shelf knowledgebanks will appear with thousands of rules (fifth-generation languages), whereas current applications use only a few hundred rules easily stored on a single chip. Such systems will become as transportable and marketable as books and software are. They will represent knowledge in an organized but adaptable manner, support knowledge in terms familiar to end users, employ user-friendly interface functions, and exploit the kinds of reasoning which are available. Analysis for such systems will be based on thorough understanding of the problem domain. Without a knowledgebank, no algorithm will suffice.

But we are not yet there in terms of implementation. Today and for the next few years what we have at our disposal are *fourth-generation programming languages*. They can be classified in five major groups (instead of the nine of Figure 2.1):

1. Programming extensions to the OS through a command interpreter

2. Database management and query

3. New programming languages such as graphics and data communications

4. Productivity-oriented tools, through precompilers

5. Spreadsheet systems

Let's always remember that technological evolution steadily changes the perception, content, and functionality of the systems at our disposal. That is just as true of software as it is of hardware, although the large majority of users seem to think more of the changes taking place on the HW side.

Nobody in his right mind would now think of using an IBM 7070 or a Univac III for data processing, yet by far the largest percentage of computer shops keep on programming in Cobol. The IBM 7070, Univac III, and Cobol were born in about the same year.

Figure 4.1 puts the chronological introduction of the different levels of software implementation into perspective. As for operating systems, we should surely distinguish between input/output control systems (IOCS) or monitor routines and OS 360. But there is also a big difference between DOS and Unix.

DBMS have had the same evolution: hierarchical (first generation), networking ("first and a half" generation), query-oriented capabilities (second generation), relational and, with them, programming language

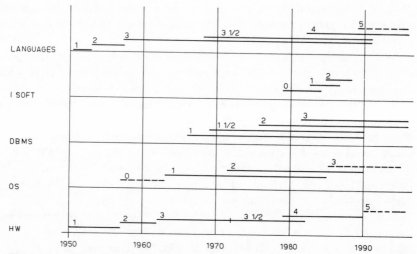

Figure 4.1 Chronology of software development and implementation: OS, DBM, integrated software, programming languages.

facilities (third generation). Even integrated software has its generations. The 0 was a spreadsheet; the first is best exemplified by Lotus 1-2-3; and the second is exemplified by Symphony, of the same software producer as Lotus 1-2-3. We will return to these subjects.

The 4GLs offered in the above-mentioned five classes are reasonably efficient and well developed; they touch fundamentals; and they are oriented to the handling of dataflow. With these types of languages, we can write programs based on data structures—rather than the other way around.

But the classes are broad enough, somewhat overlapping in the facilities they offer, and also variable in functionality and efficiency. Therefore, a decision on the choice of a 4GL has to be reached within the computer environment which has been chosen. This has two aspects:

1. The functional implementation
2. The basic software and hardware

For personal computing, spreadsheets and integrated software are the answer. But although Isoft has a DBMS facility, it is not tooled to give all the necessary support including, for example, journaling, authorization, and other security needs. Such facilities are presented by DBMSs specifically designed for those purposes. Among the relational offerings, Ingres, Oracle, SQL/DS, and DB2 are examples. In choosing among competitive software offerings, we must think in terms of the production-oriented layers shown in Figure 4.2. They provide a checklist against which facilities offered by any given 4GL can be compared.

We have also spoken of a second aspect: The basic software and hardware to be chosen. Here, particular emphasis should be placed on the operating system. Under Unix, the choices are:

- Ingres and Oracle for the larger systems
- Informix, Sequitur, Mistress, and Unify for the smaller systems

Each has its strong and weak points in regard to minimum memory needed, machine cycles, response time, and supported facilities. Table 4.1 presents a comparative evaluation of programming languages supported under Unix. Six basic criteria have been considered.

Commodity software at the PC level mainly supports spreadsheets and integrated software offerings, but also DBMS languages such as dBase II and MDBS. In addition to commodity software each computer manufacturer offers its own tools. Univac has the Mapper. IBM is richer in proprietary offerings which include:

1	END USER TOOLS
2	VERTICAL SOFTWARE
3	HORIZONTAL SOFTWARE
4	DIALOG MANAGER
5	TRANSACTION DRIVER
6	NETWORK CONTROL
7	O S
8	D B M S
9	DATA DICTIONARY
10	SECURITY

Figure 4.2 Ten production-oriented layers that comprise a checklist of software completeness.

Table 4.1 Programming Languages with Unix for Applications Development

Language	Native within environ-ment	Evolu-tionary trend	Proto-typing	Program development efficiency	Execution time efficiency	Maintain-ability
Shell	3	3	3	2	2	3
C	3	3	1	2	3	2
Pascal	2	1	1	2	2	1
C Basic	1	1	0	1	*	1
MS Basic	1	1	0	1	*	1
Fortran 77	2	0	0	2	1†	1
Cobol	0‡	0	0	0	0	0
Ingres	3	3	2	3 tops	2	3
Oracle (SQL)	3	3	2	3	1–2	3
Lisp and dialects	2	3	1	1	1	2
Prolog	1	3	2	3§	1–2	3

*Needs case-by-case evaluation of different offerings.
†Native Fortran is deficient in execution time.
‡Cobol is not operating in a native environment; compiler carries along a large structure.
§Through expert systems.

- Application System (AS)
- Cross-System Product (CSP)
- ISQL
- QMF
- QBE
- DB2I

At the same time, the choice of an HLL may be necessary for functioning similar to that of the assembler language used in a Cobol- or PL/1-oriented programming effort since the 1960s—in other words, as an exception.

This large variety of choices is a principal reason why management will be well advised to establish criteria to be used in the selection of programming languages. Such criteria should be established in advance so they can be applied objectively to candidate programming structures.

KEY POINTS WITH 4GLS

To automate software development we need a very high level language (fourth generation), an advanced database management system

(DBMS), an intelligent editor, and reusable software library. This process involves:

- Nonprocedural statements (say *what*, not *how*)
- Translation of 4GL descriptions into a set of specifications for program modules
- Retrieval of appropriate components from the reusable library
- Generation of new modules as necessary
- Elimination of file management through the DBMS
- Integration of the software components into an executable program

This mode of operation permits rapid prototyping and automatic program generation. The range of tools is impressive: spreadsheets for managerial applications, SQL, Ingres, and Mapper for business applications, APL and CAD/CAM for engineering and scientific applications, C and Prolog for compiler writing, and Unix/C-shell for system building.

A successful fourth-generation language produces applications at least an order of magnitude faster than HLL (Cobol, Fortran, PL/1). As stated, this ratio can reach 60:1 for simple routines and/or heavily database oriented applications. Fourth-generation languages employ a syntax which is typically nonprocedural, remove and automate the repetitive detail work in query, reporting, and so on, act as control language with system commands, and integrate instructions written in HLL. They are database-management-oriented—ideally in a relational manner.

A high point of HLL is that they *can be learned in 3 days or less.* They can also be understood by both the end user and the systems specialist. Add-on functions include screen support, data dictionary, and transactional, message, and file exchange. Quite often among their features are privacy and security, communicating database characteristics, and environmental recovery. Such computer-based facilities revolutionize the whole process of systems analysis.

Systems analysts, to be really good, must imagine intensely and comprehensively. They must put themselves in the places of the users and look at systems development from that perspective. Imagination can be set in action by will, and that can be trained. A person who hungers and thirsts after knowledge develops, in due course, a strong imagination.

Visual thinking capabilities enhance the analyst's imagination. Table 4.2 outlines what is meant by this term. Visual thinking leads to *visual programming.* With visual programming, "what we see is what we get." The user defines a screen and associates it with an expression without having to worry about file handling and structure. This is

Table 4.2   Visual Thinking

Principles	Features
Explicit user's model	Desktop presentation
	Icons
	Windows
Seeing and pointing	Mouse
	Menus
	Pop-up menus
Universal commands	Insert
	Delete
	Search
	Copy
	Change
	Move
	Help
	Show properties
	Exit
	Escape
	End

The principle is: What we see is what we get

accomplished through a high-level interface. Processing will be done by generators.

Systems analysis and databasing are tightly coupled with a 4GL. Banks which have programmed the automatic routing of commercial and financial paper through Cobol or PL/1 typically require 2 years of work by a group of four or five persons. Invariably, the result is a 10 worker-year investment. Four main subsystems are involved in this application:

1. The build-up of the automatic routing database (collection of the information elements is not included in the above estimate)

2. Programs for steady updating of the routing database

3. The automatic routing subsystem (basically, batch-oriented)

4. Interactive programs for the handling of exceptions and rejects

The database itself includes five sections: locality (province and postal area code), corresponding bank, branch office (loro), branch office (nostro), and limited topology (street address) around the branch office.

The writing of programs relating to regions, banks, and branch offices amounts to roughly 80 percent of the work. Topology matches make up the other 20 percent. Programs available for the automatic routing of commercial and financial paper average 40,000 to 50,000 Cobol statements—without accounting for file management routines and other utilities.

Ingres has been used as a 4GL to do the same work starting from scratch. A first prototype of the 80 percent of the required work was created by an experienced programmer-analyst in 4 hr. Its purpose was to demonstrate feasibility. The full, detailed prototype for 100 percent of the work took a week.

By using the facilities included in Ingres and its query subsets, the programmer-analyst needed only to create two read routines, one infopage format, a couple of calculation routines, and calls to the databasing macros. An estimated 90 percent of the work was done in Equel and 10 percent in C. Most important, this approach to implementation did away with the classical system analysis. The new system analysis under 4GL is outlined step by step in Table 4.3. This concept is also compared to the classical system analysis and programming (SA + P) chores.

The process being outlined resembles a *toolkit solution*. What is more, in a well-written applications environment, there will be many reusable program modules in each application. This is a vital by-product when users develop applications through toolkits. Among the facilities to be included in a toolkit approach we distinguish:

1. Screen management
2. Forms handling
3. Table construction
4. Database and data communication specifications
5. Windows for reviewing applications
6. Pop-up menus
7. Icons as graphic representations of WS artifacts
8. Standards for help and menus
9. Universal commands including help, start, move, cancel, and undo
10. Natural-language interfaces including voice input/output capabilities

First time around, these modules help the user. With practice, they become part of the toolkit for integrating new applications at the workstation. In this sense, they become the vital tools of the computer specialist.

In most user-driven systems, we first have only a vague idea of what can be created with a 4GL. The perception of what can be done is enlarged by experience, growing user population, and trial and error. The benefits increase as new users join the implementation program.

Table 4.3 Conceptual Framework for 4GLs

Classical SA + P	4GL
Formal application specifications must be created.	Users do not need to define in detail what they need until they have a version of the application to try it (prototype).
Application development usually requires months and years.	Application development time takes days or at most weeks.
Professional DP knowledge is a prerequisite.	Users can create their own applications.
	Analysts use 4GL for more sophisticated implementation.
	No classical programming staff is needed.
With procedural languages, programmers must specify *how* a task should be executed.	Users specify *what* has to be done by means of a nonprocedural language.
	The generator creates the application.
Both system analysis and programs are formally documented through manual methods	4GLs are self-document through computer support.
Maintenance work is tedious and time-consuming; it absorbs the largest share of DP staff.	Classical maintenance work practically disappears.
	The new approach is to redefine *what* to the 4GL.

The users and management may not initially grasp all the ramifications of the system, but improvements are dynamically made as code development is automated.

Such results cannot be achieved with the old type of formal systems analysis for specifications, which inherently implies a freeze in requirements (otherwise, the project would never finish), manual coding, manual documentation, and manual updating. Nor can they be reached with prepackaged software.

A new type of computer and communications professional will be born out of 4GL and 5GL usage. These new professionals will do a much better job if they keep in mind the following *twelve key factors in the new technologies*:

1. Maintenance costs must be estimated in the system's planning stage; the techniques chosen should permit their reduction to a minimum.

2. The portability requirement should be examined and understood throughout the project life cycle. We should *start at the desired end, not at the beginning.*

3. About 90 percent of the programming effort must be in fourth-generation languages.

4. The impact of database technology must be fully understood.

5. Data communications capabilities should be projected from the start.

6. Prototyping should be an integral part of the project.

7. The users should be brought into the picture from the very beginning—and be trained accordingly.

8. No home-made solutions should be applied to databasing and data communications. Only professional approaches are acceptable, and this means commodity DBMSs—particularly of a relational type.

9. Graphical presentation should be a standard, and that is true of easy text and data entry also.

10. Online help, prompt, and explanation should be supported. The environment must be reliable but forgiving.

11. Any program, procedure, subsystem, or system should be subjected to rigorous quality assurance, including program robustness and documentation.

12. Quality assurance should include system-wide tests for distributed resources, networking, and personal computing. We will return to this subject.

PROTOTYPING

Fourth-generation languages make it easy to manipulate data and to change the structure of the database. The key is successful experimentation through prototyping. Through prototyping the analyst-programmer or end user can try different ways of doing things, including the shaping of the database structure. What is more, the alternatives so developed are self-documenting. User participation, not ossified documentation, is important with 4GL.

Through prototyping, both end users and computer specialists:

1. Did away with the writing of huge specifications

2. Helped improve product quality

3. Gave for the first time in this environment real-life feedback on the results obtained

4. Kept their system dynamic and open to change

The last point is most important within a distributed environment at the WS level. At any given time, an end user workstation might communicate only with a fixed, predefined number of host applications. In those circumstances, one type of solution would be appropriate. Alternatively, user workstations may evolve into an aggregate and eventually constitute a high-performance message node. New facilities will then be required to keep track of thousands of final destinations and to dynamically respond to information about new destinations and new routes.

Properly done, prototyping projects results in increased efficiency, supports short timetables, and assures cost savings—and happy users. The classical systems analysis nearly disappears with prototyping because many system description tasks are performed automatically by the computer; the full procedure is shown in Figure 4.3. An ideal software prototyping environment has three components:

1. The 4GL, to allow quick prototype development
2. Properly managed data resources, from the database to data communication
3. End users and computer professionals knowledgeable in employing the 4GL and structuring the data

The computer professional is needed as a prototype builder. The best team will include one end user and one professional. The user is the person who needs the work done; the computer professional knows the tricks of the trade.

Let's examine the notions advanced so far. *4GLs offer a chance to break free from the rigidity of traditional approaches; they offer not only faster development but also the opportunity to provide better systems for the user. The key is the ability to adopt an experimental approach to development.*

By developing prototype functions instead of huge specifications, the user is for the first time given real-life feedback on what the end result will be like. He can look at them, control them, alter them, update them without throwing the project 6 months behind schedule as happened with intervention in the old SA + P (system analysis and programming).

A prototype will typically involve five types of modules:

1. *Identification and description of all files and records* including ID of fields, format, range of admissible values, and so on, for each field
2. *All defined outputs* and possibly alternatives to the presentation of those outputs; typically softcopy (video) presentation
3. *Listing of all programs and commands* expressed in the 4GL which has been chosen

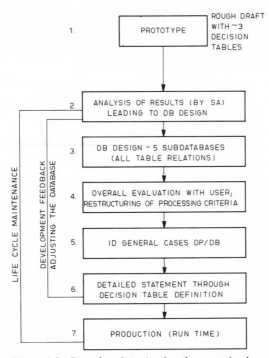

Figure 4.3 Procedure for using fourth-generation languages for prototyping purposes.

4. Identification of *the types of interactive devices* (terminals) being employed: dumb or, preferably, *intelligent*

5. *Linkages to the external world*, particularly communications routines and media

Experimentation and updating may involve any one of these key modules or a combination of them. If, for example, the routing algorithm module is designed by using a programming language such as Cobol or PL/1, both the declarations of the routing data and the algorithms for access to routing tables necessarily reflect a decision whether to organize the data by using arrays or trees.

All this is highly subjective and is left to the initiative and temperament of the artist/programmer. Past experiences make it apparent that even though codes may implement the same function, there is hardly a line in common among them. There is little chance of being able to use one source-level definition of the abstract algorithm to generate another.

The foregoing example not only illustrates the loss of portability due to the artist's temperament but also points to a precise situation in which 4GL and prototyping can be of help. This is brought about by defying the properties of an information object by relying on a sample representation of it—and also by delegating this very process to the computer and the compiler.

Several fourth-generation languages work through *metaphors*, that is, ways of describing what the computer is doing as contrasted to what people do. A metaphor helps in alluding to action: sending a message or providing an interface with common technology.

Prototyping can follow either *functional decomposition* or, preferably, the *data structure approach*. These are the two schools of thought developed since the middle 1970s with structured analysis. The latter is more recent and helps solve some tough problems. First, it is difficult to find the best way to implement a decomposing function. Second, it is even more difficult to reconcile a function structure with the data structure.

Although the automation of functional decomposition has resulted in many new tools, including application generators and definition languages, the success of those tools pales when compared with the results which can be obtained with 4GLs along the data structure line. In the mid-1970s, systems analysis tools such as PSL/PSA did increase the analyst's productivity through structured approaches. The focus on increasing the rigor of functional decomposition, however, led to much more bureaucracy in system design and that, in turn, increased project costs and lead times. This is evidenced by the massive tomes needed to provide guidance methodologies.

Decomposition strategies seem especially weak in the face of the changes occurring in the whole concept of information management. These changes are evidenced by the wide acceptance of database management systems and end user computing. At the same time, facilities supported through 4GLs have been instrumental in increasing software quality. This is particularly valuable to professionals because computer programming is governed by Murphy's law: *Any system eventually comes down.*

Testing new software is a lengthy process; often it consumes more resources than programming does, and it necessarily involves a broad range of users. Distinctions are typically made among several stages of testing. It is advantageous if each of these stages is computer-based.

To recapitulate, prototyping can be of great value in two specific cases:

1. When the user is not sure of his or her needs

Visual programming approaches help clarify those needs by providing a test bed for the description of the implementation. The prototype acts as the breadboard model of the application.

2. When the computer professional wants to experiment in order to optimize the design, file, and code structure

Optimization can be done only by specialists who are versed in the use of development tools, appreciative about the use of resources, aware of short response time needs, and able to understand the organization's information requirements.

The concept of *user-* rather than *technology-driven design* should be the cornerstone. By improving the analyst-programmer productivity an astonishing 600 to 6000 percent, fourth-generation languages make it feasible to spend the time necessary for prototyping. Table 4.4 gives some realistic estimates of 4GL productivity from a recent project involving Unix and Ingres.

In the way we have been discussing it in this book, a prototype is not a theoretical system. It is a working model which can be implemented on the machine and for the environment for which it has been conceived. The prototype may include traditional DP, WP, document handling, electronic mail, and so on. It can be created through a spreadsheet or a database-type language, and *it should be specific to the job, not a generality.*

THE NEED TO TRAIN THE HUMAN RESOURCES

The tools are there, but are we ready to use them? The big question is: Can users and computer professionals absorb all the new developments and breakthroughs? While some corporations make strong efforts to keep their information-processing systems as advanced as possible, others deliberately hang back. They are overwhelmed by the massive needs to retrain and revamp their human resources.

Table 4.4 Programmer Productivity under Unix/Ingres versus GCOS III/ANSI Cobol

Project phase	Unix/Ingres	GCOS III/Cobol	Ratio
Video format preparation for data entry and control	2 hr	3 weeks (120 hr)	1 : 60
Design of an output form			
Nonsophisticated form	7 to 30 min	2 days (1000 min)	1 : 53
Sophisticated form	100 min	3 days (1500 min)	1 : 15
Program for information retrieval	Flexible 2 to 3 min	Inflexible 2 to 3 weeks (5000 to 7500 min)	1 : 2500

Training in the new technologies is indeed an overwhelming task. Yet, there is plenty of evidence that, without massive training and subsequent hands-on implementation, the gains from 4GL will be limited.

• We must not only conceptualize *cost/benefit* of rationalization projects.

• We must also steadily *upgrade our personnel.*

Because technology moves so fast and the market orientation changes, we must always be on the alert. If we have a good system and do not update it, it will become inefficient surprisingly fast and lead to labor-intensive tasks. The same thing is true of personnel. In short, we must organize for knowledge management. In businesses that deal mostly with information and knowhow, management has to cope with a new phenomenon. A rapid divergence develops between:

• Power based on position

• Power based on knowledge

This divergence occurs because the base of knowledge that constitutes the foundation of the business changes every day. If the organization sticks to old-fashioned position power to make all of its decisions, decisions will be made by people unfamiliar with the technology of the day.

In general, the faster the change in the knowhow on which the business depends, the greater the divergence between knowledge and position power. A study by the Bank of Wachovia demonstrated that bankers who do not steadily recycle themselves lose 50 percent of their knowhow within 5 years. With computer specialists the same percentage obtains within less than 3 years.

A first-class example of management training is the *computer literacy training and professional workstations program* at Mellon Bank. In 1983, Mellon Bank, the twelfth largest U.S. financial institution in terms of assets, began a project to make all of its employees—from clerks to the chairman of the board—*computer-literate.* Training included instruction in the use of PCs and inquiry/response languages. Intelligent professional workstations were installed in the offices of all members of the bank's middle and upper management.

Mellon Bank expected to spend in excess of $40 million for the new management tools. Subsequent orders for units at its more than 300 correspondent banks could bring the total value of the order to more than $100 million. The objective was to increase the number of people in the bank utilizing computers in their day-to-day activities from 30 percent, most of whom are branch tellers, to 70 percent within 2 years. Table 4.5 presents a suggested *natal courseware* 3-day program

Table 4.5 Natal Courseware: Management Hands-on Experience

First day	Second day

1. Workstation program
   Processing engines
   Authorized database access
   Communications
   Time management
	1. Graphics
	   • Introduction to management graphics
	     and decision tools
	   • Yesterday's exercises—from tabular
	     to graphics

2. Office automation concept
   SW, HW, documentation
   Floppy with data
   Using the machine
	2. WP
	   Electronic mail
	   Calendar services

	Third day

3. Spreadsheet experience
   • Salary planning
   • Loan management
   • Current account transactions
   • Personal treasury
   • Investment accounting
   • Budgeting and control
   • Development forecasts
	1. Networks
	   Communications protocols
	   Local area networks
	   Applying Email
	   Client communication

	2. Database access
	   Authentication/authorization
	   Accessing the BPL DB
	   Accessing public databases

	3. Reactions, wishes, recommendations

for management hands-on experience. Note that most emphasis is placed on hands-on experience, not on oral courses.

An equally challenging task is *training the computer specialist.* The most clear-eyed statement I have heard on this matter came from John F. Kuemmerle, senior vice president, administration, of Guardian Life Insurance Co. He stated:

> Because computer people realize that their skills can quickly become obsolete, the opportunity to learn new skills and *apply them* is one of their biggest reasons for moving on.
>
> To counter that, *we ask* our people to *spend 40 percent of their time learning.*

But then, you may ask, is it possible to convert Cobol programmers to 4GL? The answer is emphatic: Not only possible but also profitable to all concerned—society, the company, the computer department, and the people themselves.

A recent experience substantiates that statement. A training course in Unix, C, and Ingres included 20 computer specialists of varying background in two roughly equal groups: a younger one already versatile in PC and minicomputer implementation (using Pascal, Basic, and data entry functions) and an older one that was Cobol- and mainframe-oriented. Postmortem reaction to the course was 70 percent enthusiastic approval of the new environment, 20 percent a "that's OK" to "I don't care" attitude, and 10 percent totally negative. The rejection came from the younger PC and minicomputer people, not from the older group.

For the time being, those two out of twenty persons were happy with what they had achieved in their careers. They saw no reason to change. But the older trainees saw clearly enough that they were in the Cobol pit, that their skills were becoming obsolete. And they embraced the new technology. As a matter of fact, one of them became a star programmer in Ingres. As a first implementation, he single-handedly did a fairly complex application: from prototyping to fine tuning of the programs. This happened in a small fraction of the time Cobol programming would have required. It is a good example of what can be achieved through enthusiastic approval of a new technology.

5

SPREADSHEETS AND INTEGRATED SOFTWARE

The rationale for a very high level language is simple and easy to explain: Analyst and programmer time is a very expensive commodity. If we are striving to automate the workplace and control white-collar costs, we cannot afford to spend money foolishly for programming activities which also can be automated.

One of the issues on which practically everyone is in accord is the need to improve productivity at the workplace through computers and communications. This must be done without being dependent on machines, computer programs, and computer manufacturers.

Efficiency at the workplace and also significant cost reduction can result from the implementation of modern technology. That is as true of production activities in information systems, as it is of development work. We need fast, versatile tools to deal with the new hardware products that technology has made available and to answer the ever-increasing demands for more software. We must produce software in a professional manner. That means we must rely increasingly on the new tools the software sciences have brought to the foreground.

The statistics in Figure 5.1 are based on industry projections from a study commissioned by a major computer manufacturer. They help identify the interest which the international computer community is now placing on productivity tools. From a practically zero market prior to 1980–1981, this market:

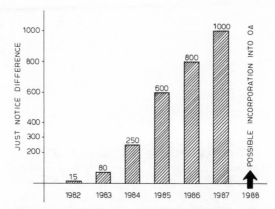

Figure 5.1 The market for productivity management tools: installed base and new implementations.

- Counted some 15 "measurement points" in 1982 (roughly millions of dollars)
- Grew by 500 percent in 1983
- May reach 1000 points (about $1 billion) in 1987

There are, however, three considerations to keep in mind. First, the productivity tools do not exist as a single integrated software offering that really does *everything in the best way*. What is available improves on some of the supported functionality and degrades some other functions which are offered at higher sophistication as self-standing packages. An example is word processing.

Second, integrated software is at its best with spreadsheets and graphics, and hence with management tools. A different way to make that statement is that some of the fourth-generation programming tools coming to the foreground aimed at improving the productivity of management rather than being addressed to programmers. Rightly so: We should think not only of programmers' productivity but also of management's.

Third, just because of the above reasons we should be careful in choosing the 4GL to be implemented. The choice should be tuned to the job in hand. Database programming languages, for instance, are more effective in using the computer resources than spreadsheets are. They are also more difficult to use. They are addressed to programmers rather than to managers.

Finally, just because the packages included in preintegrated software have strong and weak points, some software publishers think of making a living through *software integrators*. An example is Desq by Quarterdeck.

The goal of these offerings is to provide the *software bus* on which the user can hang off-the-shelf programs.

Within certain limits, a spreadsheet, word processing routine, graphics package, calendar service, and micro-DBMS chosen by the user can be subjected to a loose integration. The user does not need to learn different commands for every program. The software bus provides a set of menus the user can alter or extend through *mark and transfer*.

WHAT IS A SPREADSHEET?

Originally devised by Daniel Bricklin as a calculations aid with simultaneous update capabilities, spreadsheets have developed into very user friendly programming tools. Projected at the PC level, spreadsheets have invaded the mainframe environment (a poor practice in terms of response time), but more significantly they have grown tremendously in sophistication.

Bricklin's VisiCalc, the first spreadsheet available on the market, was born of the observation that many problems are commonly solved with a calculator, a pencil, and a sheet of paper. Computing is one pillar on which this structure rests. Simultaneous updating of the memory cells is the other.

A spreadsheet permits the decision maker, through a PC, to follow up accounting and financial data, the management of the product line, and the administration of an account. It also permits prototyping. The development staff of the computer center values management input. That is particularly true of office applications. Both at the decision-making level and at the systems and procedures level, people benefit from the capabilities embedded in a spreadsheet. That is particularly true of integrated software, which as a fourth-generation language:

1. Permits the user to work easily with a number of applicative products at one time, for instance, screen design, procedural evaluation, graphics, and database management

2. Offers a well-structured, common interface to all applications needs

3. Sees to it that man-information communications characteristics are uniformly applied to all of the user's applications

4. Makes sure that the user's applications integrate in a common work environment

5. If properly used, assures much greater productivity for the professional systems experts

6. Makes it feasible for the nonprofessional to program the computer, albeit at a lower level of sophistication

With this background let's see which possibilities are created by fourth-generation languages, first of all in spreadsheet implementation. With spreadsheet type languages, the computer's screen becomes a window which looks upon a much larger memory display. The user can scroll this window in all four directions to look at any part of the sheet.

The spreadsheet is organized as a grid of columns and rows:

- The rows are numbered 1, 2, 3, ...
- The columns are labeled A, B, C, ...

At each intersection of a row and column (Figure 5.2) there is a variable with a coordinate identifier: A1, B5, C10, and so on. Into each variable the user can enter one of three types of data:

- A string
- A number
- An arithmetic expression

When the content of a variable is changed, the system automatically recalculates all the related variables on the sheet, changes their values, and displays them on the screen, if within the window.

Depending on its design and on the computer memory it has available, a typical spreadsheet product will hold 256 rows (tuples) and

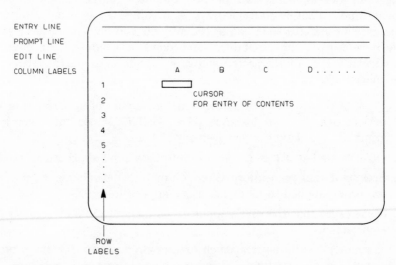

Figure 5.2 A spreadsheet screen and cursor positioning.

63 columns (attributes). A column can be one character or more wide as defined by the user through the cursor. Ten character columns are often found in applications. The spreadsheet software permits the user to scroll them through the screen or call them in a menu-like manner as pages.

The screen shown in Figure 5.2 consists of two basic areas:

- The control panel, which has three lines at the top
- The window at the middle to bottom of the screen*

At the top of the control panel are the entry line, the prompt line, and the edit line. Information displayed on the entry lines gives a full explanation concerning the variable highlighted by the cursor, including its:

- Coordinates, which act as its name
- Its contents
- The type

On the prompt line is displayed the type of entry VisiCalc thinks the user is making. On the edit line is the actual input typed by the user.

Spreadsheets are syntax-directed. Each time the user presses a key, the spreadsheet displays on the prompt line what can be typed next. The operations are either editing commands that manipulate the contents of the screen or built-in functions and operators that can be used in arithmetic expressions.

Commands include operations for clearing a row, a column, or a specific variable. They are also available for replicating the contents of variables, moving information between the screen and the file, and printing. Such commands are entered in the edit line.

Built-in functions provide easily accessible commands. They include arithmetic operations as well as function-like minimum or maximum value. Execution (or recalculation as it is called in VisiCalc) occurs each time a variable is changed. A spreadsheet recalculates by starting at the upper left-hand corner of the sheet and working its way downward and to the right until it reaches the lower right-hand corner of the sheet. Such a system allows the user to select either of two possible first operations:

- Down the columns
- Across the rows

---

*Newer spreadsheets tend to divide the control and edit lines into top and bottom with the functional operators concentrated at the bottom of the page.

The functionality supported by a spreadsheet overlaps to some extent with that of file, query, and menu management systems—and with other types of specialized computing routines. Every approach has its advantages.

Spreadsheets are not as generic as database programming languages, nor can they carry out the sophisticated functions of some generators. In exchange, they are very user friendly and easy to manipulate. Learning them is a matter of hours; it involves:

1. Cursor movements
2. Calculating functions
3. Editing
4. Labels and values

Dedicated keys on the right-hand numeric pad of the keyboard move the cursor in designated directions. The cursor itself is used to point to the appropriate position in value entry and/or commands. The entry (or command) will be executed when the RETURN key is depressed. The ; moves the cursor between windows. With the G (go-to) command, the cursor goes to designated coordinates. H (home) moves the cursor to A1.

The arithmetic operations are +, addition; −, subtraction; *, multiplication; /, division; and ˆ, exponentiation. If a coordinate is immediately to the left of an edit cue, # replaces that location's current value. Otherwise, the current value of the cursor location is placed on the edit line. When the edit line is clear, ! forces a recalculation of the entire sheet. If a formula is on the edit line, it is replaced by its current value.

The backspace key ← deletes characters to the left of the edit cue on the edit line. It will cancel a command entry and clear the prompt line if the edit cue is at the beginning of the edit line.

The VisiCalc command structure involves the following commands, many of which explode into a second layer of operations:

B	Blank; erases contents of specified cells
C	Clear contents
D	Delete cells—row, column
E	Edit (label, value); post contents of active cell on command line for editing—or edited value on active cell when RETURN is pressed
F	Format; control cell formatting
G	Global search and replace
I	Insert row, column

M	Move (from . . . to) row, column from one part of the worksheet to another
P	Print (printer, file) controls worksheet printing
R	Replicate
S	Controls storage
W	Controls windows
–	Label repeating

Multiplan has features in addition to those of a VisiCalc spreadsheet:

• The SORT command can do multilevel sort, all columns.

• NAME fields. With VisiCalc, a field is defined by row and column. Multiplan can also name the field.

Usually with spreadsheets we can multiply fields:

$$R2C11 * R2C12$$

With Multiplan we can also do price * tax, with the result to be placed in field R2C13.

It is also possible to assign a name to multiple fields such as TOTAL for the totals row. Multiplan also allows the user to connect up to eight tables defined within different spreadsheets run on the system. This is very important for management reporting, where we are interested in summary results. We can build up a hierarchy of eight different layers of spreadsheets. This, too, is a useful tool as end users gain experience and wish to extend the limits of spreadsheet programming.

Further breakthroughs in expanding the programming limits are presented by Lisa and the integrated software (Isoft) offerings: Vision, TK!Solver, Lotus 1-2-3, Knowledgeman, and MBA. Their main contribution is in end user interface technology. Integrated software is more than a spreadsheet, however; it is an entire office automation (OA) package. The new developments expand and improve the spreadsheet capabilities, but they are not revolutionary. If we know one of them well, learning the others is easy.

WHY INTEGRATED SOFTWARE?

Integrated software is a new-generation package for personal computers designed to let the end user work easily with any number of application products at one time. Typically, it is open-ended and machine-independent.

Integrated software capabilities are primarily targeted at managers and professionals. Most of the interests of this population center on financial analysis, planning, sales and distribution management, or administrative activities. Data transfer, cross-application implementation, and database management, among other activities, are made transparent to the end user. A typical example is to consider all papers and forms now used in an office environment. The object is to transfer them to the PC as they are—with minor changes or no change in form. This is greatly different from classical DP, which has steadily required changes in forms and formats. With integrated software, the same formats can be used. This simplifies procedural changes and makes the user happy. To that end it is advisable to keep Multiplan presentation no bigger than DIN A4. Use paging and no rotating screens. Think of the 80-column printer.

Applications perspectives should focus on a total integration environment in which a wide variety of jobs can be combined in feature and function. Integrated products for management come in the form of calc, graph, and word processing. The user can show financial figures on screen and in print, together with accompanying text and graphic presentation, and can experiment on:

• Return on investment
• Life cycle calculations
• Discounted cash flow

The user can even sort multiple equations, use "if" conditions, and chart the results. It is also possible to

• Do inventory control to calculate materials requirements in advance
• Perform sensitivity analysis interactively

Said a senior executive: "You can't do that with Cobol!" Added another: "With Multiplan you can write a powerful program in half a day. If an HLL were to be used, you should first count the typical 16 to 18 months backlog. Then add 6 months of programming work to it."

Integrated software further provides a comprehensively applied human interface that makes the system easy to learn and use. It includes important competitive spreadsheet features such as variable column widths, templates, and extensive formatting, and it supports cursor movement via a mouse or keyboard. It handles more extensive worksheets than the typical calc (511 rows by 128 columns), uses virtual management to ensure that the entire worksheet can be used with no performance degradation, and combines data from different worksheets automatically. Its features simplify entry of data, formulas, or labels.

Being a more recent generation than the original spreadsheets, integrated software permits the naming of cells or ranges of cells for use in formulas. It allows the entering of labels (up to 255 characters) across cell boundaries, and it provides multikey sorting whereby whole or partial columns or rows can be prearranged in ascending or descending order with sort keys numeric or alphanumeric.

Calculations are performed by row, column, or depth-first techniques. Easy-to-use display attributes, including scaling, are provided, as well as a thorough set of help instructions. There are also:

- A descriptive command menu
- Automatic text formatting
- Background printing
- A mouse to scroll, move, copy, delete, and enhance text

The documents being handled are limited in size only by disk storage. The system provides the capability to move quickly within a document by specification of the page to go to. Display status information includes current document name, page, and line number.

The system permits attribute assignment on a range basis; it provides a powerful delete function by character, word, line, sentence, paragraph, area, or document. It uses the date for headers and footers; it inserts actual DB tab separators into text; and it can present historical information on document preparation.

Sophisticated systems such as integrated software are designed to run on PCs, but they also pose memory problems. Although they may run on a 128-Kbyte system, more memory is required if large spreadsheet models are going to be used.

These programs are also excellent tutorials. They have a sophisticated command file capability. They are fast and have a superb graphics capability tied into the spreadsheet. They can:

- Recalculate the spreadsheet
- Within seconds, present with graphics what the numbers that went through computation really mean

The database uses columns and column headings as fields and the rows for records. The user can sort, select, and create subsets to design reports. The command file gives the user a lot of power.

One of the important display characteristics is the ability to dissociate:

- The scratch pad function from menu selection
- Menu selection from reporting

Another interesting possibility is the simultaneous presentation of tabular data and corresponding graphs. Color, smooth scrolling, and lack of jittering are musts.

Turning the program into a programming language, the user has the ability to write command files with conditional branching. The user can create his own menu or prepare a form letter and have it sent to selected people on a distribution list (narrowcasting). Thus, integrated software presents itself as a new generation of personal computer programs offering the manager and professional increased productivity through its ease of learning (and use) and its ability to handle several complex tasks at one time.

The user is also assured of compatibility across hardware because integrated software offerings are typically available on a wide range of personal computers. Data can be easily exchanged if the physical supports permit it, and many classical hardware differences become nearly transparent. By ensuring reasonable compatibility and upgradability, the new offerings provide a growth path as well as the basis for uniform and consistent use of personal computers.

GENERATIONS OF ISOFT

Having outlined the functionality which we can expect from spreadsheets and integrated software, we can now look into some basic design considerations. They would help explain the range within which their functionality is expected to vary.

First of all, let's be clear on what is and is not Isoft. This is shown in Table 5.1. In what I call the zero generation we have had independent horizontal packages such as spreadsheets, word processing, graphics, and DBMS capabilities. But the files that each of them managed were independent. There were no linkages except manual conversion and passage from one to the other.

Then came the in-between, or half generation. With it, software vendors have attempted to put off-the-shelf software such as spreadsheets, word processing packages, and database access programs into integrated environments. Most of these software products use a windowing technique to display different files simultaneously. However, at the basic design level, the database the different functional modules use is not integrated. There is simply a bridge, as Figure 5.3 demonstrates.

The real first generation of integrated software is precisely characterized by the integration of files through DBMS facilities. Two design tendencies prevail:

Table 5.1 Generations of Spreadsheets and Integrated
Software

Zero generation	Independent packages: spreadsheet, WP, graphics, and so on.
Half generation	Communicating packages: can exchange files, but under user command.
First generation	Integrated software: file exchange is transparent to the user.

Prevailing tendencies

Bring together existing packages Vision Easyplus	Really integrated approach Lotus 1-2-3 SuperCalc 3*
Second generation	Further integration Symphony CA Executive Intuit†

*SuperCalc 3 is SuperCalc 2 plus graphics and text editing.
†Intuit (by Noumenon) does away with the OS while supporting spread-sheet, WP, Database management, and so on.

- Bringing together existing packages
- Providing a really integrated approach

Much of the appeal of Lotus 1-2-3 is that it chose the latter road. It is not only a more elegant solution; it also leads to further-out enhancement possibilities. These have come by way of the second generation of Isoft, which followed the first in little over a year. Table 5.2 outlines the features of the second generation and contrasts them with those of the first. They are in no way a terminal point. So we have two developments at the same time:

1. One is that spreadsheets get more complex in terms of the function being supported.
2. The other is that, within the Isoft offering, they integrate with other horizontal software such as WP and graphics.

The newer generation of spreadsheets offers *consolidation*: combine data from multiple spreadsheets or parts thereof; *color display* by exception, showing negative numbers in red and protected entries in yellow; and *formatting options* such as using floating dollar signs, embedded commas, percentages, and variable decimal places.

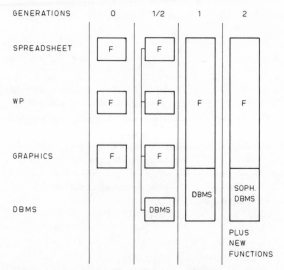

Figure 5.3 Evolution of integrated software in terms of dependence on common files.

Negative numbers are shown in parentheses, zeros are converted to blanks. *Sorting* is possible for partial or entire rows and columns in logical dictionary sort order. There is a memory manager keeping track of blank cells. Separate windows are supported for a closer look. The user can display results in one window and formulas in the other. Each window can be scrolled independently.

These are examples of an increase in spreadsheet sophistication. At the same time, the value-added functions themselves are presented at different levels of sophistication by the various Isoft commodity offerings. There is a subtle difference between charting and graphics:

Charting refers to simple bar graphs, pie charts, and histograms—means of converting spreadsheets and tabular formats.

Graphics include icons, multiple windows, and editing of charts.

In the WP line there is a need for:

WP style sheet to help edit on preferences (parameters) and, later on, to provide stepping-stone pagination.

There are also other functions to be supported as users become more demanding and software producers more knowledgeable of what they can handle. For instance, users would like to see included in integrated software:

Table 5.2 First and Second Generation of Integrated Software

Supported functions	Lotus 1-2-3	Symphony
Database	Original design	Improved design
Spreadsheet	Original design	Enlarged design
Graphics	Five graph types	Six graph types
Word processing	—	Yes (with edit, word wrap, insert and delete, erase, copy, move, search and display, substrings, headers)
Windows	—	Yes. Overlapping options; window on top is the active one.
Communications	—	Yes. File transmission, log-on to prestore, remote databases, suspend data communication session, analyze data

Functions included in other integrated software offerings

Query	By Vision
Form generator	By CA-Executive*
Tutor (Online tutorial)	By CA-Executive

Start/stop and BSC protocols become commonplace, and the DBMS facilities can be used as a fourth-generation programming language.

*Computer Associates International

1. *Calendar management* updating all calendars of communicating WS and identifying who has the right to call meetings, change calendars, and authorize changes

2. *Project management* incorporating automatic reporting on plan versus actual, update, and Pert presentation

3. *Budgetary control capability*: handling budgets, receiving financial reports, producing highlights, charts, and exception items

4. *Encryption capability* (first SW through password and ID; then SW/HW)

5. *Integration links*: WP to Email, calendar to Email, etc.

6. *Voice editing* based on voice datatypes (digital encoding) and playback capabilities

7. *Expert systems*: implementing a knowledgebank (rules), presenting conversational reports, justifying the suggested course of action

The issue to concentrate on is *added value*. That is what the customer wants: *value*. At the same time the young wizards working at the software producers' site have their own ideas about what should be added to make Isoft increasingly more sophisticated. Not surprisingly, they focus particularly on technical issues.

One example is the extension of *escape facilities* to cover the whole range of supported functionality (Figure 5.4). Another is the creation of *system commands* (shells) making all links (and other supported functions) fully transparent to the user. Other references to command facilities which have been implemented are *cursor control by context* (Lotus 1-2-3 does it), *undo complex commands* one step at a time, different *global formats, deletion recovery, variable calc order, and time trials*. That much has been achieved, but not in every Isoft on the market.

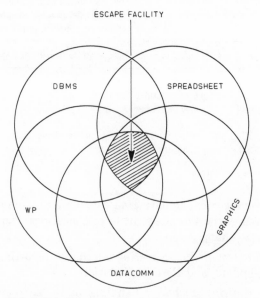

Figure 5.4 Escape facility in a range of supported functions.

Features that technical people would like to see added (and that most likely will be added in the second and third generations) include the transmission of raw worksheet data among computers, custom color attributes and flashes for text, global search functions, translation of standard print file into spreadsheet format, more advanced types of statistical analysis (chi square and t test), embedded control codes cells, better security and protection, journaling, recovery, and restart.

FUNCTIONAL EXAMPLE: LOTUS 1-2-3 AND SYMPHONY

We have mentioned commands and functionality supported by Isoft, but we have not specified the commands. Now some precise examples will complete the discussion. The command menus of Lotus 1-2-3 are among the easiest—if not *the* easiest—supported by spreadsheets. The / (slash) brings every command choice to the screen as a full word. The user can choose from the menu either by typing the first letter of the command or by moving the cursor to it and pressing the ENTER key.

The F1 key brings up one of the context-sensitive help screens. Each screen is cross-indexed to other screens, and the user has the option of reviewing earlier help screens, looking at additional ones, and then returning to the point of departure.

Spreadsheet software indicates which cell addresses should be replicated as *absolute* and which as *relative*; $ (dollar) signs identify absolute addresses. This choice is properly timed at the moment the formula is entered into a cell. Furthermore, Lotus 1-2-3 allows hybrid cell addresses which can be part absolute, part relative. It also permits the user to flexibly indicate cell ranges: The cursor can be expanded to visually identify all the cells in a range.

To name a group of cells, an available procedure enables the user to employ labels that have already been typed into the spreadsheet as *names for the values* in adjoining cells. The screen also reminds the user if the automatic recalculation feature has been suspended. Among other facilities, Lotus 1-2-3 has a handy *data fill* function that fills a series of cells with a series of numbers. The series begins with any number the user specifies, and it increments each time by whichever other number the user establishes.

Most of the special commands are grouped under the heading /D (data commands). The most vital are:

/DS. This is a sort command that allows tuples (rows, records) to be sorted by the contents of columns. The software also manages a two-key sort.

/DQ is a data query command which operates over a specified range of cells. An AND operator is established by entering multiple conditions on one line; an OR operator, by entering conditions on separate lines.

I/DT (data table) is an extension to the classical *what if*. Tables of numbers can be built through iterations.

/DF (the above-mentioned data fill) is useful for filling a range with values incremented from a starting value.

/DD (data distribution) outputs the number of call values within user-specified entities.

F (find) highlights each matching record.

D (delete) removes matching records.

E (extract) and U (unique) copy matching words to a predefined area of the spreadsheet.

@ DCOUNT gives the number of items on a list.

@ DMIN and @ DMAX search the minimum and maximum values, respectively.

@ DSTD provides the standard deviation of items in the list.

@ DVAR calculates the variance of items in the list.

The follow-up to Lotus 1-2-3 is *Symphony*. With Symphony, two of the three Lotus pieces have been enhanced: The spreadsheet is larger, and there are now eight graph types instead of five. The database is completely rewritten. But the most important features in Symphony are the word processing and communications systems. They are new, and so are the windowing facility and open-ended nature of the product.

Symphony includes not only financial management and graphics, but as mentioned, word processing and a facility for transmitting and receiving data over telephone lines. Thus it appears to be a significant improvement in integrated software: programs that combine many of the most popular applications for a personal computer.

For instance, stock data can be retrieved by telephone and analyzed through a Lotus spreadsheet, which enables users to manipulate long rows of interrelated figures for financial projections. The results can then be put instantly into a letter or a report, along with charts to further highlight a trend.

The word processing part includes such standard features as justification, automatic word wrap, insert, delete, erase, copy, move, and search and replace. The screen displays lines and character numbers at all times to indicate the position of the cursor.

Format lines can be added to the text for easy automatic indenting of subsections, single-spacing of paragraphs in double-spaced text, and so on. The format lines can be edited to change the position of margins and tab stops. Printing options include single-, double-, or triple-spaced lines, underlined or boldfaced characters, subscripts and superscripts, and headers and footers with automatic page numbers and dates.

The supported communications system is asynchronous and offers full terminal emulation, automatic dial-up, and log-on to remote databases. One of its features is capture of data and immediate user access to entered data. Other features are the point-to-point transfer of any file and full user control of all terminal parameters.

Windows split the screen into several segments and allow a user to see a letter, a spreadsheet, and a graph, for example, at the same time. The user can move from one to the other with the press of a key.

Combined with the interactive power of the Symphony window management system, the communications module lets the user instantly suspend a communications session, analyze the captured data in a spreadsheet, database, or document, and immediately return to communications mode.

THE IBM PERSONAL DECISION SERIES (PDS)

The IBM *Personal Decision Series* is an integrated set of productivity aids for managers and professionals. PC-based, it helps combine sources of information for problem solving. A family of products is available; each can be purchased separately but complements others in the series.

Designed and built by IBM's Information Programming Services department of Menlo Park, California, the Personal Decision Series is the first integrated software package with which full attention is paid to host attachment prerequisites. Composed of core programs centered around a database manager, it is modular and interactive.

The Data Edition is the database manager and the heart of the Series. It also provides asynchronous communications. The user starts the application with this central package and can then add any of the other modules to it as needed. In fact, the Data Edition is one member of a family of products; the word "Edition" is used to indicate the members of this offering.

The Data Edition loads on the PC and is a prerequisite for the other 10 Editions which are presently available. This includes the software which interfaces to hosts. Three operating systems are supported: MVS, VM, and the system support program for the System 36. With the Data Edition, files can be created, exchanged, searched, sorted, and indexed. DIF files also are operated upon with this facility. If applications produce DIF, ASCII, or other standard DOS-type files, those files can be accessed by the Data Edition for use by other Editions.

An important feature of the Data Edition is the ability to store and execute procedures. Data Edition permits the user to easily link together a series of activities, including those from all other Editions. By using this feature, scenarios can be initiated by simply starting a predefined procedure. In this manner, the user can develop mini-applications or, by using the program development capability of the Reports+ Edition, develop complete applications. At the same time, computer specialists can develop applications for end users on a customized basis with these facilities.

The Attachment Editions are a vital feature of PDS. For the first time a high level of host connectivity is provided by the family members. The Attachment Editions assure such necessary functions as:

- Transferring files back and forth, including the automatic conversion of various data types
- Host-based procedures from the PC
- The means of establishing PC virtual disks on the host
- Messaging on the S/370* Editions
- PC-host printer sharing on the S/36 Edition

PC-host interconnection is increasingly important. By using only the Data Edition, computers equipped with an asynchronous communications protocol can send and receive files. Through an imaginative approach, asynchronous lines can be defined, stored, and retrieved like macro-operations. This allows communication links to be preset, saved for later use, and chosen in an interactive manner.

In a description of Attachment Edition capabilities, it is proper to assume that communications have been established so PC and host programs can work together. Host users can perform many independent tasks, and a primary role in an interactive environment of distributed information systems is to support text and data exchanges and thereby enhance man-information communication at the workstation level.

Emphasis is aptly placed on PC-to-mainframe communications, and the software has been designed by an expert group involving both mainframe and PC specialists. At the same time, PC applications and features can be employed independently of the host. In this way, a user may continue with work in progress regardless of whether the central system is currently available. Thanks to an agile connectivity:

1. Information obtained from the host can be processed on the PC.

2. Information processed on the PC can be processed at the host.

3. Information can be shared by users of personal computers within the extended host environment.

---

*PDS uses Attachment/370 or S/370 to mean either of the host products, Attachment/MVS or Attachment/VM. But the term "Attachment/370 Edition" refers to the product on the PC. To communicate with the host by using Attachment/370 Edition, the user needs only one of the host products installed.

This is achieved transparently to the user, since one of the powerful features of the offering is embedded communications capability that assures transparent line disciplines within mainframes.

Other Editions in the PDS family are addressed to the test and data processing tasks. The Plans and Plans+ Editions are value-added spreadsheet financial modeling programs with graphics and report-generating features. Plans and Plans+ can also produce graphs directly from the spreadsheet and display and print the graphs. Options are histograms and pie and bar charts.

The strength of Plans and Plans+, however, lies in the calc features. The number of rows initially available with Plans and Plans+ is 10 to 1200 incremented by 10s. Other rows can be inserted as needed to provide up to 9999, bringing the total capacity in cells to 99 times 9999, or 989,900. Quite evidently, the number of usable cells depends on the amount of memory available to hold them, so this maximum number could not be implemented on the currently available hardware. Plans and Plans+ do, however, make good use of the available memory by not storing rows that contain no information. Therefore, these Editions can handle more data in a given amount of memory than many of the other currently available spreadsheet programs.

A separate Graphs Edition in the PDS family features useful facilities such as positioning and dimensioning of graphs. Character sizes and fonts can be altered and redisplayed on the screen. In this connection, reference should also be made to the Reports+ Edition, which acts as screen generator and report writer. Formats include heading, titles, and footers. There are four print styles and an equal number of colors which can be used.

Reports+, like the other members of the PDS family, also acts as a fourth-generation language that can be used to create basic programs. It is addressed to both end users and computer specialists at different levels of sophistication. This reinforces the major happening in the software industry today: end user programming. In 1984, an estimated 10 percent of all programs were written by end users in 4GLs, and the forecast is that, by 1994, 60 percent will be.

The Words Edition is an integrated word processor for the business professional. With it the user can easily merge information from other family members into a *words* letter or document.

6

JOBS TO BE DONE WITH COMMODITY SOFTWARE

We follow that technical chapter with a look at the applications to which we can put the fourth-generation languages (4GLs) at our disposal before again getting into the mechanics. As we will see, spreadsheets and Isoft not only are productivity-oriented languages but are also user-friendly.

The object of 4GLs is to provide a comprehensive, easy-to-manipulate system for answering the programming needs. The background issues, as has been emphasized, go much deeper and well beyond the shortage of programmers and analysts. Not only is the backlog of what is to be done rapidly increasing but also a new breed of creative probes for problem solving is necessary. People with imagination and ability to get things done are a major resource for the organization. They should not be wasted on massive programming.

The functions of Isoft should be viewed not by themselves, but as integral parts of personal computing. Despite what the term may suggest, the five top functions in personal computing are:

1. Communicating
2. Delivering
3. Presenting
4. Pointing
5. Selecting

Way down the line comes another wanted function:

6. Computing

That is why integrated software capabilities must not only be targeted primarily at managers and professionals but also be so designed as to, first and foremost, discharge the top functions.

SPREADSHEETS IN A MANAGERIAL ENVIRONMENT

We have seen that integrated software in general and spreadsheets in particular are managerial tools. Most of the interests of the managerial population center on financial analysis, planning, sales and distribution management, or administrative activities. What matters about computer assistance is the end result. Functions such as data transfer, cross-application, flexible implementation, and database management must be fully transparent to the end user.

In fact, a big difference between integrated software and classical DP is that DP has steadily (though illogically) effected changes of forms and formats from one application to another. With integrated software the same formats can be used in a variety of applications. The more we automate our applications, the more we need to standardize.

In a banking environment, for example, a spreadsheet can be employed for each type of security, commodity, property, and option within a portfolio. This enhances the ability of the portfolio manager to better the earnings from each investment. The responsible investment manager in a financial institution can use the same spreadsheet facilities to integrate an individual page for each portfolio management and get aggregate estimates. If the total return doesn't match the corporation's goal, the portfolio model can be quickly recalculated.

Experimentation through spreadsheets is typically based on changes and hypotheses, with results available interactively in a man-machine dialog. This is the sense of the what-if solutions advertised by spreadsheet vendors. The user can display, for private or group use, financial figures on screen and printout, together with accompanying text and graphic presentation. It is possible to experiment on:

• Return on investment

• Life cycle calculations

• Discounted cash flow

Multiple equations can be stored; "if" conditions can be used; and the results can be charted. In an industrial implementation, the user can experiment on inventory control to calculate materials requirements in advance, perform analyses of the make-or-buy type interactively, plan projects, and elaborate budgets.

The end user is provided with easy but effective display attributes (including scaling), together with a thorough set of help instructions: descriptive command menu, automatic text formatting, background printing, and support of mouse to scroll, move, copy, delete, and enhance text. The system permits attribute assignment on a range basis. It also provides a powerful delete function by character, word, line, sentence, paragraph, area, and document. It uses the date for headers and footers; it inserts actual tab separators into text; and it can present historical information on document preparation. The database uses columns and column headings as fields and rows for records. The user can sort, select, and create subsets to design reports. The command file gives the user a lot of power.

One of the important display characteristics is the possibility to dissociate:

• The scratch pad function from menu selection

• Menu selection from reporting

Another interesting possibility is the simultaneous presentation of tabular data and of the corresponding graphs with color, smooth scrolling, and lack of jittering. By turning the program into a programming language, the user can write command files with conditional branching, create a personal menu, prepare a form letter and have it sent to selected people in a distribution list (narrowcasting), and communicate with databases, extract needed information, and download the information to the workstation for storage and processing.

With some of the commodity offerings, the user can employ virtual management to ensure that the entire worksheet can be employed with no performance degradation. Most Isoft supports cursor movement via a mouse or keyboard and combines data from different worksheets automatically. Available features simplify entry of data, formulas, or labels. Calculations are performed by row, column, or depth-first techniques.

The services to the end user are really unique, but there are also prerequisites. Most of the prerequisites are organizational; others relate to human engineering. Organizational prerequisites primarily concern data—from data capture to reporting rates—and also procedural issues such as formatting and systems subjects such as response time evaluation.

For instance, one of the not too often appreciated subjects is the wisdom of keeping a Multiplan presentation no bigger than DIN A4, using paging and no rotating screens, and thinking of an 80-column printer so that softcopy can be mapped into hardcopy without alterations. We often say that PC and integrated software are user-friendly. Yet we often fail to recall that putting together a user-friendly system has implications for displays, keyboards, processors, storage systems, networks, and interaction devices.

System response time is the time the user waits. It is measured from the user's signal to the system that there is work to be done to the point at which the system begins to present the results to the user. A long response time is upsetting and cancels the very reason for implementing PC and Isoft: productivity. It can also have negative effects on working habits.

At least one firm is trying to solve the problem of adjusting to end users' working habits and expertise by using a time-delay activator. If a user types in a command less than 2 sec after being asked for it, the program assumes the user is proficient and skips over the menu listing of options. Users who take longer are given the benefit of directions from a menu.

Within a given operating environment, a basic system response time should be computed to identify the prevailing operating characteristics. The proper definition will typically include:

1. Job(s) being treated

2. Input needs, including formatting and error-assist

3. File access in relation to the physical media used and the logical supports

4. Logical capabilities including those relating to DBMS

5. Output characteristics and related issues (time for output and buffering)

6. Remote versus local access and chosen communications protocols

These are examples of fine tuning. They are not the only ones to take notice of. We explained how prototyping can be accomplished through 4GLs. This is a first-class example of what can be achieved by putting imagination into action and using spreadsheets and integrated software as the tools. The resulting code is structured, but the development of a new procedure is laissez faire, with the advantage of a computer-run verification practically done in realtime.

With approaches followed to the mid-1980s—including structured programs, structured analysis, and pseudocode—every development phase has been distinct. To develop a complete procedure, we had to:

- Return to point zero and start all over
- Create extensive files, often manual, for documentation
- Update the files as new developments come along

All this radically changes with 4GLs, and spreadsheets and Isoft are specific examples for management applications. Said a senior MIS/DP executive:

> With prototyping, we got an order-of-magnitude improvement in project development over Cobol. A much higher ratio was obtained at the program development level alone.

Said another MIS/DP manager:

> When we go from prototyping to production, we must do tuning. Some 10 percent of the functions can consume 90 percent of the cycles. These must be optimized.

Such optimizations are beyond the capacities of end users, but computer professionals should become versatile with them. When, through integrated software, the user has played a role, the time has come for the professional to formalize the relations, manage the information elements, and improve the response time. The program may consist of spreadsheet usage, DBMS-type operations, and macrocommands, but the person who has a problem to solve does not care about that. What matters to the user is the assurance of computer assistance, improved productivity, and the availability of decision supports.

WORKSTATIONS AND THEIR SOFTWARE

We have seen that tools should be evaluated within the context in which they are applied and used. The spreadsheet and Isoft environment is that of personal computing done at intelligent, programmable workstations. It is correct to distinguish between a logical and a physical workstation. The physical WS:

- Has a visual display unit
- Contains a single-board computer dedicated to the application being executed by the user
- Includes disk storage
- Incorporates communications devices and other I/O media

The logical WS provides:

- The addresses of all input
- Local storage (microfiles)
- Personal computing routines
- Output operations

Together the logical and physical characteristics define the functions a WS can support. Database languages, spreadsheets, and packages producing everything from financial planning to color graphics have given functionality an entirely new definition. The workstation has become much more than at-hand electronics.

Let's return to fundamentals. Executives often get where they are because of their analytical abilities, but on the job they rarely use those abilities because they lack the right tools. This is the number 1 issue to keep in mind when we talk of workstations. Analytical capability is served through personal computing. As I will never tire of repeating, *the most important thing is communications; the next most important thing is databasing.* Then comes presentation, and only then computing per se.

The service the logical and physical WS provides its user must be in direct relation to the job being performed. Here is where spreadsheets and integrated software display their versatility. Each function imposes different demands on:

1. *Information exchange*
2. *Interaction rate*
3. *Internal processing*

The power of Isoft and spreadsheets is that they are easily adaptable to the job to be done. This advances the principle that a professional workstation must be used to improve the efficiency by which data is collected, processed, presented. What is missing is the right image of how to exploit the tools in our hands. It would be an easy job to rid ourselves of the bad practices of 30 years, but we must now learn *to program the devices not on the basis of their functionality, but on the basis of the functionality of the applications we expect from the devices.*

Horizontal software and applications programs should be retained on hard disk and loaded to the central memory when called up by the user. They should then execute under a single OS in the workstation. The concept of concurrent operation allows simultaneous input, storage, processing, and output. The requirements which we place on interactive intelligent workstations can be put in four short phrases all of which are logical, not physical, in nature:

1. Software and hardware tools permitting the execution of all phases of the work
2. Proper definition of jobs: managers, professionals, secretaries, clerks
3. Clear ideas about productivity goals
4. Integration of text and data resources

The use of logical supports specifies responsibilities. Figure 6.1 suggests a certain sharing of those responsibilities by the producer and the consumer. In a physical sense, the machine comes with certain features. The user has a take it or leave it option. This should be conditioned not only by hardware features but also by logical considerations.

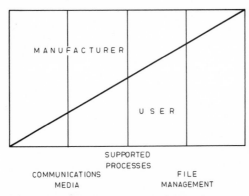

Figure 6.1 Sharing of responsibilities by manufacturer and user in terms of communications media (SW, HW), supported processes, and file management.

Communications media, for instance, are more the vendor's responsibility than the user's. The vendor should support the established protocols, whether through standards organizations or de facto (usually IBM's lead). The user should choose among the protocols. I see processes supported on the WS, from OS to Isoft and applications programs, as a 50-50 business between the vendor and the user. The issues are interrelated.

As has often been said, a commodity OS should be vastly preferable to the vendor's own version of operating system. It is a matter of respect for the clientele, and also makes good business sense, because it enhances portability. As cannot too often be repeated, the options are:

- CP/M-80 for 8-bit machines
- MS-DOS for 16-bit machines
- Unix for 16- and 32-bit machines and particularly for supermicros

The other pillar of supported processes is integrated software. In the following sections we will examine in some detail a few of the better commodity offerings in horizontal software.

When we talk of file management, the manufacturer's responsibility is rather reduced, but it is entirely his responsibility to assure standard format and compatibility. Unfortunately, it is not always met. There is, for instance, a computer manufacturer who built and marketed two products: A Unix-based supermicro (made in the United States) and a PC (made by his factory in Germany but under an American project team). Both use $5\,^1/_4$-in floppy disks. Yet the diskettes are incompatible; they cannot be interchanged. That goes beyond lack of coordination. It is irresponsibility.

But how the information elements will be organized, the files structured, and the database integrated and then partitioned and distributed is *the user's prerogative—and entirely his responsibility*. The vendor cannot and should not enter into the user's own management accounting process: neither in the structure of the general ledger nor in the distribution of the information elements in the divisional databases (Figure 6.2).

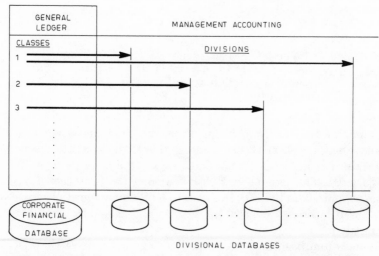

Figure 6.2 Accounting processes should provide automatic correspondence between classes in the general ledger and those in the divisional databases.

Not only should the user be looking after this subject but also the quality of the work being done will define how well the application goes. It makes little sense to choose the best integrated software if our files are in a messy form. In this as in all other cases involving human ingenuity and intelligent work, throwing money at the problem will not solve the problem. It will only make things worse.

A COMPARATIVE EVALUATION
OF "SPREADSHEETS PLUS"

With a myriad of commodity offerings among software companies in the spreadsheet market, it is only to be expected that some are doing better than others. So far we have considered only Lotus 1-2-3 and Symphony. It is reasonable to at least mention some of the competitors.

VisiCalc, so far, has had more than two dozen clones, one of the best being Microsoft's Multiplan. Like every other spreadsheet, Multiplan is organized as a grid of columns and rows. The user can scroll the window of 7 columns by 20 rows in all four directions to look at any part of the worksheet, which can be as large as 63 columns wide by 255 rows long. (We will look at spreadsheet specifications at the end of this section.) The user can automatically link the calls created at the row and column intersection, accept data from or feed information into other worksheets, and vary the column to accommodate longer words or numbers in one column and shorter ones in the next.

Like the other spreadsheets, Multiplan accepts lines of text, such as titles, across several columns, but, again like other spreadsheets, it originally did not accommodate graphics, WP, or windows. These were introduced by Microsoft in later versions.

Visicorp, which originally marketed Bricklin's VisiCalc, has marketed a new version, VisiCalc IV. It presents significant improvements over the original release, but it still does not support some of the most advanced features currently featured by spreadsheets such as help screen, calendar mathematics, block copies, and saving and loading of partial spreadsheets.

Many of the improvements, of course, have come with integrated software; we saw them in the discussion of Lotus 1-2-3. We have seen too how this 1983 product is a true first-generation integrated software in a product line in steady development. (As stated, a year after its original introduction to the market Symphony was announced as second-generation Isoft with significant enhancements, particularly in DBMS programming capabilities and new functions added to the package.)

SuperCalc 3, from Sorcim, is an expanded, reasonably enhanced version of an earlier spreadsheet program. It includes database management commands and provides for file exchange, but not in the fully integrated fashion of the other two offerings mentioned.

Series One Plus, from Executec, and KeepIt (the core module of the IT program series, from ITSoftware), are aggregates of basically free-standing programs. A system command structure has been developed to tie the aggregates together. The spreadsheet module of ITSoftware's series is CalcIt. It is distinguished, among other programs, by its building spreadsheets not only in rows and columns but also in pages.

Table Maker (T/Maker, by the T/Maker Company) was originally designed for CP/M-80 operating systems, and it was one of the first multifunction programs. T/Maker II, released in 1981, was an improved version. T/Maker III is the latest edition; it runs on both CP/M and MS-DOS; The object of T/Maker III is the creation of documents in which text, numerical tables, and graphs are integrated. It edits texts in different ways and also offers sorting and counting capabilities associated with database management facilities.

One of the advantages of T/Maker III lies in its ability to create data masks showing where numbers are to be placed in the spreadsheet. It extracts numbers from files and enters them in designated locations in a table. This function of the data masks can be useful for capturing numbers received from interactive programs.

TK! Solver (by Software Arts) disposes of a multitude of arithmetic and trigonometric functions, which can be used anywhere on the worksheet. It also includes an extensive set of functions for operating on numeric and string data:

- For numeric functions: square root, random number generation, exponentiation, logarithms
- For string manipulation: case conversion, substring manipulations, and so on

An application in which I participated with Software Arts involved seven different key variables to be combined in the study of engineering alternatives in motor design, including rotation in cycles per minute, speed, gasoline consumption, effects on steering capability, and skidding from applying the brakes on a wet surface.

Another application that demonstrated the versatility of integrated software centered on a banking environment involving loan preparation, modeling for experimentation, amortization schedules, loan control, follow-up on client repayment, form printing and reporting, and transmission to a host computer. Still another example of easy implementation comes from manufacturing operations: inventory control to calculate materials requirements in advance and the ability to perform different analyses interactively.

These examples help demonstrate that commodity offerings in horizontal software are available at various levels of sophistication in terms of database management, facilities supported, and file integration. The more advanced offerings involve four programs operating under a common command structure:

1. A calc program

2. A graphics program

3. A word processor

4. A database program

That evolution has been primarily characterized by database facilities built on top of a spreadsheet. This type of system has become an excellent tutorial aid in leading the nonprofessional user into the running of user-devised programs. But what is the range over which the capabilities supported by such commodity offerings can vary?

The answer is the wide range specified in Table 6.1. Ten criteria have been used: basic spreadsheet characteristics, central memory capacity, display, user-friendly features, worksheet format, cell formatting, built-in functions, database functionality, saving and loading files, graphics functions.

COMPETITIVE CAPABILITIES AT THE ISOFT LEVEL

The wide range of functionality among the 10 criteria outlined in Table 6.1 is more applicable to integrated software than to spreadsheets. The latter are a subset of the former, but it is appropriate to add some information on competitive offerings at the Isoft level. Not only functionality but also prices spread over a wide range. Though most new and revamped horizontal software packages make claims about a relational database, in reality the features that are supported range from simple file management to certain basic relational notions.

Relational databases are a relatively new development in a chronological sequence including hierarchical and networking solutions. The able handling of the tabular form, linkages, and associated characteristics implied in relational databases calls for significant computer power not always found at the PC level.

Nor is it necessary to have a fully relational database for the spreadsheet. The database management commands needed for arithmetic or

Table 6.1 Facilities Supported by Spreadsheets

Basic spreadsheet characteristics
1. Maximum usable memory
2. Number of rows (254, 2049)
3. Number of columns (63, 256)
   Automatic column spillover
4. Number of usable cells with 192-Kbyte memory (2000, 5000)
5. Maximum capacity of cell characters (116, 255)

Central memory capacity
1. Minimum required memory (64, 192 Kbytes)

Display characteristics
1. Use color for cells
2. Numeric precision to right of decimal (15, 16)

User-friendly features
1. On-screen help
2. Disk changing required

Worksheet formatting
1. Number of windows (2)
2. Column widths:
   • Individually adjustable
   • Minimum/maximum width (0/127, 1/32)
3. Border display on/off option (screen)
4. User-defined format tables
5. Maximum length of formula (116, 150)
6. Global command for display of formulas in cells

Cell formatting
1. Floating dollar sign ($)
2. Commas in numbers
3. Exponential
4. Percentage
5. Negatives in parentheses
6. Varying decimal places
7. Scaling factor
8. Formatting zeros as blanks
9. Hidden cells

Built-in functions
1. Mathematical
   • Basic four (+, −, *, /)
   • Sum
   • Round
   • Integer
   • Natural logarithm
   • Logarithm
   • Exponential
   • Square root
   • Module

Table 6.1   Facilities Supported by Spreadsheets
(*Continued*)

---

* Absolute value
* Power (X to the Y)
2. Financial
   * Net present value
   * Future value
   * Payment
   * Internal rate of return
3. Date Arithmetic
   * Specified date
   * Today
   * Year
   * Month
   * Day
   * Julian date

Database Functions
1. Internal to spreadsheet
2. Sorting
   * Numeric
   * Alphabetic
   * Dictionary sort
   * Single key
   * Multiple key
3. Criteria Operations
   * Number of criteria
   * Find
   * Extract
   * Selective extract

Saving and loading files
1. Automatic recalculation of load
2. Partial load
3. Partial save
4. Import files from other programs
5. Save to text file
6. Save to communicate file
   * DIF
7. Quit to another program

Graphics functions
1. Requires color/graphics adapter to view graph
2. Uses up to XX colors
3. Displays all graphs in color
4. Types of charts
   * Area
   * High-low-close
   * Exploding pie
   * Pie chart

Table 6.1   Facilities Supported by Spreadsheets
(*Continued*)

- Solid-colored pie
- Colored outlined pie
- Single-color outlined pie
- Cross-hatched pie
- Bar chart
- Outline for bar
- Outline for stacked bar
- Stacked bar
- Scatter
- Line
5. Graph positioning by quadrant
6. Interrupt plotting of graph
7. Number of variables per graph (7)
8. Independent fonts for
   - Main heading
   - Subheading
   - X-axis heading
   - Y-axis heading
   - Time labels
   - Variable labels
   - Point labels
9. User formats axis headings
10. User formats
    - Point variables
    - Time variables
    - Label variables
    - Percent variables
11. Coloring technique
    - Vertical pen movement
    - Horizontal pen movement

---

logical operations on fields are relatively easy when only calc functions are considered. At the same time, machine limitations should be accounted for.

Lotus 1-2-3, for example, limits the number of records to about 3000. That is enough for most personal applications, but for others it may be inadequate. On the other hand, keeping the entire database in memory results in very fast sorts and other data-handling functions. Another view is that a DBMS built into a spreadsheet should be balanced against what a spreadsheet is expected to do. Most commercial offerings take account of that fact.

The object of Isoft is to support integrated functions such as spreadsheets, graphics, word processing, calendaring, and data communications. It is therefore correct to cut database management off at a level that offers the assistance necessary for the performance of what has been outlined without overburdening the system.

Database management functionality should see to it that each module is able to communicate with the other modules without delays or conversion problems. System commands should provide effective passage of information from one module to another. Converting data in a tabular form to a graph is an example. System commands should be easy to execute and be specific to the function, no matter to which module they belong. This is a requirement which was practically never met with mainframe software, which has rarely been integrated.

Nor should we forget that, although it is true that the personal computer puts a limit on the number of records which can be handled at the same time, a mainframe is totally inadequate to process spreadsheet-type applications. Typically, spreadsheets work through iterations, and that process consumes so much computer power that it monopolizes the CPU and creates a lack of machine cycles for other users who are online. As a result, response time increases to unacceptable levels. In fact, one of the major advantages personal computers have brought to data processing is *a fast response time for each end user, which cannot be supported by dumb terminals under increased load conditions no matter how powerful the mainframe's CPU is.*

To appreciate the range of services supported by PCs at the personal workstation level, let's go through a comprehensive list of what is offered by the CA-Executive (by Computer Associates). This Isoft requires at least 256 Kbytes of main memory, and the programs work best with 512 Kbytes. The package comprises eight integrated programs:

1. CA-Link ties a PC to a mainframe or other PC running the same package. This communications approach permits downloading and uploading data, as well as emulating a 3270 terminal.

2. CA-DBMS is a relational database management system that includes a report writer.

3. CA-Writer is a word-processing package, including spelling and electronic mail.

4. CA-Calc is an electronic spreadsheet.

5. CA-Edit is a full-screen text editor that lets users create and edit files and programs.

6. CA-Form is a forms generator.

7. CA-Graph generates bar and pie charts and line graphs and handles composite reports.

8. CA-Tutor is an online tutorial program.

Each of these components makes use of a window manager, with commands entered through a keyboard or mouse.

Another of the competitive products at the Isoft level is the Knowledgeman (by MicroDatabase Systems). It is offered by the same people who introduced MDBS—for its time the most complete DBMS for personal computers. The Knowledgeman incorporates the capabilities of the original DBMS but adds an impressive functionality to be found in integrated software developments. (It is said that, sensing the need for a personal computer connection, Cullinet went to MicroDatabase Systems and licensed its Knowledgeman relational query software for PCs.)

The Metafile (by Sensor-Based Systems) is another package that integrates database management functionality with text processing and mathematical operations. It offers both menus and direct access to files bypassing menus. It also permits the user to create more than one database of size and number appropriate to the application and the amount of central memory available.

Three different kinds of data can be entered: alphanumeric, numeric, and date. The user describes the records contained in the database. The fields in a record can have their attributes defined: name, type, length, position, default value, range, input and output patterns, and comments. Metafile allows the user to qualify records for creating reports and browsing. The records can be called up selectively according to the user's criteria. Programming can be done with the Metafile language, which is a 4GL, and also with lower-level supported languages such as Basic and Fortran. It is also possible to set up windows for input and output.

Still another Isoft product is Decision Manager (from Peachtree/Management Sciences of America). The same software house offers Peachtree 5000, which is also integrated; it is a package of word processing, spelling verifier, and so forth, plus spreadsheet. From the same source comes the Home Library, a collection of seven disparate home-oriented products: accounting, word processing, education, and games.

These are only a sample of competitive offerings. Their brief description brings two things into perspective: first, the impressive array of supported functions and, second, a fairly large range of functionality. Selection must fit the user's needs in a factual and documented sense.

7

GRAPHICS: THE MANAGERS' SHORTHAND

Single-chip graphics display processors and the low cost of memory have been instrumental in expanding graphics opportunities and making graphics an integral part of many microcomputer applications. The growth of personal computer sales and workstation implementation ties in closely to commodity software for graphics. That is in marked contrast to minicomputers and mainframes, the graphics applications of which developed primarily in-house.

Graphics are very easy to use and require a minimum of keystrokes. At any time, the press of one key immediately initiates plotting to the screen or to the hardcopy device. In many instances, the horizontal and vertical coordinates are all the input needed to view a chart. Available graphics options include selectable typestyles (block, roman, italic, and script), horizontal grid lines, user-defined plotting colors, tick markers, point markers, and variable pen widths. In a business applications environment, graphics serve as the manager's shorthand—a personal memo with best remembrance probability.

Many companies started experimenting with graphs as part of a paper reduction program. Discussions and arguments on what reports to eliminate, shorten, and combine led ultimately to two questions:

1. How much information can be put on one sheet of paper?
2. What is the most effective way to catch the executive's attention and lead to action?

A large quantity of numbers can be crowded into a small space, but the result is not very legible. Worse, long tables hide rather than show the underlying relations among the data they include. Charts are therefore better than lists of figures. The old saying that a picture is worth 1000 words is well known. That it had not led to a wider use of graphics was due to the expense and time lag involved in charting through professional draftsmen in a specialized department.

Now personal computers have eliminated that disadvantage. Integrated software and other independent graphics packages bring the facility of charting to everybody's desk. The tools are there. The images must still be developed. A radical change is necessary *in the way we reason*. This would enhance decision-making capability. *Symbolic* rather than numerical operations characterize cognitive activities such as problem solving, forecasting and planning, and induction, deduction, and extrapolation. Graphics work in a symbolic manner.

WHAT IS MEANT BY COMPUTER GRAPHICS?

Computer graphics is the computer *synthesis* of pictures: generating charts and icons with the aid of a digital computer. In contrast, the *analysis* of natural pictures is called *computer image processing*. Though the two activities have many aspects in common, they are different disciplines and should be treated as such. Because of high-resolution graphics and visual thinking concepts, a three-way division is developing:

1. Charts
2. Complex graphics
3. Icons

Charts are of the bar, line, and pie type. They represent the more classical approach to management graphics, which, in a PC environment, is spreadsheet-oriented. A charting facility supported by a PC and Isoft usually handles format, origin point, access, labels, titles, legends, grids. Simple graphs (charts) are histograms, Gantt charts, time series, and pie charts. They can be shown in two or three dimensions and in black and white or color.

Commodity software offerings include routines for color, straight lines, and crosshatch. Pie charts are available with up to *n* sections exploded at the user's request. Line graphs offer representation of data with points connected or disconnected. High-low graphs are typically used for stock market or similar reports. They might show the high, low, and closing points for a particular stock price during the day. XY graphs allow the plotting of one variable against another variable.

Integrated software acts as a fourth-generation language for graphics. It generates the graph chosen by the user from the graphics menu. With some offerings, for example, SuperCalc 3, once the graph appears on screen, it can be immediately updated when changes are made in spreadsheet data. In that way, the screen immediately reflects the data relations in the spreadsheet.

Graphics interfaces must be used for formatting purposes to pass data to the graphics module. Here a critical variable is whether one, a few, or most graphics packages are supported. Graphics modules, for example, are included in Lotus 1-2-3, Vision, MBA, BPS Business Graphics, Graphwriter, Grafox, Fast Graphs, Graph N' Calc, Chartman, and many other commodity offerings. But the quality of the image they provide is not only a software issue. As we will see in the appropriate section, it is closely related to hardware.

Hardware and software imply limits in graphical representation. Videotex, for example, is a graphics presentation means. The original videotex alphamosaics pose no problems in making histograms or bar charts, but they produce crude pie charts, diagonals, and curves. Charting, in other words, can have different levels of sophistication in presentation. The graphic sets of the videotex standard* adopted in February 1983 in Geneva, through an international accord, foresee alphageometric capabilities. Alphageometrics give a much finer picture than alphamosaics, and still better are the alphaphotographics.

How fine the picture quality on the video will be depends on two key factors:

1. The protocol being used, for instance, NA PLPS.

2. The pixel supported by the hardware. (We will define and discuss the *pixel* in the following section.)

The software can do part of the job of creating a quality presentation. The other part is done by the hardware on which the software runs. The pixel is not the only criterion. A second important one is *bit mapping*. It has to do with the ability designed into the hardware to address every pixel on the screen of the WS.

Something similar to what has been said about software and hardware acting together as the pillars of fine graphics is valid for color presentation also. This too has procedural aspects: Smart people who use color charts *standardize the color.*

---

*North American Presentation Level Protocol Syntax (NA PLPS).

In general, more complex computer graphics call for six basic components:

1. Greater computer power
2. Appropriate software
3. Proper resolution in output equipment
4. Needed input data
5. Able user interfaces
6. A training program able to change user images

Icons should be equated to complex graphics. I treat them as a separate class for two reasons: first, because *icon* shapes can be used as standard modules in visual thinking; second, because the able handling of icon interfaces calls for an appropriate query language. *Iconic interfaces* require graphic representations of office artifacts. Designing icons for action also involves bit-map display requirements.

Under current practices, the presentation of different sets of icons can vary widely. The challenge is how the population of users associates semantics with them. The best combination is the *simple icon*; the worst combinations are sophisticated designs (because of many errors) and designs including verbal descriptions (slow reaction by user). *Graphics tests* are necessary to measure the effectiveness of icons.

Display characteristics are another aspect of computer graphics implementation at workstation level. One of the important display characteristics is the ability to dissociate:

• The scratch pad function from menu selection
• Menu selection from reporting

An interesting possibility is the simultaneous presentation of tabular data and the corresponding graphs—a windowing function. Among the advantages of windowing are visual simultaneity and reduced desk space (smaller footprint).

Among display characteristics, smooth scrolling and lack of jittering are musts. That is true also of a 4GL to enable the end user to prepare his or her own visual shorthand; but as we have already said, Isoft provides that facility.

PIXEL, PEL, AND GRAPHICS

A *logical picture element* (PEL) is the geometric construct associated with the drawing point, and its size determines the stroke width of graphics primitives. A *physical picture element* (pixel) is the smallest displayable unit on a video device.

Screen resolution is expressed in pixels (dot matrix). A given screen supports n columns and m rows, for example, 640 by 400. To make text easily visible, we need 12 to 16 rows, including 3 pixels for spacing. Today, many window displays do not offer even the necessary minimal 16 by 24 = 384, or about 400 noninterlaced pixels per row.

For the column we need 5 to 7 pixels per character, plus 2 pixels for spacing. (Usually space is 15 percent of the width.) These are minimal requirements for good legibility.

As for character design, the European Computer Manufacturers Association (ECMA) standard specifies that positive displays should use wider character stroke widths than negative-polarity displays. (Among other reasons, this is because the eye reacts primarily to luminance and emphasizes it through a process called lateral inhibition.) Furthermore, the character width should be between 70 and 80 percent of the character height. Unless proportional spacing is used, the minimum space between characters should be equal to one stroke width.

Small letters and narrow capital letters which do not fill the matrix will have correspondingly larger spaces between characters unless proportional spacing is used. The minimum space between lines should be equal to one-half of the character height; the preferred space is equal to the character height to take into account descenders of small letters and diacritical marks on capital letters.

The ECMA standard also suggests that character width and height should not vary by more than 10 percent over the entire display surface. The character shape or font appearance should not differ disturbingly from one character cell to another. Visible disturbances caused by single or multiple echoes in line direction (ghost images) are to be avoided, as are distortions of lines and columns. The perimeter line and column locations should not vary by more than 1 percent of the respective total display width or height. The observance of ergonomic and other standards should be built into system design from the drafting board up. Much needs also to be done on software.

Today's microcomputers are not projected to support in an effective manner the 640 by 400 (for 8 by 80 columns) or 720 by 400 (for 9 by 80 columns) necessary for good presentation. The same can be stated of the OS. By 1987 this will be changing radically. Although 1-megapixel screens were still expensive at the time of writing and were reserved for engineering workstations, the current forecasts indicated that by 1987 they would be part and parcel of the $5000 workstation for managerial and secretarial duties.

From a design standpoint, current practices tend to better the presentation of graphics by establishing a policy of dedicated microprocessors and software drivers. It is an almost sure bet that the graphics SW/HW will become generalized and integrated with arithmetic processors, main processor, and OS.

Also important is the support for international standards. The Videotex CEPT standard, for instance, recommends 20 lines by 40 characters of a 12- by 12-pixel matrix because it can be handled by the TV set. In observance of that standard printed-circuit boards (PCBs) which can go into one of the slots of a PC were in development at time of writing. Videotex CEPT is the European standard of the above-mentioned February 1983 international agreement, twin to the Videotex North American PLPS. Both are characterized by the following driver facilities.

A *picture description instruction* (PDI) constitutes an executable picture drawing or control command. It is composed of an OP code followed by one or more operands. The PDI includes:

- *Six geometric primitives*: point, line, arc, rectangle, polygon, incremental, each of which has four forms
- *Eight color codes*: reset, domain, text, texture, set color, wait, select color, and blink
- *Sixty-four character positions*

The PDI character set does not consist of predefined patterns, one per character; it consists of executable *drawing functions*.

The *dynamically redefinable character sets* (DRCS) allow the user to take advantage of the resolution capacity of the TV screen. A DRCS contains 96 custom-definable *text* characters, whose patterns can be downloaded from the host. These text characters are PEL patterns which, when called, are drawn with a set of preselected attributes at the screen. Their position is indicated by the cursor.

A *unit screen* represents the virtual display address space within which text characters are deposited and all PDIs are executed. Horizontal (X), vertical (Y), and depth (Z) dimensions are defined, the latter only in 3-D mode.

A *G-set* is a graphics set comprising up to 96 character positions arranged in 6 columns by 16 rows. With PLPS:

- Operation is in both 7- and 8-bit environments.
- ASCII alphanumerics, a set of supplementary graphics characters, and the DRCS are provided for the encoding text (Figures 7.1 to 7.3).
- Both alphamosaic and alphageometric primitives can be used to create graphic displays.

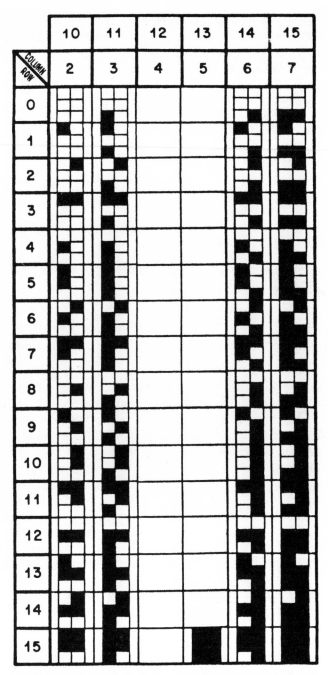

Figure 7.3 Mosaic graphics (for alphamosaic presentation).

A G-set repertory is the collection of available code sets subject to designation as one of the G-sets. A *geometric graphic primitive* is a locally stored picture-drawing algorithm that can be called through a specific opcode and associated operands.

The object of a *C-set* is control functions. With PLPS/CEPT there is a basic control sign inventory (C0) and an additional control sign list (C1). Supported services include:

- Format control
- Cursor and other machine controls
- Protocol handling (ACK, confirmation)
- Code extension (such as shift to change the meaning of a coming sign)

The protocols at the *presentation control* level belong to the sixth layer of ISO/OSI. The objects are to:

- Follow up on session establishing, maintaining, and terminating
- Request the creation of a process
- Notify a process upon receipt of data and thereby make data more understandable through segmenting, blocking, and so on
- Assure message management beyond the level of buffering and error controlling

If virtual terminals are used, the presentation level protocol(s) adapt(s) requests to the specific machinery at that location. If programs use local names, they translate them to a common reference, and vice versa. Finally, they provide for information enrichment, encrypting/decrypting, and compacting/decompacting. The NA PLPS protocol uses picture description instruction analogs to the *virtual device level interface* (VDI) output primitives of the ANSI standard, though they do not have the same syntax.

The ANSI VDI is important for *graphics portability*. Intel, Xerox, DEC, and DRI pledged their support for this graphics kernel standard. Digital Research implemented VDI in its GSX offering. A GSX standard may be implemented under Unix, which lacks graphics exchange. Among technical characteristics to be observed are the speed-of-display update, the role of the input/output devices, and the availability of reasonable computing power at the workbench. The speed-of-display update is critical because primary output device(s) will often be on the CPU bus. The role of input media is important because the typical user will employ graphics input for interaction.

The power of microprocessors is steadily increasing, and so the impact of computer power on future graphics development should not be a limiting factor. However, a large overhead of software systems is not acceptable at professional workstations.

THE MANAGER'S VIEW OF THE SYSTEM

As an end user, the manager will not necessarily be concerned with the technical details of pixel, PEL, NA PLPS, and the different graphics drivers. But like many end users today who program their own machines, the manager may wish to develop graphics through a 4GL. In that case, the preceding section becomes a prerequisite.

Managers do appreciate that a good chart can make complex relations much clearer than numbers presented in a tabular form. Inherently, graphics have much less ambiguity than tables. The eye and mind can more quickly visualize a trend in a chart than in a table full of columns and rows.

Banks were among the first to introduce computer-based charting into their daily operations. One of the earliest applications I saw was in a Forex room; it was provided (through a Micom switch) by a few Apple II computers in the online database access the dealers had available. The Apples supported charts, and they were in high demand for that reason. "The combination of charts gives us a concise overview of our business," a Forex executive commented. "We can easily compare two or three elements at the same time."

Graphs had previously been available through mainframes by use of Tell-a-Graph software, but taking them down to the Apple II level made the difference. The graphs were easy to update and be made promptly available merely by adding the latest points to the master.

This example is particularly important because, historically, the availability of good-resolution graphics on the Apple II provided the first high-volume color graphics system. To be sure, there have been many contributions in this field:

- Apple made available a portion of random access memory as a bit map for the video drivers.
- Atari designed special-purpose processors into the 400/800 computer that executed graphics display, listed instructions, created the video signal, and processed analog inputs.
- Other machines made limited graphics available through user-definable character blocks that were typically 8- by 8-pixel grids stored in a reserved portion of RAM for the video driver to access.
- Xerox Smalltalk technology made it feasible to manipulate text and graphics with a single kernel operation called bit block transfer

(BitBlt), performed by special-purpose hardware for high-speed combination of blocks of pixels into structures that make up a display.

- The IBM PC made available a bit map in RAM that can be configured for monochrome high resolution (640 by 200) or four-color medium-resolution (320 by 200).
- The IBM AT adopted the VDI standard.
- The NEC PD7220/Graphic Display Controller has been configured with four 1024- by 1024-pixel memory planes. It draws lines, arcs and circles, rectangles, and characters at the rate of 800 nsec/pixel and provides lightpen detect and zoom as well as pan.
- Quite important, Apple's Macintosh presented a dedicated 32-BPW architecture (16-bit external, 32-bit internal) based on the Motorola 68000 processor that made the handling of icons possible.

Indeed, to reduce the number of commands that a user must memorize and type into a computer to get it to work, Macintosh enables users to communicate with the machine through *icons* and *menus*. Macintosh replaces commands with an array of tiny icons such as a file folder to indicate filing. To tell the computer what to do, the user points to the appropriate picture on the screen by moving a pointing device such as a mouse over the desktop.

Options are presented by a *pulldown menu* which looks like a window shade over the upper-left quadrant of the screen. Macintosh shares icons and windows and has an upward compatibility with Lisa, its sister product. Visual interplay is the key concept behind this approach. Apple's engineers believe pictures are more quickly recognized than words, and Macintosh's bit-mapped graphics make black-and-white pictures quite appealing.

As graphics become more popular, their range of possible applications increases, as Figure 7.4 demonstrates. The actual use of graphics expands, and it extends from weapons systems to management decision making. The range of implementation steadily expands.

Software to drive graphics systems was originally developed on a machine-by-machine basis, but commodity-type graphics applications run on more than one machine. Interpreted basic with graphics features is available on a variety of equipment. Graphics subroutine libraries for compiled languages have appeared on the market. Transportability of applications to many systems without custom installation is one of the principal objectives of commodity graphics systems for PCs. The availability and observance of standards will be helpful in that direction.

Graphics standards activities at ANSI and ISO are providing a basis for machine independence in minicomputer and mainframe graphics

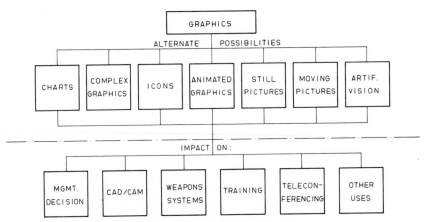

Figure 7.4   A range of possible graphics applications.

software. The ANSI Technical Committee has an active interest in co-operating with international efforts. The German graphic kernel system is expected to become an ISO standard.

For business applications at the workstation level, software support tends to include features beyond the popular chart types: text annotation, merger with WP, chart overlays, and series editing. In combination with menu commands, some offerings use a mouse to select menu items, place annotations, scroll plot windows, and so on. They facilitate an integrated applications environment by supporting transfer of data directly into graphs, rescale graphs to any window size automatically, permit scrolling of graphs within windows, and allow hardcopy preview. They also produce graphs to fit paper size, combine, for instance, up to four graphs per page and twelve series per graph, include format option sheets and thereby permit manual and automatic changes in the current graph, and contain help instructions to ensure ease of use.

The market for graphics applications is itself in full expansion. With only seven reference points (say, millions of dollars) in 1983, it grew almost fourfold in 1984 and is expected to reach up to 100 reference points in 1987 (Figure 7.5). (These estimates are from research by a computer manufacturer.) After 1987, graphics offerings are expected to be integrated with office automation (OA) products.

For greater efficiency, some graphics products are written in the microprocessor's assembly language to provide the highest possible screen support speed. Once they have been loaded, they attach themselves to the operating system and intercept the control codes that drive the high-resolution screen. In one graphics offering, the high-resolution screen consumes 40 Kbytes of RAM to provide the bit map for the

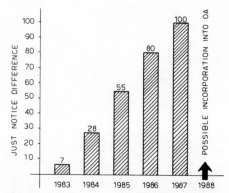

Figure 7.5 The market for graphics applications: installed base and new implementation.

320,000 pixels available on the screen. Each additional screen in memory will consume an additional 40 Kbytes. Screens can be stored on disk and retrieved under program control as required. Frequently used screens may be left in the system RAM to provide a faster display under program control.

Some graphics packages allow the user up to 10 different character sets of 128 characters each and up to 8 full screens. The exact number of screens available is determined by the amount of central memory. For example, in a system with 512 Kbytes, all 10 character sets and 8 screens may be used, leaving 128 Kbytes for program use.

Background screen support modes permit the loading or design of a high-resolution screen without a display on the video. This prevents operator fatigue while waiting for the screen to be drawn. Once the screen is completely drawn, it can be quickly displayed with one control sequence. A window technique allows the screen to be sectioned and supported in portions, which makes it possible for a text or graphic viewport to be created under program control.

By use of an escape character sequence, a program can control all aspects of the high-resolution screen. For instance, it could send a command to the graphics package to clear the screen and draw a line from the current cursor position to an absolute screen position. With that control sequence, the following can be accomplished:

- Circles
- Shading
- Arcs
- Windowing

- Dot-level addressing
- Cursor type selection
- Character set load

The width of the line and its attributes can be selected by following the proper sequence. Once completed, the screen can be saved to disk or output on the system printer.

Software for business graphics is typically menu-driven, and therefore no programming knowledge is necessary. Specific characteristics include the drawing of diagrams according to direct input data or files which have been created from other programs, the changing, completing, or rearranging of files with a built-in data editor, and the automatic calculating of all diagram details.

Examples of supported facilities are securing, editing, and printing of all diagram definitions, enriching the graphs with headlines and explanatory text, handling row and column tables, and providing for row and column arithmetic. Also supported are curve fitting (linear, exponential, geometric, and regression analysis) and data transformations.

Fourth-generation graphics languages are commercially available with:

- Built-in editor
- Calculation routines for diagram details
- Ability to output on one of three different graphics machines (screen, plotter, printer)
- Enrichment of the diagrams with headlines, dates, and explanatory text
- Scaling capabilities and division of axes of reference

The graphics wanted are defined by software in an interactive manner, the input being managed by functional commands. The result is available on the screen and can be changed any time. Since the graphics are stored in files, they are callable any time.

WINDOWS AND POINTING DEVICES

Graphics software should incorporate display windows, pointing devices, and bit-mapping facilities. A pointing device, such as a mouse, controls movement of data between several applications on the screen. Other graphic input means are the graphic tablet and the touch-sensitive screen. Choices must, of course, be made. At least one manufacturer decided against the touch-sensitive screen because of arm fatigue during extensive hours of use, easy dirtying of the screen face, and questionable accuracy because of alignment problems.

The track ball, popularly known as the mouse, is at present the favored device. Moving the mouse causes the cursor on the screen to move directly to the desired location. This is a simpler approach than pressing keys on a keyboard. The mouse does not present the problems of the touch-sensitive screen. It offers easier adaptability, but there are disadvantages too; for example, the mouse is on one side of the PC and the hands must also be on the keyboard.

From an applications view there are also limitations. The mouse is usable only as a relative pointing device. The big advantage of the graphic tablet is the much greater freedom it offers in allocation of functions. The use of a mouse as a pointing device is no cure-all solution to the input problem. It is most useful for spreadsheets and for anything relating to menus and windows. It is not recommended for heavy-duty word processing and precise graphics.

A somewhat more sophisticated track ball approach may be to include on the casing of the track ball up to three special keys: one to move the cursor, a second to do scrolling, a third to open windows on the softcopy. (Vision uses the first and the second keys; Lisa and Macintosh have only one key.)

Alternatives do exist. We can present the information through a graphic tablet. A graphic tablet entry is both faster and more accurate than the track ball. A graphic tablet (or graphic pad) is a printed-circuit board (PCB). Its elements have numeric codes defined by PCB records in the database design file. First appearing in computer-aided design (CAD), such pads provided user-friendly capabilities for:

- Scaling
- Rotating
- Zooming
- Volume accumulation
- Error message diagnostics
- Generally programmable formats

Graphics tablets now find a range of applications in management in connection with personal computers. They make feasible the elimination of keyboards and assure user-friendly reporting and input, provided the input can be fairly standardized. The limitation of the graphic tablet is that the work environment must be reasonably stable. For that reason the tablet is not a solution when there are highly variable professional requirements.

An operating system and its associated routines must also take care of such bread-and-butter items as the keyboard, which, as offered by many vendors, has limited possibilities. Pointing devices and prompts are two different concepts, but they do integrate in a number of activities. When equipped with the appropriate software, a display screen prompts the user for information. For all prompts, characters or signs entered by the user will trigger certain actions. These are the arrow keys, the function keys, some combinations of upper- and lowercase letters assigned special meaning at initialization, and the RETURN and ESCAPE keys.

Although the pointing device permits the user to command what is seen, managing the screen also demands windows for viewing applications. In turn, that brings up the need for window sizes, standard window formats, standard placement of help and menu facilities, and the ability to design new windows as the occasion demands.

Windows are independent format-handling devices which respond to standard input/output calls. They answer commands to manipulate such attributes as location, size, font usage, exposure, and keyboard status. Typically, a window is associated with the raster-scan device upon which it is displayed. It may or may not have a one-to-one relation with processes. Every window has an independent multifont map.

Window management makes feasible a distinction between *physical* and *logical windows*. A physical window displays one or more pages of a document which can be manipulated in a logical sense. A *page* may be defined as an area of specific length. Within this area there can be one or more subareas of fixed length. If there is never a partial subarea on any page, then the subareas are said to be blocked within each page. Otherwise, the subareas are unblocked. In a file, a disk block can therefore be thought of as a page containing logical records as its subareas. File access modules use commands to determine the position of pages and subpages.

Logical support should include a multiwindow manager able to:

1. *Scroll*:   Up, down, left, and right
2. *Command windows*:   Insert, delete, shrink, expand
3. *Turn pages*:   Next, previous, by one, two, three, or more steps

The latter makes it feasible to *browse* through documents. It helps in running menus, and it enables the handling of embedded applications.

A window attaches itself to a process group to which a signal is sent whenever the window:

- Changes size or location
- Becomes exposed or covered
- Gains or loses current keyboard window status

Only the user has control over the windows in the system, but a window can be manipulated by a process in its operations group or by a process with write permission on the window. All windows, upon creation, are entered in the file system as special character devices. In the directory they have filenames specified by their user-supplied labels.

A window is dynamic in that its location, size, exposure, and font map can be modified at any time under user or program control. When a window is created, it can be used in a variety of ways by the process that created it. When a window is covered, output to it can be saved in a buffer and displayed when the window becomes exposed again. A process will not be halted because it wants to output to a covered window.

With a multiwindow capability each program can handle its own window. As windows overlap (except in the filing approach), the one on the top is the active one. Window commands include open new window, switch windows, rearrange window, close window, file and print, learn, mark and transfer, install and set up, help, view, script, and exit.

Windows lead to the implementation of a simulated virtual memory environment that allows concurrent running of combinations of applications which would never fit into ordinary personal computers. User creation and control of windows is accomplished through a set of calls. They make it feasible for a user process (operator, machine, or program) to:

- Make and initialize a new window
- Draw or erase a window
- Insert a selected window
- Obtain the current state of a window
- Modify the current state of a selected window
- Select and manipulate the fonts utilized by a selected window
- Read the state of the mouse device in a selected window
- Obtain the current state of the display to which a given window belongs
- Switch keyboard input to a selected window

Windows may occupy independent and changeable rectangles of video-screen surface and may overlap each other. They help users move easily among spreadsheet, word processing, graphics, and other packages.

The evolution of screen design must be studied experimentally on the machine until a set of screens that satisfies user requirements is developed. The screen's convenience in use, format, and vocabulary must be tested. The user should experience immediate response from computer support, and the response must be understandable.

User friendliness is inherent clarity based on simplicity. The system must respond to the determination of the user's needs. This calls for an imaginative grasp of the problem; it begins with clear design and ends with clear documentation.

A DATABASE
LANGUAGE FOR PCS

Since data processing and word processing have merged and graphics and spreadsheets have come to the fore, a database programming language must serve all areas of interest. It should also provide an agile and secure means for interacting with the information stored in the computer.

DBMS languages like ISQL and DB2I are for mainframes; Ingres and Oracle are for supermicros. At the PC level there are other candidates. We have reviewed some of them, including Knowledgeman/MDBS and Metafile. Other examples are dBase II and dBase III. Originally projected for CP/M-80, dBase II is now available for many PCs and OSs as a fully implemented version. Used as a programming language, it not only improves productivity and ease of use but also helps in adapting the software environment to the particular needs of the user.

Announced by Ashton-Tate in mid-1984, dBase III offers greater functionality and simpler commands than dBase II. According to its designer and vendor, the new release can handle millions of records in the database and is essentially limited by the hardware and software features of the PC.

Among the advances over dBase II (which is treated in this chapter), dBase III handles, apart from the alphanumeric and numeric information, a *date* field which permits the execution of arithmetic calculations on chronological data. It also features a *memo* field that makes feasible the insertion of up to 4000 characters of text.

Another new facility is the *dBase Assistant*, a command with prompt and menu to guide new users in the most common applications of database manipulation. Also provided are function keys for color display and online help. These examples are typical of both the growing range of supported features with successive software releases and the user-friendly characteristics of programming through database languages.

The point has already been made that some DBMSs have become programming language products. Statistics can further substantiate that statement. A major German software distributor reports that, in the product line he offers:

- dBase II sells better than any other product, including traditional HLL compilers.
- dBase II sales amount to several hundred per month.
- Next to dBase II, the best-selling item is Multiplan.
- C Basic edges up as a classical programming language.
- Pascal comes right after C Basic.

Several factors may account for these statistics; for example, dBase II is in German and Multiplan is in English. The mainframe users don't know what a spreadsheet is, but many know the DBMS.

These observations may help explain dBase II popularity over Multiplan, but they don't answer the question: "Why are the sales of the classical languages lagging behind?" The real reason for this fact was given by one of the users: "There is no need to program the personal workstation the old way. The use of a database language is not just the best choice. It is the only wise one." Added to that is the fact that many management services—for which the PC will predominantly be used—have to do with file access and database handling, for example, query capabilities.

PROGRAMMING WITH A DBMS

Database management languages are complete, structured programming systems able to produce not only lines of code with greatly improved programmer productivity but also full documentation, which is often passed over in classical programming because of time pressure. It is quite important that the documentation is kept by the computer and is updated automatically by the machine when the programmer changes an instruction, redefines a table or alters its contents, or adds, modifies, or deletes any sorts of records handled by the language.

Indeed, other programmer productivity–oriented languages may be a vanishing species replaced by the database programming languages such as Ingres and dBase II. The latter offer increasingly similar capabilities, but the DBMS programming approaches are more fundamental. The new generation of DBMS query facilities is typically relational in nature. This generation can run on a variety of equipment from PCs to mainframes, although not necessarily with the same package structure or types of supported features.

The new DBMSs present a sophisticated command file and are reasonably fast. They can be looked at as the forerunners of a new species of operating systems which will integrate the classical monitor functions with databasing, query, and transaction processing. (The system is *transactional* if it guides the terminal and, through it, the end user. Query is typical of an *interactive* environment, in which the end user guides the system.)

In this type of support, the query features are simple but effective. Together with the command file capability, they turn the software into a powerful programming language. The user:

• Can create a menu

• Has the ability to write command files with conditional branching

• Can access any information element in the database without knowing its address

The experienced user has no need for a computer specialist to guide this work. The user can interact with the deliverable system through a scenario simulation and can also use various types of input as long as they are acceptable by the machine. This makes the DBMS and query system a powerful tool, though not necessarily as easy to use by nonprofessionals as the spreadsheet. The component parts of a structured query language are shown in Figure 8.1.

Database languages can also be used effectively to provide office automation features.

▪ *Calendar* is a program and a file.

The calendar function can be automatic or solicited. Routines can guide access to the appropriate database, provide authorization for reading and writing, and assure a journal as well as recovery and restart.

▪ *Electronic mail* is a way to send letters to mailboxes. It can be networked.

This service can extend over an impressive range depending on the sophistication of what is supported: from videotex to computer networking. Database-oriented programming languages can take care of mailboxes. Depending on the way they are used, they can be the springboard to a

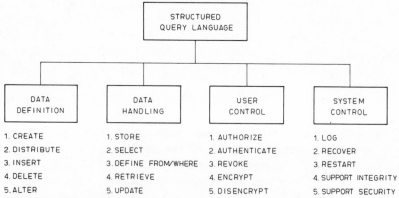

Figure 8.1 Component parts of a structured query language.

number of value-added services. For both calendar and Email, file saving and deleting are key necessities.

Facilities to be expected in the near future are voice mail and digitizer usage for teleconferencing. The latter involves a blackboard electronically connected to a communications device, a TV screen, and database access (Figure 8.2). Writing on the blackboard in one location shows on the TV screen in the other location. It can also register in the database—or access it for information enrichment.

Such applications are vital to the development of computers and communications. It is useless to spend time reinventing the wheel through classical programming when we can be helped through database languages—and are thereby able to invest human ingenuity in advanced implementations.

RELATIONAL DATABASE TECHNOLOGY

The details of relational database technology are beyond the scope of this book. The object of this discussion is to investigate the degree to which relational methods are now an influence on the PC level. Several factors are behind the adoption of relational technologies for software intended to equip the workstation. One of the most important is the premium placed on the ability to manage unforeseen changes in requirements.

Relational models are good at handling complex, dynamic data that has many interrelationships. Workstation equipment must further be able to handle data of a variety of basic types: formatted, unformatted, matrices, pictures, and digitized maps.

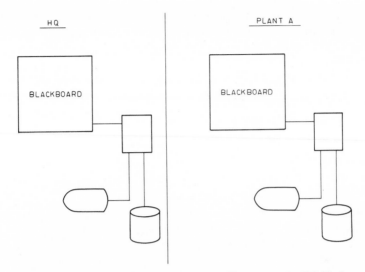

Figure 8.2 Teleconferencing arrangement. Writing on the HQ black-board appears on the plant A screen, and vice versa.

Basic approaches to man-information interaction tend to involve three levels of database activity:

- The highest is the external level. This is the data the applications program sees.
- The middle level is conceptual. The records are logical although the fields are the same as on the lower level, albeit without implementation signs.
- The lowest level is physical. This means the storage level, the way data is physically stored on a support medium.

The data model projected by an application and supported by a DBMS is the method by which data is structured and accessed. Relational models involve data structures and an access mechanism, along with the necessary linkages included in the finer programmatic interfaces. They also involve a set of integrity rules.

The structural part of a relational model consists of flat tables: The tuples represent rows; but there is no notion of one column (attribute) succeeding another, and the same thing is true of the rows. The linkages are provided by a collection of operators (commands) such as join and select. They are used to interconnect tables and thus derive, modify, or simply retrieve data from the tables.

Through the available commands the user specifies *what* the system is to do. Unlike classical procedural languages, the user does *not* say *how* the system should be doing it. In that way, database programming follows a nonprocedural approach. The more powerful the database language is, the better this nonprocedural approach can be followed and the greater the number of machine cycles it will consume.

The more sophisticated the database language, the better the user will be able, through English-like commands, to:

1. Add, delete, edit, display, and print data from the database.

2. Have a minimum of data duplication on file.

3. Gain a significant measure of program and data independence—so that when the user changes the programs it is not necessary to change the data—and vice versa.

4. Use a full-screen editing capability to set up screen formats.

5. Evaluate what will appear on the screen and enter data by simply filling in the blanks.

6. Generate reports from one or more databases, automatically.

7. Do multiplication, division, subtotals, totals, and other data manipulation every time it is needed.

This is a considerable evolution from the original DBMS concept, which began as a solution to specific access problems. The point, of course, is that only slowly were the common features recognized, a theory developed, and a nomenclature (often several nomenclatures) developed. (While the theory for central databases was not yet fully established, minis and micros arrived on the scene. At the same time, networking also was becoming widespread. Both smaller machines and networking influenced DBMS development.)

Today the polyvalent aspects of a micro-DBMS are so well recognized that it is projected that by 1987 there will be no PC sold without a DBMS routine. Most of the offerings will tend to be relational; eventually they will be cast in silicon.

dBASE II

In the way discussed in the preceding section, a relational system like dBase II can offer significant advantages to the user as well as flexibility in usage. Add-on programs are available; they enlarge the functionality through generators, menu guidance, and evaluation procedures.

Standard commands help the man-information communication in accessing and managing tables, change of data, and searching for established criteria. Operations such as the combination of several tables into a new table are some of the more than 50 commands available in dBase II. Daily use, however, requires very few commands. For example:

- [ ] = optional items
- < > = user-defined items
- ? <exp [,list]>
  Display the value of an expression.
- CREATE
  Make a new database.
- DO WHILE
  Standard while loop.
- EDIT
  Edit records in the database.
- FIND <key>
  Locate a record in an indexed database based upon key value (no quotes are needed for character keys).

Other database commands permit the user to:

- Input a character string from the console, no quotes
- Format console screen of printer output
- Add to a database from operator input or from file
- Make multiple changes to a database
- Copy data from a database to another file
- Create a new file whose records define the structure of the old file
- Create an index file for the database in use
- Add a new record to a database among other records
- Generate a database that is sorted on a field
- Modify a file directly, with screen editor included
- Write memory variables to a file for future use
- Generate a report

  With the command:
  CREATE <Filename>

dBase II asks for name, type, width, and length of field (decimal positions, if numeric). The total records may be 1000 characters in length. They can be divided into 32 fields. For over 1000 characters it is necessary to build a secondary data file to be joined to the primary file.

Once a data structure is created, the following command can be used:

```
INPUT DATA <A/N>
```

Alphanumeric (A/N) fields can have up to 256 characters; strictly numeric fields have only 10 characters. It seems possible to use A/N and hide the numeric characters.

After a file is built, it can be called by command

```
USE <filename>
```

With the command

```
LIST
```

all records in datafile can be displayed. The LIST command has many options.

The command to add new records to a file is

```
APPEND
```

To edit a record in a data file, use

```
EDIT <record number>
```

Edit subcommands are *mark for deletion* and *cancel edit*; with the latter, the system returns to normal dBase II mode.

```
DISPLAY <record number>
```

has the subcommands display all and display next *n*. To go to the next record, dBase II uses

```
SKIP (+ or - n)
```

To insert positions, use

```
INSERT
```

To show name of current record, use

```
? <fieldname>
```

To selectively use records from files, use

```
LIST for <criterion>
```

Criterion identifies specific conditions, for which the LIST command is used. This command offers a good possibility for selecting specific records.

To locate first record meeting specific criteria:

```
LOCATE FOR <criterion>
```

To count all records in the database meeting the given criteria, use

```
COUNT FOR <criterion>
```

To sum up references (or units) in the database, use

```
SUM <fieldname> FOR <criterion>
```

Another dBase II command,

```
REPORT FROM <report name>
```

calls into action an integrated report generator.

The interactive screen gives considerable freedom in defining the form of the report and also setting headings.

```
FIND <fieldname>
REPLACE <fieldname> WITH <expression>
```

For example, a given price can be replaced with a certain amount, such as a new price. With one command all the prices in a list can be adjusted.

All commands which are available serve in an interactive mode or for specialist programming except for

```
MODIFY COMMAND <filename>
SELECT PRIMARY/SECONDARY
```

With them, two files are open at the same time. For example, the primary database can be last name list; the secondary can be a location list.

To combine data files, all that is necessary is a common field in both files.

```
IF ... ENDIF
DO WHILE ... ENDDO
```

are used to program loops. Examples are

```
DO WHILE NOT EOT; DO WHILE n<10
```

Quite similarly,

```
DO CASE
   CASE <condition>
```

is very helpful in menu selection.

```
MODIFY STRUCTURE
```

allows the user to modify the content of the database and change names, types, and width.

COPY

permits the user to copy files, whether the whole file or part of it. It is possible to copy a given file from dBase II into an OS-compatible (CP/M, MS-DOS) format.

The summary of dBase II functions includes: #, record number function; *, delete record marker; EOF, end of file; &, macro substitution; ! <variable/string>, convert to upper case; and TYPE (<expression>), data-type function. Also included are integer function, string to integer, integer to string, string length, substring select, convert number to ASCII, and so on. dBase II can define up to 64 variables which can be transferred into another application environment through memory variables.

Some commands are alternatives. For instance, SORT and INDEX can index fields ascending or descending and thereby essentially create an index key. The procedure can automatically update up to seven files at the same time. INDEX is a faster process than SORT. How far this type of application can go depends on the supported facilities. dBase II specifications include:

- Records per database file, 65,535 max
- Characters per record, 1000 max
- Hence, dBase II can master 65 Mbytes of disk storage
- It is possible to spread files across multiple disks
- Fields per record, 32 max
- Characters per field, 254 max
- Largest number, $\pm 1.8 \times 10^{63}$ approx
- Smallest number, $\pm 1 \times 10^{-63}$ approx
- Numeric accuracy, 10 digits
- Character string length, 254 char. max
- Command line length, 254 char. max
- Report header length, 254 char. max
- Index key length, 100 char. max
- Expressions in SUM command, 5 max

dBase II is written in assembly language. It was specifically designed for microcomputer implementation. The original version was developed for 8-BPW machines (8080, 8085, or Z-80) and it required a 48-Kbyte-minimum memory. It worked with the CP/M (version 1.4 or 2.x), CDOS, OR CROMIX operating system, and it needed one or more mass storage devices (usually floppy disk drives). The newer version was designed for 16-BPW microprocessors and MS-DOS.

SOME APPLICATIONS EXAMPLES

Through easy-to-master English-language commands, the DBMS offers good possibilities of file and data treatment: capture, change, integration, sorting, merging, and searching. There is a built-in mask generator (currently only in 8-BPW version) that facilitates the development of templates and a report generator. The schema and content are defined in the documentation.

The user can bring up dBase II by typing ^dBASE^. A prompt line asks for the date. If the user enters a date, it will be recorded in the files as the last access every time there is an addition to or deletion from the file. It can also be useful for keeping track of updates.

dBase II loads into memory, displays a sign-on message, and shows the prompt dot (.) to indicate that it is ready to accept commands. Escapes from certain possibly long-running commands, such as DISPLAY, COUNT, DELETE, INPUT, LIST, LOCATE, RECALL, REPLACE, SKIP, and SUM, are done through ESC, which also serves as an escape from ACCEPT, INPUT, REPORT (dialog), and WAIT. In all cases, ESC returns control to the interactive monitor and displays a dot prompt.

When in a command file execution, the system checks for an ESC character before starting every command line. The escape capability can be disabled by the SET ESCAPE OFF command.

- *Lowercase* in the screen representations indicates material that the user types in.
- *Uppercase* indicates the dBase II prompts and responses.
- In text, uppercase is used for dBase II commands.
- [. . .] (square brackets) are used to indicate parts of a dBase II command that are optional.
- < . . . > (angle brackets) indicate portions of a dBase II command that are to be filled in with real information.
- < . . . > (angle brackets) are also used in text to bracket field names and file names.
- <enter> means press RETURN or ENTER key on the keyboard.
- ^. . .^ (circumflex accents) are used in screen representations if needed for clarity.

An application example is dBase II usage for internal correspondence. The data entry follows the sequence:

`Last name, first name, title, department, location`

Location is looked up in a location list to obtain the full address. The needed files reside on the same floppy. Every addition to the file updates the "last name" and other portions of the data.

There is also menu guidance that permits menu entry by end users, administrators, and application developers. It handles menu-driven forms and also provides access to other software functions. A valid approach to the use of this facility is the creation of a master menu frame exemplified in Figure 8.3. dBase II develops a menu and restricts the user on choices available on this menu.

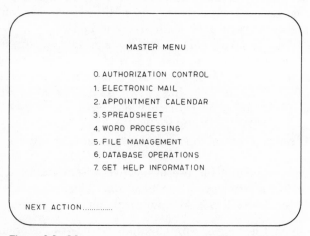

```
                        MASTER MENU

                    0. AUTHORIZATION CONTROL
                    1. ELECTRONIC MAIL
                    2. APPOINTMENT CALENDAR
                    3. SPREADSHEET
                    4. WORD PROCESSING
                    5. FILE MANAGEMENT
                    6. DATABASE OPERATIONS
                    7. GET HELP INFORMATION


        NEXT ACTION............
```

Figure 8.3 Master menu frame implemented by an electronic merge service.

When using a database language, the programmer has several degrees of freedom and can specify:

- *Fixed fields*, for instance, headings
- *Variable fields*, the actual values by column and row

In this sense, from an operational viewpoint a database language is different from the programming facilities offered through a spreadsheet. The latter make no distinction between the end user (operator) and the programmer, because the professional programmer in developing an application cannot specify what is fixed and what is variable.

A database language makes it possible to write programs with both:

- Database commands
- WP commands

They can not only coexist but also interleave. That is not possible with spreadsheets. But a database language also requires more skill in its use. Therefore, executives will rather go for spreadsheet-type applications because with them they can see immediate results. Stated differently, with a database language we must first create the file and then implement the function. Once that is done, the rest is easy.

Calendar-type applications, once programmed by a professional, become quite simple for the average user. They are also a good example of implementation. A typical calendar agenda to be developed through database language support is presented in Figure 8.4.

```
A - ABORT        F - FORMAT    M - MOVE CURSOR    S - SHUT FILE
B - ADD TEXT                   R - REPLACE        ? - HELP
C - DELETE TEXT
-----------------------------------------------------------
3/25    8:30 AM      ROOM 1      EXECUTIVE COMMITTEE
  "    10:00 AM      ROOM 5      STAFF MEETING
  "    12:30 PM      LUNCH       WITH BUSINESS PARTNERS
  "     3:00 PM    OWN OFFICE    WORK ON PROPOSALS

3/26    8:30 AM      ROOM 2      BUSINESS BRIEFING
  "     9:30 AM    OWN OFFICE    APPOINTMENT WITH MR. X
  "    10:30 AM      "    "          "         "  MR. Y


TYPE COMMAND:
```

Figure 8.4 Typical calendar agenda developed through database language support.

The user who is working with a single drive should employ the COPY or BACKUP command and follow the screen prompts. Backups are essential, and they should be made frequently. If the computer session is short, once a session may be enough; otherwise, it should be done much more frequently. A user can balance the cost of doing the backups versus the cost of losing the data. This cannot be overemphasized.

Let's also recall that dBase II is a low-cost even if a powerful enough system. As such, it does not pretend to offer facilities greater than those that can be supported on superminis and mainframes. dBase II is available for use with Unix. It is also possible to transfer Multiplan applications into the dBase system; but once defined, records and fields must be fixed in length. If variable records and fields are used, then it is necessary to convert to a fixed through a maximum length approach. This conversion is not difficult, but it poses limitations.

USING THE AVAILABLE FACILITY

As we have seen, dBase II restricts the operator but also distinguishes between end user and programmer. In the latter mode, we delete files, records, and fields and we can also restructure. As with every system, there are limitations. The fact that dBase II is for a single user is perfectly acceptable. Indeed, this feature is good, which cannot be said of another: that it operates without security routines for multiple users. As a result, there are possible risks when it runs in a LAN environment.

One of the negative features is that recovery is not provided by dBase II. Indeed, two of the basic differences from Ingres are that:

• dBase II is not designed for sensitive files; Ingres is.

• dBase II is a single-user DBMS and query; Ingres is multiuser.

It is, however, proper to add that some deficiencies can be overcome. For instance, to assure recovery, a manufacturer uses the dBase II feature of menu selection to force the program to have a backup. With that approach, the user can't take any data from the system unless a copy has been made. That is not a transaction level recovery, but it provides good guarantees.

One of the positive features is that all relational operations can be applied. There is no restriction on key-based searches; hence, there is no need to specify in the design the types of keys which will be subsequently used. Specification of data structures is done in dialog form with the computer. Since, as stated, dBase II has its own VHLL for programming, there is no need to use any other programming language.

We have reviewed some of the available instructions. It is important to recall that in a very high level (fourth-generation) language like dBase II some 50 basic HLL instructions can be replaced by one command. That, plus agile file manipulation, is behind the fact that some 3 worker-months of Cobol programming can be done in 1 worker-day with dBase II.

One example of programmer productivity with dBase II is a purchasing application that involved a main program and 20 subprograms. The total represented 70 percent of the manual work in a company's purchasing department. In all, it required 10 worker-days of dBase II programming. Management estimated that classical programming approaches, had they been followed, would have required 80 worker-days of system analysis and 200 worker-days of programming plus time for installing the system. Added to that would be the tremendous work in adjusting the main database to the application. Even without counting the latter, the difference is an impressive 1 to 38 in favor of dBase II. It's evidence that cannot be ignored.

A second example is an order-handling and statistics application that involved one main program and 15 subprograms including all report formats. The total time necessary with dBase II was 12 worker-days of work. The ratio to classical Cobol programming, management found, was 25 times more effort for the Cobol solution.

However, if the work had been done on the mainframe, it would have been necessary to work out a complicated access to the big database. That would have been so involved that it would have brought the ratio to double the estimated figure. There is also the structural delay aspect to be accounted for. It takes a few days to get an application on PC; it may take months or years to get something on a mainframe.

Another example of programmer productivity attained with dBase II is that it took the DP specialist one day to learn how to work with the system, and in that one day he also did an applications routine. Afterward he worked for 2 hours with the database languages to write the program. It consists of 40 lines of code. With Cobol, the specialist said he would have needed 400 lines of code. More important still:

- 400 lines of Cobol code, compiled, tested, and documented would have required at least 10 days work by a good programmer.
- The 40 lines of dBase II code were written in 2 hours after experience was acquired.
- The difference in productivity is 1 to 40.

Furthermore, add-ons can be easily implemented. In one application, data communication software was used to transfer from the central information files to the PC and for reporting purposes. This application was in a manufacturer's shipping department that was using dBase II and the Personal Computer Transfer System (PCTS).

Being a program and therefore a file, dBase II can be stored on the file server of a mainframe and downloaded to the workstations. However, if the applications programs are written in the dBase language, it is necessary to have the program at each WS in resident fashion.

Another add-on is the so-called dBase Window. It simplifies working with dBase II because it functions as a translator. The user informs the program what is wanted of the data, and the dBase Window transforms the request into a database language statement.

Among the dBase Window implementation characteristics it is notable that no prior knowledge of dBase II is necessary. The add-on guides the addition, change, search, finding, deletion, and printing of database sentences, and many functions which in dBase II are executed through several commands are carried without programming.

Supported functions can be integrated directly into existing user programs. The add-on is interactive; it makes feasible the interleaving of more than two databases (for instance, the report generator can exploit two databases simultaneously); and it assures control through passwords, thus complementing a function in which dBase II is rather weak.

Another product by the manufacturer of dBase II is *Friday*, which offers management-oriented query capabilities. This product is easier for use by the nonprofessional than dBase II. Its main purpose is custom-made reports, but it needs a whole floppy for storage.

9

PC LEVEL OSs:
MS-DOS AND CP/M

Each level of microcomputer has its own operating system (OS). As has already been mentioned, CP/M-80 is a first-class OS for an 8-bit microprocessor and Unix for the upper-level 16- and 32-bit machines. In between is situated the main market for MS-DOS. Processor power, central memory size, and functionality wanted by the user are behind this near specialization of commodity OSs for microcomputers.

Another way to make that statement is that, rather than be linked to the vendor's label on the machine, the market voted with dollars for some types of commodity operating systems. Let's also keep in mind that the 16-BPW machine is the typical PC-level choice for every executive desk. The 32-BPWs are coming. The greater number of bits per word provides greater microprocessor power and has a radical influence on both hardware and software design.

What are we going to do with more microprocessor power at the executive desk? To answer that question, we must look into the main trends in workstation design. Here is what the PC should be doing for the executive and the professional in the coming years:

1. *Multimedia support*

Traditionally, the computer service offered to the executive has been based on data; now we must integrate text and graphics. For graphics, we first think of ouput, but we should also look increasingly at input.

Image-processing capability and speech input/output will also be important. Another very vital issue is

2. *Communications, both local and long-haul*

The importance of machines able to communicate among themselves and with databases is becoming more evident every day. A basic ingredient of progress is shared information, and that is true of competitiveness also.

Decision support systems rest 90 percent on data and only 10 percent on mathematics. Valid, vital, actual data is distributed; computing is only a small part of the total. The really important issues are communications and databasing.

3. *Flexibility for expanding future requirements*

Requirements for more power, greater central memory, hard disk support, and the existence of communications as primitives are growing every day. The fact that technology can meet them at an increasing pace is the engine behind the acceleration in demand. Resolution, for instance, has become a key issue in handling data, text, and graphics in a nice way. Reasonable as it may look from the user's viewpoint, the request for higher resolution impacts on all the HW and SW components of the system.

4. *Software ergonomics*

Many issues come under this heading: the facility of use, the ability to learn the system easily, the support of help functions, and adaptability, and also consistency in design and security. The system should see to it that a small mistake by the user does not become a big disaster. This capability is software-based, and it consumes machine cycles.

"We buy software based on these considerations," said the senior executive of a PC vendor. "Companies like Microsoft and Visicorp have learned these principles and follow them." That should be true of the users also.

COMMODITY OPERATING SYSTEM: MS-DOS

Like all OS structures, those designed for PCs are basically monitor and control programs. They are bootstrapped from floppy disk and may reside on the same support or on hard disk. They also use the above-mentioned auxiliary memory for backup storage.

The functionality of a commodity operating system for personal computers sees to it that rapid access is provided to stored programs through a comprehensive file management package. Such a system:

- Supports named file structures
- Allows dynamic allocation of file space
- Provides for different types of accesses (random, sequential)

This file system will handle both data and programs—the latter in source and machine-executable form, depending on whether interpreter or compiler techniques are being followed.

The Microsoft Disk Operating System (MS-DOS) consists of three separate files:

- IO.SYS
- MS-DOS.SYS
- COMMAND.COM

The I/O module includes the primitive disk and character routines, reading and writing a physical sector, console input and output and status check, getting and setting both time and date, and tables which describe the disk format to the OS.

The MS-DOS.SYS includes the program interface, disk file manager, and character I/O handler.

- The program interface processes system calls.
- The file manager updates the directory and file allocation table whenever read, write, erase, open, close, or rename occurs.
- The character I/O handler retrieves or sends the requested number of characters.

COMMAND.COM interfaces between the user and the MS-DOS module. It has internal commands for file manipulation; it will load and run any external executable file or batch file when the file name is entered; and it is itself an executable file which may be replaced by a menu-driven command processor. Among the built-in commands are:

DIR	List directory contents.
REN	Rename files.
DEL	Delete files.
COPY	Copy or concatenate files.
TYPE	Display file on console.
DATE	Get and set current date.
TIME	Get and set current time.

MS-DOS is entirely in the microprocessor assembly language. This assures speed improvements over other operating systems. Furthermore, this OS uses 4-byte XENIX* operating system compatible logical pointers for files and disk capacity up to 1 Gbyte.

A small professional PC configuration and most home PCs will not use hard disks. Within a single floppy, the user of MS-DOS can have files with different logical record lengths. MS-DOS is also designed to block and unblock its own physical sectors. If the user opens a file with a logical record length other than the physical record length, MS-DOS recalls where the file ends, rather than round it to 128 bytes. A directory format can provide for duplicate allocation of information.

There is no need to log in floppy disks, as long as no file is currently open. This helps improve usability by single-disk system users. The OS also simplifies the I/O to different devices by assigning a reserved file name to each. File names are built in and are detected by the file system. Programs designed only for disk file I/O can have their input come from the console or their output sent to the printer.

MS-DOS also provides error recovery procedures. If a disk I/O operation cannot be completed successfully, the system will return an error message and then wait for the user to enter a response. Another feature is operation through a "template" in the input buffer. This template is simply the last input line entered and is used for editing purposes. The advantage is that a new line can be edited immediately and a command can be edited before retrying it in case of an error.

MS-DOS also assumes program relocatability. This is necessary because the microprocessor architecture (Intel 8088) limits each segment to 64 Kbytes and requires intersegment references to be fixed for a given load address.

Among the weaknesses of MS-DOS, the following are the more important.

1. When a file is printed in the background by using the spooler while data is handled on the screen in the foreground, data will be mixed.

This happens if we use only one printer and try to work with two types of information that can intermix.

2. MS Basic 86 and MS-DOS eat up about 64 Kbytes. Hence, the minimal configuration should be 128 Kbytes.

---

*The proprietary OS version of Unix by Microsoft.

The same difficulty is found with the macroassembler. Let's also keep in mind that MS-DOS cannot directly address more than xxx Kbytes* (see the Xenix reference).

3. A rather inconvenient way to back up the Winchester disk.

The backup utility requires a whole Winchester backup if selected storage is in excess of one floppy. This full backup in turn calls for 16 floppy disks.

It is, however, correct to add that for the IBM PC there is an IBM program permitting multivolume. This is one of the differences between MS-DOS and PC-DOS. The major one, however, is the proprietary ROM by IBM, particularly in regard to the hardware-dependent basic I/O system (BIOS).

4. No easy out-of-order indicator on input.

As a result, errors will be caught by sequence check, but overlays can happen if floppies are out of order. This does not apply when a DBMS—for example, dBase II—is used because backup is under database control. Besides, there are basic precautions the user himself should take, such as not removing a floppy when the file is not closed and the application is running.

Several of the most important precautionary steps have to do with interfacing: If we write any driver and do so according to MS conventions, we can use the mechanism (system driver) provided by MS-DOS. This means:

- Define a device header.

Pointers, interrupt routine, and device name are necessary and are very important for later access. Bits in the device header provide for the definition of standard input and output.

- Observe I/O controls.

These include transmission speed, parity, number of stop bits, internal or external clock, and so on. The user has to benefit by closely following the vendor's instructions on OS usage.

The utilities are fairly complete. In addition to COMMAND, the following is provided:

- CHKDSK

---

*Original versions were limited to 128 Kbytes; the rest was done through indirect addressing.

The utility checks and corrects the integrity of the disk directory and reports the amount of storage allocated and available.

- DCOPY, to format and copy diskettes
- EDLIN

The latter is a line-oriented text editor, including commands to insert, delete, and list lines and to make corrections within a line.

Global search and commands allow the user to confirm that the correct text string has been found before proceeding. By paging parts of the file in and out of memory, EDLIN can edit files of any size.

- FORMAT

The object is to format diskettes and optionally transfer the system tracks and COMMAND.

- RDCPM, to copy files from a CP/M format diskette
- SETIO

This sets and displays the logical to physical device assignments and, for example, allows output to the printer to be sent to the screen.

- UDCCALC, to permit a 10-key keypad to function as a calculator

Furthermore, during program development, the Microsoft linker can combine object modules from the Basic, Fortran and Pascal compilers and Macro 86, the macro assembler, into an executable module of up to six segments.

An MS-DOS multiwindowing capability has been available since the end of 1983. This is a Lisa type* but works faster than Lisa, which is rather slow. Release 3.0 is multitasking; it makes a user shell available to both Xenix and MS-DOS users. (Some Xenix-type calls have been supported with release 2.0.) It also requires another 10 Kbytes of central memory. Portability is enhanced through Xenix-type calls, which essentially means a user shell.

As for DBMSs working with MS-DOS, the market offerings look very similar. Many packages have been designed for both CP/M and MS-DOS environments.

- TIM runs on MS-DOS
- dBase II runs on both, but it was primarily designed for CP/M.

---

*The now discontinued line of Apple computers.

One should also take into account the fact that 16-BPW-designed applications are still maturing in the market.

CONTROL PROGRAM FOR MICROCOMPUTERS: CP/M

In spite of the provision of some first-class enhancements such as the VDI-compatible graphics kernel GSX for CP/M-86, the CP/M family had been fading away from the market. Then, in early 1984 came the announcement of the accord between AT&T and Digital Research to develop an applications library for Unix (which eventually would mean porting of a good deal of the rich CP/M library to Unix).

With this, the interest in the commodity products coming out of Digital Research revived. Besides, there are still a great many 8-BPW microcomputers around, many of them with limited central memory. For them CP/M is an interesting subject. Originally designed for 8-BPW personal computers, CP/M was the first OS made by a third party able to establish an industry standard. Its designer, Digital Research, projected a whole family out of this product which is now called CP/M-80. The list includes:

- CP/M-86, for 16-BPW machines
- Concurrent CP/M (CCP/M), for multitasking
- CPNET, as a networking OS
- MP/M, multiuser multitasking for 8 BPW
- MP/M-86, for multiuser multitasking with 16 BPW

CCP/M, for instance, is a single-user multitasking OS for 8086- or 8088-based PCs. The concurrency feature sees to it that it is not necessary to finish one job before starting another. That creates a relative multitasking environment that is particularly important if a PC is to handle data processing and data communications at the same time.

Personally, I would be cool toward MP/M. A multiuser environment is not to be implemented at the PC level. The PC is a one-user machine. Multiuser environments call for supermicros, preferably with 32 BPW, and for them Unix is by far a better choice.

CP/M is, however, more economical than other commodity OS offerings of central memory requirements. CP/M-80 requires about 12 Kbytes, but it also manages a maximum of 64 Kbytes. Another limitation is that, with CP/M-80, 8 Mbytes is the upper limit on disk. MS-DOS goes up to 1 Gbyte.

Organizationally, CP/M is composed of four parts:

- BIOS, the basic hardware-dependent I/O system
- BDOS, the basic disk operating system
- CCP, the console command processor
- TPA, the transient program area

BIOS assures the primitive operations necessary to access the disk drive or drives and interface standard peripherals such as video and printer. In other words, BIOS represents the physical portion of the operating system that contains the system-dependent input/output device handlers. BIOS defines the hardware environment in which CP/M is executing.

BDOS is the logical, invariant portion of the operating system. It performs system services such as managing disk directories and files. The object of BDOS is to provide disk management by controlling one or more disk drives containing independent file directories. It implements disk allocation and file construction while minimizing head movement across the disk during access.

This subsystem has entry points that include the following primitives which can be accessed by programming: *search* for a particular disk file by name, *open* a file for further operations, *close* a file after processing, *rename* a particular file, *write* a record to a particular file, and *select* a disk drive.

The CCP is a symbolic interface between the user's console and the remainder of the CP/M. It reads the console and processes commands, including listing the file directory, printing the contents of files, and controlling the operation of transient programs. Assembler, editors, and debuggers are examples of the latter. The CCP interfaces between the user and the operating system that executes the user's commands. It includes built-in commands: ERA (erase), DIR (directory), REN (rename), TYPE (display), and USER (set user number).

The TPA holds programs that are loaded from the disk under a CCP command. During program editing, the TPA holds the text editor machine code and data areas. Programs created under CP/M can be checked out by loading and executing them in the TPA. Once a user's program is loaded into the TPA, the CCP, BDOS, and BIOS areas can be used as the program's data area. A bootstrap loader is accessible whenever the BIOS portion is not overlaid.

CP/M-86 allows up to 128 Mbytes of online disk storage, multiple programs in memory, and a file structure compatible with CP/M-80 for 8 BPW. It manages noncontiguous memory areas for application programs. CP/M-86 files are completely compatible with the CP/M-80 and Z-80 versions. Commands such as DIR, TYPE, PIP, and STAT respond the same way in both CP/M-80 and CP/M-86. Calls for system services have the same function numbers. Application software on CP/M-80 must, however, be upgraded to run under CP/M-86. Assembly language programs will require recoding; higher-level language programs will recompile with some modification.

CP/M-86 can support up to 16 logical drives each containing up to 8 Mbytes of online storage. Any one file can reach the full drive size, with space dynamically allocated and released. Each device has a directory of file control blocks that map the physical locations of files on the disk. Disk definition tables in the BIOS translate logical drive, directory, and file structure to the physical characteristics of the disk.

By using a memory configuration table, CP/M-86 manages noncontiguous memory locations. It allows multiple programs to reside in memory simultaneously. A transient program can load additional programs for execution under its own control. The OS keeps track of the order in which programs are loaded. If an abort command is entered, execution of the program most recently activated is discontinued.

Language processors may specify up to eight independent program units. Each command (CMD) file has a file header that specifies the application's memory requirements for each independent unit. There are also minimum and maximum buffer sizes. CP/M-86 uses the header information to allocate memory for the program to be loaded. An executing program requests additional buffer space from the OS during processing.

For relocation purposes, dependence on absolute addresses has been minimized. CP/M-86 uses a reserved software interrupt for system entry. To make a call for system services, an application program need only place the required call parameters in the appropriate registers to execute the correct microprocessor instruction.

Control passes to the operating system, which performs the requested service and then returns control to the calling program. Among the utilities we distinguish the following:

- BOOTCOPY. Copies the system tracks from one diskette to another and is useful in creating new system floppies with empty directories.

- DCOPY. Copies the entire contents of one floppy onto another and formats the destination disk as it copies.

- ED. A text editor that allows creation and modification of ASCII files by using string substitution, string search, insert, delete, and block moves. ED permits text to be located by context, line number, or relative position. A macro makes test changes with a single operation line.

- FORMAT. Formats new floppies or disks for reuse.
- HELP. Displays the command syntax and options of the CP/M-86 commands and utilities.
- PIP. A peripheral interchange program that provides file transfer between devices and disk files. PIP also performs various reformatting and concatenation functions. Such options include parity-bit removal, case conversion, file validation, tab expansion, and line number generation.
- STAT. Alters and displays I/O device and file status including free-space computations, status of online diskettes, and physical-to-logical device assignment.
- SUBMIT. Allows the user to batch a parameterized group of CP/M-86 commands in a file, and then submit them to the OS, with a single command.

There are other add-on utilities, such as the Very Easy Graphic Application System (VEGAS) for business graphics. It supports the creation of line, bar, and pie charts and outputs them to a printer.

VEGAS works through menu selection, one of the options being data entry to create a new graph. Values are entered by row. There is, however, the limitation that no integer larger than 32768 can be entered, which basically means handling four-digit numbers. A menu provides the user with a choice of the type of graph wanted. When all the information is entered, or recovered from memory, pressing the RETURN key leads to the compilation and presentation of the chart.

DEVELOPING OS FUNCTIONALITY

To survive, a commodity offering needs steady development effort to back it up. Both CP/M and MS-DOS have had this development, but since the announcement of MS-DOS 3.0 has been delayed and this book cannot benefit from a description of its features, CP/M is used *as an example*.

First the bad news: Many problems of CP/M 2.2 have stemmed from the relatively barebone version that Digital Research provided to ensure portability. It was left to the individual hardware manufacturer to come up with operating systems enhancements, including user-friendly interfaces. And, as we will see in a Unix example, there are cases in which the HW manufacturer could not care less.

Eventually, Digital Research did come up with CP/M 3.0. This release has user-friendly features, including:

- Time and date stamps on files
- A help facility
- Prompts for each part of a system command
- File searchers that automatically extend over all disk drives

CP/M 2.2 lacks error recovery facilities; CP/M 3.0 provides not only automatic diskette log-in but also extended error recovery. CP/M 3.0 also has other improvements, such as multisector disk reads and writes and larger maximum file sizes.

Although the multitasking idea is powerful, it has made little progress. Because of the current level of software offering,* users find that rapid switching from one program to another emphasizes the inconsistencies in the interface—the way programs use:

- Screens
- Keyboards
- Commands
- Syntax

For example, the same key might save a file to disk in one program but erase a line in another.

Because of these shortcomings, concurrent CP/M has been designed with a *single-user* environment in mind. In contrast, MP/M (by the same software manufacturer) is addressed to multiuser applications. This point has already been mentioned.

Now let's look at the Digital Research releases of its commodity OS. The CP/M and related systems include:

- CP/M 1.4 and 2.2, CP/M Plus, and MP/M, and MP/M II
- CP/M-86, Concurrent CP/M-86, and CP/M-68K
- CP/M for other processors
- CPNET
- Graphics add-on

There are routines associated with the CP/M structure: IOBYTE assignments, CP/M disk format, and CP/M Memory Map. Quite important as well are the replacement user interfaces. For CP/M, they include:

- Taurus CP+
- Epic Computer Supervyz

---

*See also the discussion of the different versions of integrated software.

- Durant Software Simplifile
- Computing! CP/Power!
- The Information People Organizer
- KIAI Systems Okara
- Pluto Research Tools

In an effort to regain its lost market leadership, Digital Research has put emphasis on graphics supports—but only for 16-BPW machines, and initially only for the IBM PC. CP/M-86 incorporates a graphics kernel that:

- Takes standardized descriptions of graphics from the software
- Draws the corresponding image on the screen, within hardware capabilities

Also included are:

- The Graphics Package GSX
- Drivers for different types of printers

Although a multiuser environment on the same PC should be avoided, concurrent operations in terms of tasks serving the same user can present particular interest. CCP/M's advantage rests in its ability to manage concurrent processes simultaneously. This permits the user to run more than one *virtual console* in realtime. Such a facility is necessary at the advanced workstation to make it possible to use one's PC to write a letter on one video while the second shows the results of a query and the third shows a graphic presentation.

For *concurrent presentation* as contrasted to concurrent processing, the OS requires a multifunctional realtime monitor (RTM) for process dispatching. The dispatcher:

- Selects a waiting process of higher priority
- Suspends process in execution
- Traps the data
- Returns the suspended process when the CPU is available

The projected need for concurrent processing in the mid-1980s has induced Microsoft to release version 3.0 with concurrent features. Eventually, there will be a merger of the basic features of this OS with those of Xenix, the Microsoft-designed Unix choice. By this strategy the software manufacturer will avoid having to translate every horizontal or vertical software program for every OS which it supports. It will also open up a new avenue in operating system design.

Concurrency in information handling underscores the wisdom of incorporating a hard disk in the PC for program storage if not for data. This is further enhanced by the fact that one of the most significant effects of technological development has been the sharp cost reduction per bit of information on storage.

The effect has been to open new perspectives in the utilization of memory support in personal computing. Auxiliary storage devices for all types of computer gear can be classified into:

1. Hard disks

2. Add-on memories

3. Flexible disks

4. Magnetic tapes

5. Optical disks

The hard disk category can be subdivided into classes of rigid devices: fixed versus removable, large versus smaller capacity, classical versus supercompact. The most advanced in terms of low cost and low error rate tend to be the classical, very large capacity, Winchester type. Here the competition between American and Japanese companies is very tough. NEC claims to have achieved a bit error rate (BER) of 10^{-6} for the 3.5 Gbytes, and it projects the introduction of a 10^{-7} BER. Diameter is a basic parameter. 1982 was the year of $5^{1}/_{4}$ in, which is now subjected to fierce price competition. 1984 was the year of the under 4 in disk. Older dimensions are now represented by new families of storage devices with increased capabilities. For instance, the 14 in moves toward very high capacity and the 8 takes the place of the 14 in the "established" capacity market for minis and midis.

These developments may appear to be particularly HW-oriented and outside the scope of a discussion on OSs, but exactly the opposite is the case. The OSs should not only account, through native routines, for file management (Pick has an embedded DBMS layer) but also fit within a broader architecture of distributed databases.

THE PICK OPERATING SYSTEM

As stated in the Preface, Unix is the subject of a companion volume to the present one, but there are other commodity operating systems to be included in this discussion. For instance, SofTech Microsystems' p-System approach starts with the language choice. This operating system and its utilities are written in Pascal and translated into the binary machine code of a pseudo-machine from which the system gets its name. A p-machine emulator enables the system to be run on a variety of microcomputers. Sof Tech claims that portability is maintained at the object code level.

The p-System began gaining momentum in the 16-BPW arena in 1982, when IBM announced its availability on the PC and Displaywriter. It is said that IBM introduced the p-System for its PC as a means of luring Pascal-based applications from the Apple II computers already installed. However, although the p-System runs on 13 different processors, ranging from the Intel 8080 to Digital Equipment, there has been no rush to adopt it. If anything, it has lost momentum since 1982.

We should also take notice of other operating systems for PCs:

- Apple II DOS, Apple II ProDOS, Apple III SOS
- Radio Shack TRS-DOS
- Commodore DOS
- Phase One OASIS
- Alpha Micro AMOS
- Convergent Technologies
- FORTH, Inc. FORTH

But again there is no particular market trend toward any one of these OSs, although this or that installation may employ them.

The real market desire is for portability, and portability rests on two factors. Both are important because the bigger the population, the more portable the applications written on a given OS become. The two factors are:

1. The number of computers adopting the commodity OS and the number of installations employing it
2. The technical features of the commodity OS that determine its portability among microprocessors, BIOSs, and finally computers

Factor 2 is not an alternative to factor 1; it is a *basic supplement*. Both factors are determinants.

In a 1984 meeting with MCC it was stated that the two really portable OSs are CP/M and Pick. But the market support for CP/M is weakening and Pick never really got the momentum needed to become established. Yet it has first-class technical features. The Pick OS was first developed in the late 1960s, as an application package. Its designers were Dick Pick and Don Nelson. Its characteristic feature is natural-language storage and retrieval—within an environment dominated by project management and project accounting.

At the University of California, Irvine, this special software was redesigned and revamped into a generalized information retrieval system (GIRLS). It was also run on different mainframes: IBM, GE, and Xerox. In the early 1970s the whole system was once again rewritten, this time in microcode. It was streamlined and expanded to cover the whole range of OS functions. (DOS and CP/M are also written in microcode; Unix is in C.) The market to which Pick particularly appealed was the 16-BPW microprocessor.

The Pick operating system is multiuser, database management-oriented. It features a virtual disk approach and supplies a nonprocedural query language. Pick PS allows the operation of online terminals simultaneously, controls data access through a security system, records user name and date of access, permits concurrent processing of the same database, and permits records, fields, and subfields to be variable in length. It defines the information elements of the database by a data dictionary and assigns a user-oriented name to each information element.

Operating system security sees to it that there is an individually defined command file for each user. This allows sensitive commands to be restricted to privileged users. The security system also includes:

- A four-level hierarchical code stored in the user's log-on profile
- A set of passwords for both read and write access to further protect the database

Before read and write operations, the passwords being used are compared to passwords in the user's authorized command file. Multiuser access of the same file is coordinated through special system calls.

Pick works on virtual memory principles. It separates the low central memory into sections reserved for 512-byte *pages* and a table of *page addresses*. It keeps track of the pages most recently used and replaces the least-used pages with new ones when it runs out of space. This is the way virtual memory works: automatically changing storage for the user. Information is written in whichever storage medium is available. Track is kept by the system. Upon request, information is automatically retrieved and, if necessary, converted, formatted, and delivered to the process asking for it.

Each file is divided into two parts: First, the *dictionary* contains records describing the fields within the file. One record points to the location of the file in memory. Second, the information carrying files, records, and fields is variable in size and is addressed by unique, user-assigned names.

Pick uses ACCESS, a nonprocedural language processor. It allows the user to identify the data desired, and the system determines exactly how the data is to be extracted. If the syntax of the language processor is properly followed, the extracted data will be correct. ACCESS makes feasible data retrieval from one or more files based on selection criteria and relational operators. The latter may be described on an attribute-by-attribute basis. It also includes a number of extended functions such as sorting, counting, statistical analysis, and complex printout formatting.

PROC is a procedure processor that allows the creation of system commands which can then be invoked with a single name. Such stored procedures simplify system operation for the typical user, whose command vocabulary is tailored to the requirements of the application.

PROC also offers screen formatting, argument passing, keyboard data entry validation, and access to virtually all system programs including the editor and the database manager. An operating system EDITOR permits the online, interactive modification of database file items. The EDITOR can be used to create, modify, or delete records within any data file or data file dictionary, including BASIC source programs, and PROCS. It uses a current line concept: A field within a record can be listed, altered, or deleted or new information can be inserted at any point within a record at any time. Two other utilities are RUNOFF for text editing and JET for word processor.

Had PICK instead of Unix been adopted by the Department of Defense, it might have obtained the latter's prominence and market appeal today. That is not the case, and the reservations about PICK are in the commercial, marketing, and portability areas. Technically it is valid.

10

COMPETITIVE OS FEATURES

The basic operating system characteristics for PCs, MS-DOS, CP/M, and (to a lesser extent) Pick, have been described. Also identified were the available functionalities. Not yet brought into perspective are the competitive OS features and how they apply to the job at hand.

First the fundamentals. An operating system can be seen in either a limited perspective or a broader one. The more limited view covers only what an OS represented in the 1960s: monitor, input/output control, scheduler, and some drivers. The broader view includes those features and also DBMS transactional routines, system shells, and fourth-generation language capabilities.

Prior to a comparison of features and possible advantages of particular OSs, it is advisable to look at the features in common. In a generic sense, the way we look at them in the mid-1980s, they include:

1. Monitoring functions
2. Input/output control system
3. Scheduling of jobs and memory usage
4. New commands of all sorts, particularly graphics orientation
5. Systems calls
6. Library routines and utilities
7. Transactional programs
8. Protocols for file formats and conventions
9. File access

10. File management
11. Macro packages for specific applications areas
12. Maintenance procedures

System commands are programs to be invoked directly by the user. Subroutines are intended to be called up by the user's programs. Commands are generally mapped into a directory to be searched automatically by the command interpreter. System calls are entries into the supervisor. Each system call has one or more language interfaces. Subroutines are available in libraries, are callable by programs, and perform utility and/or generating functions. They also handle specific issues such as those related to I/O devices.

File formats and conventions reflect the structure of files, for example, the form of the output of the loader and assembler and storage and intermediate files. File access features are necessary for security and protection. File management routines might have been part of the reference to "others in the library," if it were not for the great importance of this subject. If it is projected to function as a DBMS also, an OS needs a rich repertoire of file management facilities.

Macro packages exist to extend a language's functionality and for special purposes, for example, typesetting. Maintenance procedures are not intended for the ordinary user. They often involve special commands, whereas an attempt has been made to single out peculiarly important maintenance characteristics.

Among the common characteristics of advanced commodity OSs is log-in. The user must call the operating system from an appropriate terminal and must also have a valid user name and procedures to specify log-out.

LAYERED OPERATING SYSTEMS

The levels of functionality described in the introduction to this chapter identify logical supports which can be organized nicely in a layered fashion. Eventually some of these routines will be converted into hardware and be replaced by others in response to the growing demand for new features.

The OS is no longer a monolithic structure; it is a flexible aggregate. OS functionality reflects the experience we have had over several decades with compilers, generators, and languages. The development of the latter is shown in Table 10.1.

The principle of the layered operating system offers a novel and efficient approach to the management of computers and communications.

Table 10.1 Compilers, Generators, Languages

1950s	ML to symbolic assembly languages Macros and open subroutines Flowmatic, Sōap, Sap, Fortran, Cobol, Algol Interpreters

1960s	Better-structured compilers APL, PL/1
	Among the new concepts in compiler design:
	  Fast vs. optimization
	  Edit vs. nonedit facilities
	  Run time vs. one-shot production of object code

1970s	Beginning of OS language association, Basic, Pascal, C Introduction of analysis-level languages First appearance of solid-state software
1980s	Language integration into OS shell Emphasis on program portability and robustness Very high level languages (Focus, etc.) Nonprogrammable computers Silicon software

The functions embedded in an OS can be partitioned into layers, each implementing a class of real or virtual facilities and managing:

1. Processes and jobs
2. Virtual memory
3. Text and data search and retrieval
4. Files and messages
5. Communications disciplines
6. Directories and definitions

In this way, programming languages, horizontal software, classical OSs, transactional routines, and database management systems will be merging into an aggregate. Care must be taken that the resulting system is user-friendly and surely leads toward open-ended approaches in integrated software evolution. Each layer must be implemented with interfaces both toward the lower-down level and the higher-up one. This principle is extendable to permit the design of cooperating processes within an integrated methodology.

Though the semantic gap from the outermost to the innermost layer may be great, that between any two successive levels is small. Each layer is characterized by a protocol, and many layers may be converted to firmware. The more a given layer takes a hardware form, the more effective the total system becomes and the more the system resembles an integrated DP/DB/DC machine. Fitting nicely within such an environment is the new family of two-level compilers which features:

1. A common front end for all compiled languages
2. A universal back-end module developed for each CPU

Typically, the front end is written in C and can be *rehosted* to other CPUs and other OSs. Its job is to convert the *syntactic* constructs of the user's source language into a common intermediate language. Such an approach was successfully used in 1955–1956 with Perlis' IT, and it was projected for Uncol. After that, it was forgotten.

The *back-end* module is able to emit native machine code. This solution makes it feasible for a user's application program to travel unhindered from PC to mainframe. Hence, it breaks down the classical maxi, midi, mini, and micro barriers.

The programming language best suited to the environment we have been discussing will be of the fifth generation (5GL) and will be designed to respond to the SW and HW features of the OS for which it was projected. Generic processors and solid-state software (SSS) will also bring the user another important benefit. With VHL, Cobol, Fortran, and the like, we experienced an uncontrollable explosion of programming languages. Cobol alone is said to have 250 dialects. Even ANSI Cobol is not the standard it is supposed to be. (In one project in the early 1970s, the cost of converting from Honeywell ANSI Cobol to IBM ANSI Cobol amounted to 30 percent of the original programming investment.)

With generic processors and solid-state software we can expect an implosion of languages and dialects (Figure 10.1). Front-end compilers should provide the needed infrastructure for this approach, which will eventually benefit both users and vendors, particularly the stronger vendors.

The way the working environment develops will influence future OS design and microprocessor-supported capabilities. Standards are welcome, even if norms may be slow in coming, because it is very difficult to qualify and quantify the factors which come into play in the total aggregate we have been considering.

The whole field of man-information interfaces is still in its infancy. Some evaluation work is now done through applied experimental psychology. One example is the Software Usability Test (SUT). After a battery of tests is established and gets industry acceptance, we can use statistical methods. (SUT was originally devised to help evaluate masks in data processing presentations.)

Adaptability of the hardware and software features has to do not only with ease of frame presentation but also with the structuring of

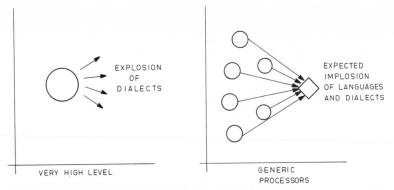

Figure 10.1 Expected implosion of languages and dialects.

the form itself. This is an issue that should be carefully considered in connection with 4GLs. It is also a sure prediction that the experience obtained during the next few years will find its way into the framing of the fifth-generation languages.

Let's recapitulate the notions discussed in this section. The first is the layered approach to OS design. The second is the advent of generic processors. The third refers to the fact that, by the end of this decade, we may be moving out of the plurality of the 4GL and into a 5GL perspective. This will feature a convergence of programming features and artificial intelligence orientation, as we will discuss in the following chapters on natural languages and expert systems.

Such an evolution will be the right follow-up to microprocessors getting more powerful and operating systems being increasingly cast in silicon. (As for the OS perspective alone, Intel is said to be working on such a solution for CP/M with its 80186 processor. For the 80286, Intel has developed its own Xenix and C.) Several approaches will stress interfacing. An example is the Universal Development Interface (UDI), a software bus (a group of specifications) to be observed by every language to be OS-independent. Figure 10.2 presents a layered approach: universal development interfaces (UDI), libraries, and OS. Above UDI it will be necessary to have end user interfaces—both for easy man-machine communication and for an increased resolution on the screen.

PROGRAMMING EXTENSIONS TO THE OS

Extensions to the OS are not only feasible but also necessary. The question is which way they should go. Taking as a point of reference the PC used to equip the interactive workstation, the de facto industry

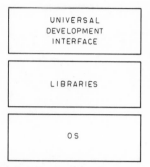

Figure 10.2 A layered approach to more powerful personal workstations.

standard has moved from single user, single task to single user, multitask. Programming extensions should evidently proceed that way, and we have spoken of data communication and databasing routines.

Another example of necessary OS extension is the construction of shells, both generic and specific, by projected applications area. Among the generic offerings, the best example is the Unix shell. The *shell** is a command processor with the ability to test the results of a preceding command and perform decisions like *execute* and *terminate*. Communication with Unix is carried on by the shell.

The shell also helps in multitasking. It has the ability to substitute parameters and construct argument lists. This makes it possible to execute commands conditionally on character string comparisons and on the existence of certain files. As an interpreter of Unix commands, the shell is often confused with the OS itself. Commands are sent by the user through a terminal, and the interpretation for the Unix-based system takes place with the expression of an execution command.

When a shell is started, it will automatically execute a file called Profile in the log-in directory. This contains initial commands the user may wish to have executed to establish a proper log-in environment and start working with Unix.

Rarely, if ever, does the interpreter of commands take part in the execution of what has been requested. Its job is that of an interface between the user and the OS. This gives the shell two basic characteristics:

• Handling the shell commands, which are very simple

• Providing interface support through interactive procedures

---

*This discussion focuses on generic characteristics and therefore does not distinguish between the Thompson, Mashey, Bourne, and Berkeley shells, and so on.

The user, having logged in successfully, may see a message specifying the arrival of mail or other news items. The Unix user can execute the Mail command to send mail to other users, read mail from the general mail file or from a saved mail file, and specify the Mail command disposition of a letter, such as deleting, forwarding, or saving. The user also has available a:

1. *Write* command to establish a one-way or two-way dialog with another user
2. MESO command to either permit or deny writing to the user's terminal
3. *News* command to read items from the system newsletter

If either the log-in or the password has been entered incorrectly, the user will receive a message which says *log-in incorrect*. This is followed by another line prompting reentering of the log-in name. The "log-in incorrect" message does not mean that the log-in was necessarily incorrect; it may mean that *either* the log-in name *or* the password was incorrect. Following some possible local messages, the user will receive a shell prompt. This may be $, %, or some other symbol or word.

All Unix versions implemented on different equipment *have the same kernel*, but they *may have unique shells* oriented to the *particular features* of the machines on which they run. This is very important because some operations reach the shell level, at which they are interpreted or modified prior to being presented to Unix. Although a major part of the inter-activity between processes is centered on the Unix shell, there are also references to the C language which should be clarified by studying the C language structure.

At the same time, the Unix shell is a fourth-generation language working as an add-on to the OS with interpreter functions. Programming through shell is a valid alternative to using the more conventional programming languages. Among the major advantages are:

- A very high level language approach
- Simplicity in usage
- Immediacy of results

Programming in shell is good for prototyping, not for run time routines and particularly not for interactive programs because of the high consumption of machine cycles. Programs executed by the shell work in a modular manner. They start with two files which have descriptors O and I. As the program begins execution, file I is opened for writing and file O starts off open for reading. In Unix, the lowest level of I/O provides no buffering. It is a direct entry into the OS. All I/O is done by these two functions: *read* and *write*—their first argument being a descriptor. The concept of a *pipe* was born out of this simple notation.

A different approach is taken with IBM's Advanced Development Facility (ADF). This is a superstructure to IMS/DB, DC and works as a precompiler. ADF modules permit the reading of messages from a terminal, the implementing of segment layout rules, the retrieval of segments from the database, the application of handling rules, the updating of information elements in the database, the provision of logic for processing segments, the input of transaction rules, and the writing of messages to a terminal.

As an integrated instrument of IMS, ADF is able to develop database-oriented applications that can benefit from these facilities:

- *Sign-on DB* controls the mode of access.
- *Audit DB* controls the updating of single fields.
- *Message DB* controls the automatic and user messages.

IBM promotes ADF as an advanced program structure for expert programmers, not as an alternative to, for example, query language capability. Table 10.2 makes this point by comparing ADF and Standard Query Language (SQL).

Other programming extensions to operating systems work through menus and options. But although they are generally discussed as transaction drivers, they offer significantly greater capabilities to their user. One of the most vital of those capabilities is a great improvement in programmer productivity, the way 4GLs work. The schema handled by transactional tools allows frames to be used in more than one application. Often, the resulting environment can be represented pictorially. By using their catalogs, 4GL programming tools build executable files that implement the application.

Table 10.2 ADF versus SQL

ADF	SQL
ADF is a generator of transactional capabilities.	SQL is a data manipulation language with logical and arithmetic capabilities.
ADF is oriented to computer professionals.	SQL can provide challenging features for expert programmers.
As of today, ADF is not used under DB 2.	The end-user-oriented programming language capability is embedded in the query management function (QMF).

There are also objections to the different OS extensions. The one I consider most valid is that experience is as yet thin on the end effect this type of language can have on computer power. A quantitative example is given by IBM's transaction simulator used to project the computer power necessary at clients' sites. One result I have in mind indicated that the number of transactions to be handled by a given number of millions of instructions per second (MIPS) machine under SQL is half of what could be processed if Cobol were used. This means that SQL not only doubles the overhead but also consumes half the available computer power.

Another example of how much more time an interpreter type of implementation may require is given by a comparison of the demand on machine cycles by an interpreter versus that needed for compilation:

- A benchmark done on Basic showed that the interpreter needs 3.5 times as much machine time as the compiler.

- In a benchmark done on Cobol (no I/O included) a given machine under interpreter handled 2 kIPS (kilo instructions per second) and under Compiler 6.5 kIPS.

Is the exchange between machine cycles and programmer's time fair enough? Most DP/MIS managers and a great many specialists think the answer is yes. The answer is so much more reasonable when we talk of the workstation level, at which so much machine power is available and fast programming and user-friendly interfaces are of so much greater importance.

Another thing not to be overlooked is optimization. In practically all cases, the early versions of a complex software system are slow. It is first necessary to stress functionality. Only after functionality is proved can we direct our attention to performance. That is why it is quite reasonable that the developers take some time to learn how to tune a software system.

They also need to produce the tuning tools. Some techniques used with current technology may be used, but new tuning techniques will usually have to be developed. And it is also necessary to first gain experience with the programming language, which can be done only by widening its implementation.

COMPARING OPERATING SYSTEMS AND LANGUAGES

To start with, the term "alternative" should be seen only as relative. CP/M and Unix are surely not alternative OSs in any case. But CP/M-

80, CP/M-86, and MS-DOS do overlap over certain implementation areas, and that can be said of MS-DOS and Unix also.

We mentioned on several occasions that as bits per word tend to increase (Figure 10.3), so do the capabilities supported by, and required from, the commodity operating systems. This does not cancel a current OS offering in one stroke, but as sales decline, less money is available for new features and the user community thins out.

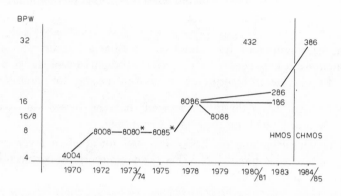

*DIFFERENT FUNCTIONALITY, SPEED, NUMBER OF REGISTERS

Figure 10.3 Microprocessor bits per word (BPW) capabilities.

The operating system market for this and the coming years is totally different from the one we knew in the 1963 to 1983 timeframe. Over two decades the OS features (particularly for mainframes) changed very slowly. Whatever features were added were pasted on. Few new developments appeared, and this was one of the reasons for the success of Unix. (Actually, Pick has excellent features but no market thrust, which limits both computer choice and application program portability.)

CP/M and MS-DOS have been new departures in operating systems design. Yet, just as mainframe manufacturers made the mistake of trying to squeeze their proprietary OSs for the big machines into the mini, so micro OS producers hope to explode their commodity offering from the low-end PC into the supermicro. The squeeze failed miserably, and there is no reason to believe the explosion will succeed either.

Every type of machine needs basic software from monitors to input/output control, timing, and synchronization. At the same time, the user, for an application, requires for the larger machines types of services and protection unneeded for the smaller PCs. With Unix, for example, when the user has successfully logged in, the shell is listening to the user's terminal. It:

- Reads typed-in lines
- Splits the lines up into command names and arguments
- Executes the commands

A command is simply an executable program. The shell looks first in the user's current directory for a program with the given name. If none is there, it then looks in a system directory. The command name is always the first word on an input line; it and its arguments are separated from one another by spaces. When a program terminates, the shell will ordinarily regain control and type a $ to indicate that it is ready for another command.

Other OSs use different signs and do not necessarily support the same procedures. The better these procedures are designed to help the end user, the more sophisticated the operating system is. Also, the greater the inventory of routines available to an OS, the more flexible the OS is. In this sense, it can be stated that MS-DOS is more flexible than CP/M because it provides a nice mechanism to:

- Install drivers
- Replace the command processor
- Handle files
- Define the blocking rate

Such functions are not provided (as of the time of writing) by CP/M. Similarly, on comparing Unix with MS-DOS, we can say that Unix has file locking, security, and log-in, whereas MS-DOS is lacking them.

Still, no OS monopolizes the facilities needed by the user, and these facilities have a price. For strictly character I/O, CP/M has some advantages because of reduced overhead. MS-DOS is fast with blocked I/O, but the user will be well advised to work on a character basis. Sometimes the original writing of a package gives an advantage to a certain OS. WordStar was written for CP/M; translated into MS-DOS, it has twice the overhead.

Languages, too, are primarily projected for a given OS and, beyond that, for a computer size. A commodity OS for PCs, a certain brochure advertises, supports Basic, Pascal, CIS Cobol, Fortran, and PL/1.

Basic and Pascal are languages for PC implementation; that is not true of Cobol, Fortran, and PL/1. It is better not to use personal computers than kill them by implementing Cobol—apart from Cobol's being a deadly obsolete language.

Let me digress at this point. The question is often posed: "If Cobol is obsolete, then what should we do with the hundreds of thousands of Cobol programmers around the world?"

That is a good question—if turned the other way around. In my opinion, we need not worry about the Cobol programmers, *but we should train them in the new technologies.* As the computer becomes the central nervous system of companies, they should be put in a position to find work in the brain functions rather than in the legwork of Cobol code. I know a few ex-Cobol programmers who refused to return to Cobol even on an interim basis. They said it distorted the image they had acquired with their new experience.

Today there is a crying need for computer specialists with imagination as well as for able managers who can make creative use of technology to address business objectives. There is work in graphics (both management and engineering), in robotics, in office automation, and in structural studies within the organization.

We need a new sophisticated class of computer and communications technicians who are also able to have the perspective of business people. Rewriting the huge library of Cobol, Fortran, and PL/1 programs should not be a mechanical job. The new applications software should, at long last, make business sense. The new generation of computer technologists must be knowledgeable not only in, say, Unix, Ingres, C, MS-DOS, Lotus 1-2-3, and dBase II but also in the choices which must be made. C, for instance, can run on MS-DOS, but in reality this is a C subset which misses several powerful functions.

Much depends on microprocessor power and also on the way the processor has been projected. Hardware design characteristics may fit one language implementation better than another. Figure 10.4 makes this point by presenting benchmark results by Intel. Pascal by Intel is a better implementation than Pascal by DEC. The opposite is true of Fortran, though the larger part of the difference may be due to the superiority of Unix over the other OSs.

Another test by Intel was C versus Pascal and Fortran. The results obtained with C were better than with Pascal and Fortran:

- C versus Pascal, by 30 percent
- C versus Fortran, by 35 percent

Table 10.3 suggests programming languages and database management systems for PCs and supermicros. Let's add that the user who compares different machines with Unix should surely look into what the vendor has as add-ons. The add-ons can have both positive and negative effects: They ease programming and improve operations, but they also reduce portability.

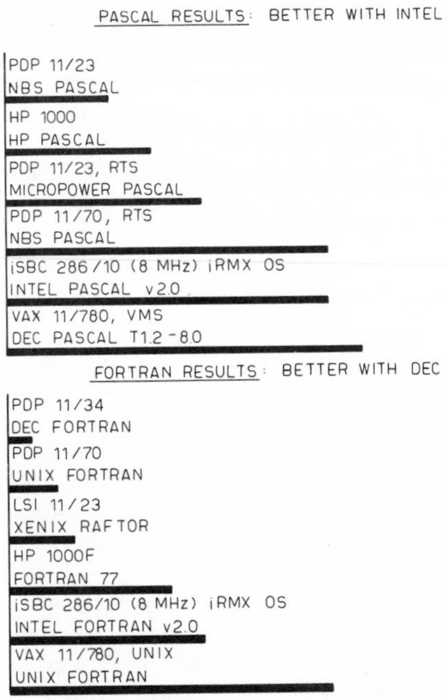

PASCAL RESULTS: BETTER WITH INTEL

PDP 11/23
NBS PASCAL

HP 1000
HP PASCAL

PDP 11/23, RTS
MICROPOWER PASCAL

PDP 11/70, RTS
NBS PASCAL

iSBC 286/10 (8 MHz) iRMX OS
INTEL PASCAL v2.0

VAX 11/780, VMS
DEC PASCAL T1.2-8.0

FORTRAN RESULTS: BETTER WITH DEC

PDP 11/34
DEC FORTRAN

PDP 11/70
UNIX FORTRAN

LSI 11/23
XENIX RAFTOR

HP 1000F
FORTRAN 77

iSBC 286/10 (8 MHz) iRMX OS
INTEL FORTRAN v2.0

VAX 11/780, UNIX
UNIX FORTRAN

Figure 10.4   Benchmark results by Intel.
Note the difference in machine power depending on the language being used.

Today none of the commodity OSs are really user-friendly. CP/M
is poor in this respect; Unix is not easy. More work is necessary to
define end user interfaces at the WS level. The principle must be
that executives, professionals, and secretaries should *not* know which
OS they use. Functions must be equivalent, and equivalent functions
should be implemented on the different operating systems. Both vendors
and users will be well advised to look into migration policies. This
includes processing characteristics, databasing developments, and, above
all, *compatible communications.*

Processing compatibility can be assured through database structures,
management systems, and language choices. We have spoken of these
possibilities and have given as examples a whole range of offerings
distinguishing between PCs and supermicros. This can be said in conclusion: Commodity OSs are now on their way to maturity. Even if this
maturity is not yet a confirmed fact, PC and supermicro vendors will
be well advised to avoid proprietary OSs. That is the way to spend $30
million to get where they already were prior to changing machines or
microprocessors.

Table 10.3 Suggested Language Choices for Machines of Different Capacities

PC	Supermicro
Intel 8088, 8086, or 80186	Motorola 68000, 68010, or 68020 or Intel 80286
MS-DOS	Unix
Languages	
Spreadsheet and integrated software	Integrated software
dBase II, et al.	For Ingres: Query by Form (QBF), Report by Form (RBF), and Report Writer (RW)
C or Pascal	C and other relational languages
DBMSs	
dBase II and Friday (query) MDBS Other PC-level offerings (Mistress and Unify are possibilities)	Ingres or other relational DBMSs (Oracle, Informix, Mistress, Unify)

ADVANTAGES AND DISADVANTAGES OF COMMODITY OSs

For supermicro and PC users, commodity OSs may not have the capabilities of an IBM MVS/XA, but neither have they the cost of it nor the need for it. In their current status, and for the level of machines we are talking about, commodity offerings are by far a better choice than proprietary OSs, and their use is most advisable.

Not everything is rosy with commodity OSs, however; the greatest worry is the way some of the OSs are used by the hardware vendors adopting them. Let me give a specific example. To mount Unix, Ingres, and some utilities on Tower, the Motorola 68000–based supermicro, NCR employs 40 (!) floppy disks (25 for Unix, 10 for Ingres, and 5 for other software). For the user, this is a nightmare—and users have made that known to the vendor. Although lame excuses can be made, such as "this is done as a way to protect the software," the result is to disgust the user rather than protect the vendor. Furthermore, given its complexity, the load operation takes a long day of work by a specialist and demands uninterrupted attention.

For instance, when loaded, each floppy asks questions that even a software specialist would find difficult to answer. When the user is confronted by such a hostile environment, the only reasonable way out is to *drop the OS* and choose something more friendly. (AT&T should at least appreciate that, when its resale network acts as it does, Unix will have limited market penetration.) Easier ways of doing business should be urgently sought at the source. Unix takes some 6 Mbytes of hard disk. It can be loaded at the factory once and for all before shipping. New releases can be sent through streamer, and minor changes can be downloaded at the vendor's risk and guaranty.

While it is conceivable that, at a central computer center, specialists might be around to do the job described above, it is *out of the question* to send a mess like that to a bank's branch offices, the industrial sales offices, and the factories. Better not to use Unix (and the Tower) than to be crippled by the vendor.

The use of a commodity OS is a good choice, but it should not make the vendor lose his sense of responsibility. If by moving into a higher-up, more sophisticated operating system the user would be disadvantaged in terms of supporting basic software in a fully distributed environment, it would be better to settle for a simpler OS. Although we wish to train the end user to be able to program and manage the PC, we surely don't want to pile on any unnecessary chores. So the first piece of advice is this: Within the open vendor policy, get a competent supplier, one who can deliver.

The second piece of advice stresses the need to be precise: Choose the OS fitting your current and projected needs over a 3- to 4-year timespan. Remember the 5-year life cycle for any system installed today. Within that perspective, and speaking strictly of the workstation at your desk, let's make a competitive evaluation of MS-DOS and Unix.

An MS-DOS (or PC-DOS) advantage is that it is and has been addressed from the beginning to the industry standard 16-BPW microprocessor. A second major advantage is the availability of commodity programs: horizontal and vertical software. There are also disadvantages.* A lot of available programs are tied not to MS-DOS, but to IBM standards: ROM, direct disk address, and video bit mapping. Whether this is a brief market trend or becomes a permanent feature remains to be seen. Within current perspectives, programs are not always transportable from machine to machine, including direct access to peripherals and writing into user space. Because the software was not fast enough, ways around it were developed, such as the BIOS which is in ROM.

---

*Though at the time of writing the multitasking MS-DOS was still delayed, no reservation is made on this subject—on the assumption that version 3.0 will soon be available to users.

What are the Unix advantages? Support by the Department of Defense and major user organizations is a positive one. It helps make its vendors more responsive to the market trend. Other things being equal, this offers a better return on the supplier's R&D funds. For the user, a major plus is the (within limits) portability: The user is not locked to any vendor. Another advantage is the 4GL tools developing around Unix. For a personal programming effort, the user has a great range of available fourth-generation languages—among the best in the industry.

There are also disadvantages, such as the vendor's clumsy and insensitive 40 floppies. But Unix has other problems also. First, from the beginning Unix was not a commercial offering. The vendor must now do a value-added job. Second, the not yet optimized system commands cannot guarantee absolutely predictable response time. Because some programs are on disk, the user must know the environment and nail them in central memory. One little known but effective approach is the "sticky bit." Third, priority driving is not a native Unix characteristic. The system is time-slicing. This is a bad answer to some applications requirements at the WS level.

Fourth, flexibility, which is a Unix advantage, can lead to overtooling if the developers are not controlled. A fourth-generation language, like any other tool, must be managed. Fifth, Unix has high overhead. One estimate places it at 3 times as high as DEC's VMS, which is not an optimal system. These points are made, not to discourage the use of Unix, but to make the reader aware of requirements and pitfalls.

Every one of the leading contenders in the commodity OS race has its place. At the current state of the art, I would rather put MS-DOS at the WS level and use Unix with Ingres as the back-end machine managing the larger database. Let Ingres manage the local database, the 100 Mbytes to 1 Gbyte needed at the branch office and the factory. If a limited number of PCs is necessary for the workstations, connect them to the back-end database machine as a cluster. (With six or more attached WSs, response time deteriorates drastically.)

If a large number of terminals are needed, install a local area network. There is Ingres/Net, and add-on routine which permits the sharing of data by computers. Use this facility. But above all the terminals you put on the cluster or the LAN should be PCs. *Don't* use dumb terminals. They cost just as much and return less than 10 percent as much. Dumb terminals crowd the system, increase the response time, and seal any possibility of future growth in applications and their sophistication. Even if the need for PCs is not apparent at the time the installation is made, it will become so as experience is gained. Dumb terminals are only for dumb people.

11

NATURAL-LANGUAGE PROGRAMMING

Speech recognition and natural-language programming are not yet everyday tools and may take years to become such, but icons and English language menu selection are a good beginning. A key issue is semantics and words the machine can understand. Vocabularies are becoming comfortably large with decreasing speaker dependence. New technologies can accommodate more flexible approaches even if the background is structured.

A basic issue with new developments for software productivity is formalization. An example with very efficient structured approaches is the visual hardware description language (VHDL),* a very high speed programming approach for integrated circuit design. The interest in high-power, high-productivity programming developments is not coincidental. It is a reflection of the fact that the best organized, managed, and funded project will be a failure if the end result does not satisfy requirements—and the best person to thoroughly understand the effort is the end user.

The job of a natural language is to help translate users' needs into statements, but precision in stating the requirements is essential. Furthermore, reports must be conversational, not cryptic, and the communication channel should work satisfactorily in a sustained two-way mode. Japan's fifth-generation computer development project is noteworthy.

---

*VHDL is a hardware description language which is deliberately extendable.

A knowledge-information-processing (KIP) computer is being designed. It follows non-von Neumann architectures. KIP-based application systems are expected to handle many forms of input:

- Speech
- Handwritten characters
- Video images
- Printed text

The systems will be able to extract meaning from information they are given, answer user questions, and offer advice leading to solutions.

Natural-language (NL) programming must handle, in an able manner, visualization, graphics presentation, and algorithmic expressions—the latter in a way transparent to the user. Its employment imposes prerequisites. We must also assure compatibility between system structure, communications solutions, supported processes, databases, and relations between the information elements in the databases. It must offer the end user considerable powers of calculation without requiring classical programming experience. The user must be able to incorporate volumes of information in a given model, change a condition of the processing model, or redo the entire evaluation, analysis, and presentation with little effort.

Though the investment in user training can be higher than for simple functions like electronic mail, the benefits can also be much greater. Eventually natural-language programming will converge toward knowledge-based, problem-solving systems.

HIGHER-ORDER SOFTWARE

Higher-order software presupposes the existence of powerful processors able to handle sophisticated user-oriented command structures. This is within the forthcoming capabilities of large-scale integrated circuits. Forecasts indicate that the present multichip 32-bit microprocessors will soon be available in single-chip versions, 64-bit multiprocessors will be available in multichip versions by 1986, and one-chip versions will be available by the end of the decade.

Technological advances have seen to it that, in terms of hardware, the 4-BPW microprocessor now costs about $1 and the 16-BPW microprocessor has dropped below $10. The 32-BPW microprocessors should drop steadily to below $10 per unit by the mid-1990s as volume production increases and the 64-BPW machine conquers the market.

Within that perspective, the potential of problem-solving systems is very promising, though they may, in the beginning, be oriented toward discrete subject areas. At the same time, the realization that higher-order software needs an overstructure, a main structure, and an understructure promotes fundamental research on all three levels. Processing layers can be served both by software and by hardware. Provided we have clear ideas about what we wish to achieve, supporting this functionality poses no problems because, as stated, VLSI promises up to 500,000 components for a few dollars.

As stated in an earlier chapter, the basic building blocks will no longer be gates or multipliers; they will be units capable of speech synthesis, probabilistic reasoning, and so on.

- With time and experience, off-the-shelf knowledgebanks with thousands of rules will appear.

- Current applications use only a few hundred rules, easily stored on a single chip.

Such systems will become transportable and marketable in the way books and software are. They will:

1. Represent knowledge in an organized but adaptable manner
2. Support knowledge in terms familiar to end users
3. Employ user-friendly interface functions
4. Exploit the kinds of reasoning which are available

Analysis for such systems will be based on thorough understanding of the problem domain. This means the ability to develop a knowledgebank in which methodology and rules dominate.

Within the context of higher-order software, natural-language programming will allow fast development of algorithms, which are the most valuable assistance for computer program development. At the same time, emphasis will be placed on relational databases, user-generated computing, and the use of nonprocedural languages. The user will be able to specify the result wanted, and the relational database will ask the questions and do the job of software creation. Natural-language programming is expected, typically, to provide 15 min turnaround versus the 7 months needed with classical approaches.

Sperry's MAPPER and the approaches followed at the PC level by Texas Instruments are examples of the above solution being applied in the mid-1980s. Though the resulting software consumes machine cycles, we should not forget that about 80 percent of the programs in a computer facility use only 2 percent of the machine cycles, but their existence is crucial. All these programs should be developed in fourth-generation languages (4GLs).

Other major advantages offered by 4GLs, such as natural-language programming, are flexibility, low-cost maintainability, and the possibility of reshaping the application with minor effort. IBM surveyed people exposed to software with successful programming features and found that 80 percent of most beneficial characteristics were *not* in the initial releases.

In a design sense, simple, linear program restructuring is most important, and new programming technologies make it feasible through the proper language interfaces expressed in a natural language and supported by expert systems. By the time we have established the formalisms, we will be basically through with the project. The rest will be done by the expert system.

Symbolic rather than numerical operations characterize cognitive activities such as:

• Problem solving

• Forecasting and planning

• Induction, deduction, and extrapolation

The expert system approach capitalizes on this finding and on the fact that computers are processors of symbols and not just fast calculators. At the same time, as has been emphasized, very large scale integration makes it feasible, at a reasonable cost, to program machines and make them able to exhibit intelligent behavior.

In man-machine communication, we have to go beyond tools; we also need metrics. We must be able to quantify all measurable entities and tune the system. A similar statement can be made about sophisticated checkout and debugging aids. The aims of interaction during compilation are automatic correction of syntax errors, compile time diagnostics, and corrections of complex errors without recompilation.

In interaction during execution, the goals include inserting and replacing source statements, saving changes in source data sets, direct execution of additional statements without recompilation, and, upon program termination, resumption of execution from the beginning. Equally important are the automatic checking and symbolic display of data overflow, cross-reference for critical variables, and object time diagnostic messages with source statement identification.

Intelligent systems will be data- and demand-driven, and the software they employ must reflect that fact. Higher-order software should put the project in a position of gaining firm understanding about knowledge systems and their representation. Knowledge representation needs to be done in a formal way to map it within the machine. This is understood by those who are developing the new software. For instance, ongoing DBMS work looks beyond data structures and into a dataflow machine.

Data resides in a knowledge system. Access to data is an integral part of what we can do with the programming language. We also need very high level capability for modeling and techniques for dealing with data naturally.

NATURAL-LANGUAGE FRONT ENDS

Natural-language programming follows the constructs of higher-order software. It enables users to compose English queries for remote databases, with the software translating the query into the code needed to access the database. Natural-language interpreters translate English requests into formal database inquiry commands. Some offerings act as a DBMS with natural-language query facilities and feature fourth-generation application generators.

Although opinions differ as to whether these natural-language systems will catch on in the short term, the predominant thinking is that English environments will be common. Some system specialists consider a natural-language capability critical in developing applications for database management packages. Opponents of that view argue that the advantages of natural-language systems are offset by help facilities inbred into packages on several levels. A similar argument is made about more complete and better written documentation and other easy-to-use technologies like voice input and touch-sensitive screens.

Those arguments, however, miss the point. A natural-language approach is open to development and can incorporate different sorts of man-machine interactions including voice input, touch-sensitive screens, and icons. Besides, natural-language support on a micro is a significant leap forward in user assistance. Since the micro is the base of the intelligent workstation, the natural-language interaction serves as the process by which the software learns what the user wants to accomplish. Programs can become adaptive.

We ought to expect sophistication in the use of tools for man-machine interaction. The more knowledgeable the end user becomes, the more the user will find ways of using systems that no software or hardware manufacturer has foreseen. The user is now the key driving force in pushing forward. There is more to come. A mere 5 percent of the knowledge workers in America own and use personal computers, and the percentage is even lower in Europe.

Growth can be phenomenal if the industry can break through the barrier of the 20 to 40 hours of work it takes to master current software. "More packages" cannot solve the problem because understanding the needs of the users and being able to meet them are not the same thing. We must be alert to new advances in technology for man-machine communication. Natural languages and expert systems open the way. Several components are necessary:

1. Screen and windows
2. Grammar
3. Message builder (and screener of a legal set of choices)
4. Interfacing
5. Lexicon
6. Parser
7. Translator
8. Formal query processor
9. Response formulator
10. Report writer and formatter

The grammar will be that of the natural language. It will contain rules describing a given language (but not restricted by it) and will be used to parse and possibly generate linguistic strings. To facilitate grammar writing, we must contain syntactic variety. A most important aspect is the understructure. The system must permit the user to easily identify, modify, insert, and delete and generally interact with the natural-link software. The latter has access to the description of user's natural language and interfaces with the translation to system language.

This process suggests what we already know from higher-level languages. The underlying system cannot directly understand the user's NL; it is necessary to map the natural language into the system language. A *lexicon* will facilitate the mapping of the user's input language into the target language for the computer. In this sense, the access to the description of the user's NL can be seen as the primary input to a translator process. This proceeds in the following way.

The user selects an English word or phrase from an active window. The *parser* initiates a process of resolving the user input into grammatical components. Typically, the parser accepts the actual linguistic text from the user and performs a syntactic analysis. The result is an annotated parse tree, indicating the parts of speech (noun, verb, and so on) and the syntactic relations between constituents of the sentence.

As the user input is built, a tree structure describing the syntactic relations of the input is passed from the parser to the *semantic/pragmatic translator*. The latter:

- Looks into the lexicon for the text into which the grammatical component is to map
- Saves the mapped text for future display or submission to the underlying computer system

The translator basically uses knowledge about the

- Conventions of language use
- Previous dialog
- Domain of the particular database

to interpret the user's request. It can also provide advice to the parser to help guide the parsing process or engage the user in a dialog when further information is required.

The interpreter's output may be a program, query, or series of queries in a formal language. There is also a *paraphraser* capability. The system will paraphrase the chosen interpretation of the request and present it to the user for approval.

From these observations it can be appreciated that the translator plays a decisive role in determining the information that must be kept in the lexicon. A valid lexicon must contain the translation text for grammatical components defined in the grammar as requiring translation. The parser calls for certain information that can also be stored in the lexicon. To control the manner in which the user constructs a natural-language statement, the parser causes changes to occur in the states of windows and in window contents. Interactivity is also pronounced, because the selection of an item from a window may cause that window to become inactive and cause another window to be activated.

To have control over this process, the parser must know both the window and the location within the window of each component of the user language. This information is part of a grammatical definition. Thus, the lexicon must contain:

- A list of words known to the system
- The syntactic properties of the words
- Meaning in the domain

Content of the database itself may function as an extension of the lexicon, and morphological analysis may be performed. The latter regards the recognition of word forms. Figure 11.1 shows the interaction between grammar, file description, and lexicon.

Now let's recapitulate. In the natural-language interaction, the parser uses the NL information to build parse trees. This is a structure like a sentence diagram recording grammatical choices. The translator completes the parse tree by using the lexicon and building commands for target applications. A driver handles the interaction.

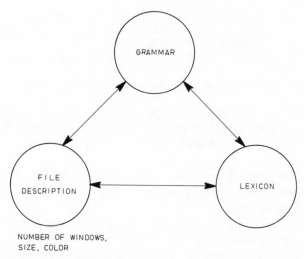

Figure 11.1 Interaction between grammar, file description, and lexicon.

Other vital components include the *formal query processor, response formulator*, and *report writer and formatter*. The formal query processor is similar to an English-like query system. It acts as an interactive query processor or program interpreter and may be part of the DBMS. The response formulator interprets the results of execution against the database and selects an appropriate form for presenting the information to the user. The result usually requires the generation of a linguistic response. The report writer and formatter is a module to compose and label retrieved data in an appropriate form.

By limiting the *concepts*, that is, the nature and relations of the data it references, and the *linguistic forms* it must understand (form of the user input), queries are guaranteed to be valid in the context of the referenced database.

As can be appreciated, the whole structure is a fairly complex system. Part of the complexity can be offset by training the system and also by providing it with specialized knowledge about the database being referenced. *System training* calls for considerable knowledge about the algorithms that drive the natural-language interface. In this sense, solutions closely approximate those of expert systems.

TOOLS FOR USERS AND SOFTWARE DEVELOPERS

Natural-language programming and expert systems are not competing, but reinforcing technologies. In both cases artificial intelligence (AI) components interpret the user's choices. Such approaches bring a new perspective and give fresh meaning to both hardware and software. They assist in improved end user productivity, accelerate management awareness, and also provide more efficient internal operations for the computer system.

Starting with screen management, the NL typically provides software that handles all interaction with the screen. Here the AI contribution is the software which interprets the user's choices. The parser is one of the components. It takes a user's choice, checks the grammar to determine what sentence(s) the user could be building, and employs the grammar to determine the user's next step of admissible choices.

The parser is intelligent. It uses the information it obtains to build a structure, much like a sentence diagram, which records a particular set of grammatical choices. This is what we have called a *parse tree*. However, depending on the grammar, a single choice can lead the parser to build more than one parse tree. The parser modifies the description of the screen and thereby impacts on the presentation of windows and their contents. The screen appearance is controlled through contents of the grammar, the lexicon, and the progression of phrases selected by the user from the active windows.

In a fundamental sense, this is the means by which the natural-language interface assures that only valid choices are presented to the user. Valid choices are those permitted by the grammar specification. Validity is a function of the grammar and tools needed to assist in developing an error-free grammar.

We also spoke of the translator and defined it as the software which takes a completed parse tree and, using the lexicon, builds a command for the target application. Reference has been made to the driver. This is the software handling all interaction among the parser, translator, window manager, and user's application.

The sequence of handling steps and system components involved in each phase defines a process that tells the computer how to solve a problem. This is what we have always called a *program*, but the way it is built is nonprocedural. Working in a nonprocedural way, intelligent machine components handle all screen management, compute the next set of choices, and perform the translation of the English language command. This is a reasoning process, and the step-by-step approach is not outlined by a human programmer. What is more,

• The program is expressed in nonambiguous terms
• The program's coding can be 100 percent error-free

If the system to be referenced by a natural-language interface is sufficiently self-descriptive, the interface generator can automatically produce much of the lexicon and screen description. For a relational database this is frequently the case. In this sense, data definition utility could elicit information and build a lexicon accessible by the interface generator. The latter could be packaged with the natural-language software so the user of an application could potentially develop a personal variation of an interface, with the differences tailored to needs.

Though the semantics and the syntactical considerations are different, writing a grammar for a natural-language interface can be seen as analogous to the task of writing a program. Tools are therefore necessary to help produce an error-free grammar and to assist the analyst in the task of synthesizing the model for a grammar.

To operate successfully within this environment, the user must become familiar with the command language and its functionality in terms of the target application. In a way resembling structured programming, the user must devise a set of English sentences that correspond to these commands—and be sure to constrain the syntactic variety to facilitate grammar writing. But the user also has freedoms: to design a screen for use with this set of sentences, to actuate a grammar subset which will generate this set of sentences and only this set of sentences, and also to use the interface builder to build the lexicon, develop the interface file, and debug the program.

The interface builder can also be employed to test the file in order to assure that the interface produces both the desired natural-language sentences and target language commands. The user interaction with the system is shown in Figure 11.2, where a distinction is made between end user and software developer. In some cases, the two may be the same person. The user and NL software developer will be the same person in the case of building packages, professional expert systems, and other applications requiring significant expertise. Both users and developers, however, require an environment able to provide database administration in the creation and usage of natural-language menus.

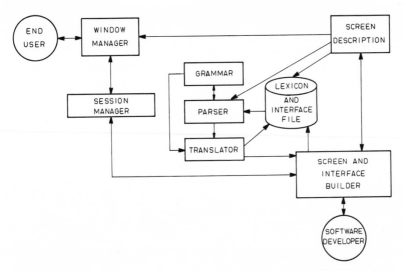

Figure 11.2 Interaction between user and the facilities provided by his or her workstation.

The database administrator must determine the details of a specific interface. This includes the user's log-on command, files and interfaces to which the user should have access, permission to the user to generate his or her own interface, and revocation of permission. Another example is whether a link should be used with remote databases.

After the appropriate decision is made, the interface should be tailored to a particular user who, upon receipt of the generated interface, typically begins to access the contents of the database. The user will communicate with the computer in a natural language and be assured of the creation of only valid queries. The creation and execution of single queries is only one aspect of the system, which should also provide the user with

- Features to save queries for future use
- The ability to format data retrieved from the database

The user must be able to save database commands with or without accompanying formatting operations. An easily remembered title could be created by the user and associated with the saved query. This assures identification for future reference.

The simpler the man-machine communication becomes, the greater is the need for security. This poses the questions: What users are authorized to employ a given interface? What phrasing should appear on the screen. Also, default answers for many questions should be provided by descriptive information from a lexicon.

For protection purposes, the database administrator must specify what data the interfaces can reference. He or she should be provided with the tools to generate an interface, modify, show, list, or delete existing interfaces, restrict access within the interfaces, and package one or more of the interfaces for a particular user.

The database administrator should be assisted with system commands for association, pattern matching, and extrapolation regarding the use of the database and knowledgebank (methodology, rules). At different times during that work these characteristics will be combined in various mixtures according to how the administrator decides to allocate and/or protect the resources under his or her authority. The administrator should be able to add further facilities, such as charting capabilities, icons, and voice input/output, and should also be able to create closed user groups with exclusive access rights to certain files, menus, and screen formats.

Tools must be put at the disposal of the database administrator to simplify the task of managing a natural-language interface, though this task will remain nontrivial. Other tools at the developer's side could simplify the design perspectives and increase the power of the generated interfaces. New departures are necessary because most of the currently available software tools, languages, and techniques are still tangling with 35-year-old problems. Images are still limited to sequential processing. Available approaches cannot yet manipulate patterns and combinations of patterns; new departures are needed.

AN INVESTMENT ADVISER SYSTEM

Intelligent man-machine interactive approaches follow the path of examining a problem, decomposing the problem into its sequential and associative parts, and altering, in a logical sense, the organization of the computer at each instant of the solution. This capacity for adaptive restructuring inherent in every piece of software is particularly pronounced with expert systems.

Natural-language programming can thus be seen as the front-ending of the user interaction with the intelligence residing in the machine. High-resolution graphics, windowing, bit-mapping, agile pointing device, keypad (for numeric entries), and voice input/output are tools within the broader communications problem.

Emphasis on both NL and expert systems approaches is practically synonymous with the ability to recognize both the content of a problem and its procedure-independent solution sequence. Expected advantages from this approach include the fact that the user:

- Has only to formulate logical constructs
- Can easily structure acceptable queries
- Uses the system to eliminate unanswerable questions and be informed accordingly
- Has available system prompts and guides

The underlying code is very efficient; errors are minimized; the knowledgebank grows through self-learning; and, most important, the expert system justifies the opinion it gives.

Specialization is a competitive advantage. For instance, an expert system can be built for each type of security, commodity, property, option, and so on within the portfolio, leaving to the portfolio manager the task of making reasonable future earnings for each investment. The judicious investment manager can use these facilities to integrate vital components and get estimated aggregates. If the total return doesn't attain the corporation's goal, the portfolio model can be quickly recalculated based on changes and hypotheses with prompting and smart questions asked by the expert system.

We will follow, as an example, an investment advisory model. The top issue is dealing with the expert system while believing we deal with a person behind the machine. This is a bold approach, basing designs on the *needs of brains* instead of the constraints of silicon. Let's look at the fundamentals. An expert system is accomplished through:

1. Nonprocedural methodology, by computer-based knowledge
2. Inference mechanism and justification
3. Learning capability

The first step is *knowhow-through-showhow*. The further-out goal is a *knowledge refinery* through an integrated suite of problems for deriving, transforming, testing, and measuring machine-oriented embodiments of useful knowledge.

The *reference rules* are the best understood part of the knowledgebank. The Esystem has a large number of rules to produce a small number of answers. That's the way a human would behave. For a small number of rules, we don't need such a system. What's more, the smart software should be personalized. An investment advisor should run on the executive's personal computer.

As this example demonstrates, a learning, adaptive computer is not only possible but has already been created. The targets are low-cost delivery and availability of a precise goal within a wide range of conventional applications. This extends the usefulness of the PC as a managerial workstation.

The *investment decisions* included in this program involve:

1. Types of investment
2. Financial analysis
3. Capital financing
4. Tax consequences

These are *knowledge domains* that need to be integrated. An expert system helps do that. In terms of priorities, the first effort is to find some niche in which the system can be used. Don't try to cover everything the banker would do. We are not ready for such a broad approach.

Typically, a specialized system asks questions regarding:

1. User's reason to pose question (why)
2. User's answers (or no answer) to the system queries
3. More information needed to form opinion

Queries and answers lead the expert system toward knowing the user's reason for posing the original question. In the investment application, the system's top commands are rules, parms (parameters, variables which the system is to satisfy), and go. The investment application runs as a *superspreadsheet* able to make up its mind. The expert system is sophisticated in the type of questions it asks in order to:

• Analyze type of investments
• Get to know the capital markets, including interest and taxation
• Learn about alternative investments
• Evaluate ROI for all alternatives
• Give an opinion on contemplated investment
• Justify this opinion

The end product traces through the logic (rules). In doing so, it provides good justification. In this process, the job of the *rules editor* is crucial. The database administrator should be the only person to change the rules, not the end user.

12

EXPERT SYSTEMS AND KNOWLEDGEBANKS

Knowledge-based systems provide facilities well beyond the decision support capabilities we have had since the late 1970s. They make feasible the creation of *knowledgebanks* (KB), consultations, inferences, and the operation of other systems such as robotics. Their general character is that they are less mechanical; they exhibit a learning behavior. Examples are programs simulating human memorization performance and human-like reactions: trial and error, relearning, forgetting, and adjusting to parameters.

Knowledgebanks are, usually, organized collections of rules represented as *knowledge networks*. Knowledge nets are also known as *inference nets*. They typically relate symptoms, or known inputs, to diagnosis or advice. The facilities provided by a knowledgebank can be employed to assure new system capabilities. When such knowhow-dependent processes are useful for solving problems related to a class of objects, we talk of *expert systems* (Esystems). The functionalities of several expert systems may be combined to formulate new design tasks. This is particularly true when all subsystems of the new aggregate are based on the same nucleus.

An expert system may use open exits and leave some parameters for further specification. The parametric user will specify the capability to perform variations, test alternatives, and proceed with the analysis of supported features to obtain desired results. The technical development of an expert system calls for:

1. The able development of knowledgebanks
2. Significant stress on methodology
3. Design decisions on presentation sequences
4. Procedural choices and priorities
5. Object transformations
6. Schema, subschema, and design planning
7. Process resource management
8. Interfacing of resources
9. Increased insight into the effects on man-information communication
10. Ability to implement training sequences

To a very substantial extent, Esystems make use of concepts and rules developed in research on *artificial intelligence* (AI). Therefore, it is proper to start this discussion with the state of the art in AI, then treat expert systems as a new discipline, and conclude with a comparison with what has been made available so far in decision support facilities.

ASSUMPTIONS, RULES, AND ARTIFICIAL INTELLIGENCE

There are two ways to look at the artificial intelligence effort. The one is theoretical and has to do with basic research which to a substantial extent derives from automata theory. The other is practical and rests on the development of systems which can exhibit at the computer level characteristics we usually relate to human intelligence.

To start with, a major distinction should be made between intelligence and cunning. To be cunning is to be clever and shrewd and skillful in deception—although perhaps pleasing or attractive. But intelligence involves much more than that. The pillars of intelligence are perception, understanding, memory, and inference. Inherent in intelligence is the ability to learn from experience, to acquire and maintain knowledge, to respond quickly and successfully to new situations, to use reason in solving problems, and to use skill in directing conduct.

Also inherent in intelligence are the process of applying rules and the ability to find inappropriate actions and specify a correct course. Practical implementations of AI tend to use:

• A knowledgebank of component descriptions.
• A description as a set of attribute-value pairs.

Each constraint is represented as a rule, and rules are grouped by subtasks and assumptions. One of the basic strategies has been to propose extensions of current configuration and proceed with accept/reject decisions.

Practical implementation of artificial intelligence suggests the need to learn about and exploit possibilities by building a small demonstration system, establishing criteria for a suitable application problem, and involving intellectual tasks as candidate applications. A priori assessments have been made by using human information processing and human memory characteristics. Research has often focused on knowledgebank size and its relation to training.

Cooperative experts have been a critical component of this process. At the current state of the art, the knowledge is not in books; it is in the heads of practitioners. To write it down correctly is an arduous task. Information must be teased out bit by bit. A reasonable way to exploit AI is to select a small in-house application. The first goal should be to obtain staff competence in artificial intelligence, verify the technology, and get a simple application system.

The objectives should not be too ambitious. It is wise to consider problems for which there are no known effective computational procedures that provide solutions but there are existence proofs. These will typically be found in humans able to provide satisfactory performance.

Several daily intellectual tasks are good candidates for AI applications. They fall naturally into knowledge-based systems; a domain knowhow and expertise already exist; for some of them conventional algorithmic approaches are ineffective; practitioners provide existence proofs; and, therefore, value and level of success can be determined. An in-house staff can be anything from a handful of developers to a large laboratory. Either can be justified depending on the mission and the expected benefit—provided the organization has a clear need for an application or for experience with AI.

A company's computer operations may themselves be a good ground for an experiment because software products related to knowledge-based systems are about to appear. Database technology, including natural-language query capability, is related to this effort. Teknowledge, a Palo Alto, California, expert systems builder, developed a knowledge engineering package to enable relatively untrained systems programmers to build knowledge-based systems without having to become experts themselves in the working of Lisp. Lisp is the language of choice for AI work:

- At the $30,000 to $80,000 level, there are Lisp machines on the market, with MacLisp (from MIT) and InterLisp.

• There are also Lisp systems for personal computers that are available for $2000.

The former are designed for major tasks involving substantial capabilities. But the existence of offerings at the microcomputer level—though more limited in power—is good news in view of the range of applications which will be developing at workstations.

One example of implementation is oilfield log interpretations. An expert system by Schlumberger, the oil well drilling equipment company, analyzes well logging data for patterns that indicate likely deposits of oil, a task that once required highly trained experts. Another example is Dendral. Its field of operations is chemistry. Its mission is to analyze mass spectograms by using substructures, both those necessary and those forbidden, together with a nonredundant algorithm to enumerate remaining possibilities. Dendral uses chemical knowledge in the form of rules describing how molecules with given structures will fracture. This helps predict the fragments that will result. The mass spectogram to be expected from the given structure is therefore extrapolated.

Still other applications examples include fault diagnosis and response for medical applications, equipment operation and maintenance, manufacturing, robotics, and controlled processes at large. "Artificial intelligence will change, by an order of magnitude, the size of our business," Jean Riboud, president and chairman of Schlumberger, has said.

Mycin is an expert system for medical diagnosis with the facilities of English language interviews between physician and patient, diagnosis of certain infections, explanation of reasoning, and prescription of antibiotics. The possibility is open for accepting new rules from the user. This is one of the best known and well-developed AI systems, and it has spawned many other developments.

From a design standpoint, Mycin uses the information from the physician and a knowledgebank of a few hundred rules to deduce a diagnosis. A similar process leads to a prescription. In terms of diagnosis, Mycin can, for instance, tell if the site of the culture is blood, the identity of the organism is known or unknown with certainty, and so on. It can also identify the strain of the organism and its morphology.

This reference is very important because it helps identify the difference between the knowledgebank and the database. An expert system structure is shown in Figure 12.1:

1. Knowledge-based systems make a wide use of methodology and specifications integrated into the components forming the aggregate.

2. Such a methodology implies a rigorous discipline that both the

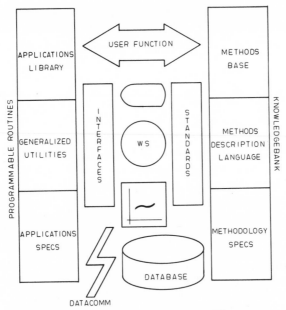

Figure 12.1 Structure of an expert system. The computer becomes an automated knowledge-based problem solver.

machine software/hardware (SW/HW) and the human user should follow.

3. In this sense, a knowledge-based system acquires a fourth dimension, beyond the three already provided by DB/DC/DP.

In the case of Mycin, the system has knowledge in the form of a few hundred rules. For example: *If* the infection type is primary bacteria, the suspected entry point is in the gastrointestinal tract, and the site of the culture is one of the sterile sites, *then* there is evidence that the organism is a bacteroid. These rules are resident in the knowledgebank and make it feasible to connect evidence such as symptoms and laboratory tests to possible diagnoses. Rules attach certain factors to conclusions. But the calculations and extrapolations that the expert system does may employ probabilistic reasoning.

SOFTWARE ENGINEERING AND COGNITIVE PSYCHOLOGY

Weapons systems, war games, modeling, simulation, pattern recognition, robot vision, database management, natural-language questions and answers, and computer-aided instruction are implementation areas which have attracted considerable attention in artificial intelligence studies. In fact, some of these fields have seen such breakthroughs that they are getting out of the basic reach level and into expert system implementation.

Knowledge-based systems are not only feasible but available. Diagnostic structures in medicine include Mycin, Casnet, Internist, Pip, and Puff. In engineering there is Sacon, and in geology there is Prospector. Among the systems designed for knowledge acquisition within the diagnostics domain we distinguish EMycin, Expert, Kas, and Teiresias. For instance, EMycin is a large, comprehensive, productive tool for building knowledge-based systems. EMycin is built in InterLisp, a research system that is fairly difficult to get access to. Others are more accessible, however. Computer-aided instruction in medicine has a system Guidon, and that in engineering has Sophie.

Search problems in chemistry are handled by expert systems like Dendral, Sechs, and Synchem. Problem solving Esystems are:

- EL, for circuit analysis
- Molgen, for genetics
- Mecho, for mechanics

R1 is an Esystem for configuring computers; Pecos, for programming; and Age, Hearsay III, and Rosie, for system building.

These efforts nearly have a background in methodology in common. Their strength lies in lessons learned. They see, for instance, a pattern: direct representation, simple method, refinements. From there, the methodology resident in the Esystem leads to pattern recognition, speech understanding, or board games—depending on the objectives.

In pattern recognition, the fundamental concept is feature extraction, combination, and selection. Then come refinements: feature construction from components and weighted combinations. Further refinements may involve adjustment, learned extrapolation, breadth and/or depth, redundancy control, and large-scale searches.

To write a search-based game program, such as chess, the expert system must look into the expanding current position, within specified rules, evaluate terminal localities, and simulate to select moves. In this process:

- The *basic concept* is search.
- *Refinements* include general heuristics, evaluation techniques, and learning.

Heuristic search is a kind of algorithm adequate for some games, but not for all. Expert system design starts with working principles and follows an application-oriented path. Since the building of the first expert system in the early 1970s, several successful projects have demonstrated that, when equipped with the appropriate knowledgebank, methodology, and set of rules, computers are capable of expert performance.

Typically, this implementation path involves the convergence of many disciplines to make an artificial intelligence product. At the foundations are two disciplines:

1. Software engineering
2. Cognitive psychology

In software engineering, structured approaches have made yesterday's risky projects simple routines. Application systems are becoming reasonably intelligent: database management systems and fourth-generation languages are examples.

Now available is a range of programming environments that multiply productivity and program sophistication. Their features include *help*, *undo* (reverse the effect of the last transaction), and other operations. One of the most intriguing is *dwim* (do what I mean). Syntax and spelling correctors are other examples.

Like structured programming, artificial intelligence is possible in any system or language, though some languages are easier to use than others. The methodology is fundamental: All successful AI systems are based on good systems analysis. The tools of structured analysis complement AI; they isolate and focus key issues in a system.

The other pillar of expert systems is cognitive psychology. In the foundations of its implementation is the *emerging understanding of thinking as information processing*. As we understand it today (rightly or wrongly), a major difference between humans and other animals is that humans can pass on knowledge. But knowledge is cumulative for machines as well.

At the same time, humans are limited to a fixed endowment of memory capacity, whereas in terms of multiaccess and multiprocessing machine storage, access and processing power can be expanded at will. Perception, complex information processing, and large-capacity storage complement cognitive psychology and lead toward machine intelligence. Another way to look at the subject is that expert systems are the first concrete attempts to industrialize the production and distribution of knowledge.

Addressing computational tasks that are ill-structured, without known algorithmic solutions, and in which the logic and organization of the tasks present significant difficulties requires powerful SW/HW engines. To this is added the challenging task of interpreting cognitive psychology for the computer system, whose main mission is understanding human cognitive processes through modeling and experimentation.

Cognitive models yield methods of representing knowledge and inference making in practical ways. Yet, in most cases, intensive computation is warranted or even necessary. Perception requires large amounts of processing. Current chess-playing programs, for example, explore up to 10,000 continuations at a time.

Chess is a good example because, at the start, it is simple to represent by computer. The algorithm is straightforward: look ahead to the end of the game and select the optimal move. The problem is that there are estimated to be 10^{120} chess games. To enumerate the games at one per microsecond would take 10^{107} centuries, or more than 10^{98} times the current age of the universe. Hence, the way to go about it is to limit the extent of the search by heuristics. In the same way, computer models are used to verify theories. The process involves seven steps:

1. Define the cognitive task
2. Observe humans performing the task
3. Record behavior in protocols
4. Study protocols to formulate a theory of subject behavior
5. Write programs according to theory
6. Run program on same problem(s), keeping trace
7. Compare protocol to trace; evaluate theory

Heuristic solutions and the observance of rules and of forbidden moves leads to two lists commonly known as *goodlist* and *badlist*. Using goodlist and badlist reduces the search space. Goodlists include structures known a priori to be contained in the unknown structure. Badlists contain structures which are not allowed, perhaps because they are known to be unstable. A structure generator is a sophisticated algorithm for enumerating these possibilities without redundancy.

Such rules and the lists which they imply are fundamental for converting human behavior piecemeal to computer behavior. The same is true of the representation of knowledge and of process abstracted from particular software and hardware.

KNOWLEDGEBANKS VERSUS DATABASES

The knowledgebank containing the rules and lists relates type-source pairs to data. Examples are frequencies, ranges of variation, dependencies, changes of all types, and terminal states. Methodologies have been available in procedural systems, but they have not been formalized. They are formalized with the knowledgebank.

Stated differently, information handling through classical voice-oriented and paper-based means does not require a formal representation. That is not true of information processing through physical and logical machines serving computing and communications purposes. The process of formalization, from the establishment of formalisms to their implementation and policing action, calls for a specific methodology which is part of the knowledgebank. A key question in establishing such a methodology is whether all information:

- Text and data
- Graphics and images
- Edited voice (for input, transport, output)
- Design specifications
- The rules governing the methodology itself

can be completely formalized. While this process is still in evolution and can be handled only at the level the state of the art permits, the need for using formal languages and formatted information element (IE) structures is beyond doubt, and the means for meeting the goal do exist.

Through algorithms and representations, rules of all kinds may be used when they help. Studies in artificial intelligence closely resemble systems analysis with *representation* and *process* as *free variables*. Anything that works will be acceptable, and this is called an *opportunistic strategy*. Opportunistic programs are introspective. They have reasons for their actions and can even explain their actions to users. However:

1. The form of the program does not necessarily reflect the structure of the problem (at least not directly).

2. Processes are not composed of hierarchies of one- or two-page modules.

3. Processes accomplish goals, but pieces must be understandable individually—which also facilitates development and maintenance.

Typically, the structure of a process will employ connection matrices and decision trees. Changes in specifications modify the structure of the program, or they invalidate it. Based on those notions, Table 12.1 contrasts a database and a knowledgebank. The relations list between information elements will, for instance, help in the match process by eliminating candidates having necessary features that are absent from

Table 12.1   Contents of a Database and of a Knowledgebase

Database	Knowledgebase
Information elements subject to: Input Update Retrieve	Relations among information elements Decision rules Consistency control Access control Propagation actions Dynamic extensibility

the experimental spectrogram and ordering the remaining candidates by the number of peaks accounted for.

A set of rules with single-cycle interpretation is equivalent to a decision tree but is more intelligible if less efficient. It is also easier to alter without introducing errors. In a sense, a decision tree is a compiled form of rules. A knowledgebank might handle the rules it stores through multiple cycling. Interpretation would then require its own rules to govern the flow of control. This would typically be accomplished by manipulating markers. Such programs are currently the best detailed models of human cognition.

Certainty factors in methodology are associated with assertions and with ways of deriving new assertions. Such certainty factors connect confidence in a hypothesis to the dependability of a rule and the certainty of a conclusion. However, the use of certainty factors can also be tricky and misleading.

In consultation, knowledge-based systems:

• Interact with users in problem-oriented, naturalistic languages

• Display what looks like verbal reasoning in the use of knowledge

In the creation of knowledgebanks, knowledge-based systems accept instruction from humans who understand the application. As a model for learning, they apply a production rule to a task and, if an error is made, identify the rule that committed the error. They can also insert a new rule or new rules.

Expert systems use the kind of knowledge that a human does; they can justify their judgments in terms intelligible to users; and they bring all the benefits of computer-based processes to the tasks being executed. That is why *cognitive psychology, complex information processing, and machine intelligence are different perspectives of the same aggregate.*

Table 12.2 divides hardware, software, and knowledgebank features into three reference groups:

Table 12.2 A Comparison of Hardware, Software, and Knowledgebank Features

Hardware	Software	Knowledgebank
	Memory features	
1. Magnetic disks	1. Databases	1. Methodology libraries
2. Optical disks	2. Data validity checks	2. Knowledge-intensive
3. Controllers	3. DBMSs	references
4. Channels	4. Drivers	3. Learning functionality
	5. Program libraries	4. State representation
	6. Security locks	of processes
	7. Update algorithms	
	8. Consistent images	
	9. Downloading capabilities	
	Processing features	
1. Central processing units	1. Applications programs	1. Procedural system
2. Peripheral units	2. Modules and routines	analysis
3. Means for data flow	3. Control identification	2. System design
(intelligent channels)	and verification	3. Program design
	4. Means for program	4. System and program
	portability	documentation
	5. Error handling	5. System and program
	6. Recovery and restart	test references
	7. Monitoring and scheduling of resources	6. Means for device and applications
	8. Setting of priorities	independence
		7. Authentication
		8. Cryptography
	Interactive devices	
1. Video display (color, graphics, image)	1. Cursor	1. Man-information communication
2. Printer	2. Text editor	2. Expert system
3. Plotter	3. Character strings	features
4. Graphic tablet	4. Case constructs	3. Inquiries
5. Light pen	5. Image file	4. Menu techniques
6. Keyboard	6. Graphical presentation	5. Keyword search
7. Functional keys	7. Text, data, graphics, image integration	6. Message handling
8. Mouse	8. Electronic mail capabilities	7. Presentation technology
	9. Videotex send/receive	8. Prompting and help assistance
		9. Training sequences

- Memory capability
- Processing power
- Interactive characteristics

Selectively, these features are available to a variety of applications, which themselves are subject to steady development. Initially, such applications involved board games (checkers, chess), language translation, simple problem solving (puzzles, combinatorial problems). In each case performance is a matter of making the right choices and the goal is a reasonably intelligent process. As experience accumulated, the concept of knowledgebank became important to conserve and present expertise in problem domains. An example is voice understanding based on semantics. By adding sensory capability (robots) and increased intelligence on chips, the frontiers of knowledge-based system technology are pushed forward.

A word of caution: Don't listen to people who tell you: "An expert system needs 100,000 or more logical instructions per second (LIPS). Otherwise, forget it." The basis is a guesstimate of a military project with computer vision and complex robotic activity.

Very powerful computers are necessary when artificial intelligence engines run other machines, but when an intelligent machine interacts with a human person, a PC can do the Esystem job well. Besides, at the current state of the art, what we have available for business applications are *adolescent* expert systems with 100 rules, more or less.* It will be years before these adolescent Esystems reach the age of maturity in business. Yet, they can already be of help.

There is also bound to be a convergence of approaches. Although there have been diverse schools of thought on how to go about artificial intelligence, almost all researchers in the field followed the same sequence of developments, applied similar concepts, considered the same kinds of applications, and obtained parallel results and experiences. Therefore, they also developed a common outlook.

The key question for the future is not being for or against artificial intelligence; it is how we can put AI to work in a valuable way. *Expert systems are based on long human experience. They should serve to augment it rather than substitute for it.*

---

*See also D. N. Chorafas, "Applying Expert Systems in Business," McGraw-Hill Book Company, New York, 1986.

13

DEVELOPING AND USING EXPERT SYSTEMS

With artificial intelligence, the computer is shifting from being a *power-based* to being a *knowledge-based* machine. The expert system (Esystem) is no number-cruncher; it is a construct able to think and reflect about fairly complex situations. Expert systems research is an outgrowth of work done on artificial intelligence (AI)—practically, the first concrete example of its implementation. This field is still in full evolution, and AI interests include speech, imaging, natural languages, seismic interpretation, robotics, artificial vision, and investment analysis.

"The key thing about expert systems," said Donald Michie of the University of Edinburgh, "is that they not only provide accurate answers but also justify their answers in terms that make sense to the human user." That explains the interest we have in Esystems research.

The development of expert systems began at Stanford University. As mentioned in the preceding chapter, the first working prototype was Dendral. The best known project which followed Dendral is Mycin. We will review some of the other examples in the following sections. The success of an expert system is measured by whether the system captures not only textbook knowledge but also the way the mind of the human expert works. This means

- Intuition
- Informal rules

- Formal rules
- Experiential knowledge

All that is necessary for the knowledgebank of the system. The system's effectiveness is actually determined by the quality of its knowledgebank: completeness, usefulness, expandability, validity. Esystem's *inductive engine* is built on these premises.

The task of codifying the expert's judgments is called knowledge engineering. The knowledge engineer must understand the expert's field, brief the expert, debrief the expert's understanding, translate the expert's rules into if-then statements, and then formalize the rules.

A narrowly defined technical performance is not the only criterion of acceptability. Conceptual simplicity is important, and so also are the built-in mechanisms which allow the accumulation of knowledge and the correction of the system's own deficiencies.

SOLVING PROBLEMS

The greatest contributions of Esystems research go beyond the development of high-performance intelligence programs. They impact on the systematic handling and codification of knowledge and on the way and means we use to solve problems. Improved approaches to formalizing and managing knowledge processing are highly important in a variety of medical, scientific, and economic sectors. To solve problems, people not only possess but also handle knowledge and employ it in different ways:

1. Clarifying the issue(s)
2. Judging the dependability of facts
3. Developing alternatives
4. Making choices
5. Deciding on acceptability
6. Developing a plan
7. Suggesting the procedures to be used

Whether man or intelligent machine, the problem solver must know explicitly how to use knowledge. General approaches must be supplemented by knowhow specific to a given domain.

From research in artificial intelligence we have come to realize that not all fields of knowledge are suitable for a strict methodological approach. A task can qualify for an Esystem development if there is at least one human expert who is acknowledged to perform the task well. The primary sources of the expert's abilities must be special

- Knowledge
- Judgment
- Experience
- Ability to formulate rules and methods

In other terms, knowledge, while necessary, is not enough. The expert must be able to articulate the special knowledge and explain the methods used to apply it to a particular task. Also, the task must have a well-bounded domain of application.

One precise example is the extension of decision support systems (DSS) toward artificial intelligence solutions. Figure 13.1 details the transition from DSS to Esystems, and from there to the further-out perspectives of artificial intelligence. Management discipline, business problems, and goals are the criteria used in this comparison.

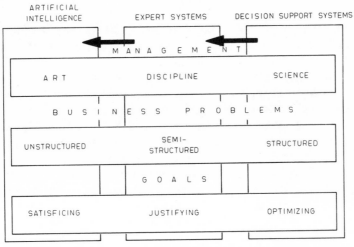

Figure 13.1 Transition from decision support systems toward artificial intelligence solutions. ("Satisficing" is a coined term meaning satisfying within an AI context.)

Observers of AI research often note that the most difficult part of solving a problem is converting the problem from a vague initial statement to a form that is sufficiently precise to allow formal problem solving to begin. Successful expert systems research is disclosing additional new problems, many of which are sociological. The limitations of current expert systems have exposed unsolved problems in such basic areas as:

- Knowledge representation
- Inference
- Perception
- Learning

Progress in solving these fundamental problems would lead to significant advances in the capabilities of artificial intelligence to add value to the faculties the human intellect can support.

The processing of knowledge is often tuned to the requirement imposed by the time in which we live and the tools at our disposal. Current technology is best suited to diagnosis or classification problems whose solutions depend primarily on the possession of a large amount of specialized knowledge, whether factual or empirical.

Progress is also being made on synthetic problems such as planning and design. Success in those areas not only points to the potential of the expert systems field but also helps define the most important subjects for ongoing research.

Diagnosis is often based on differential approaches. Examples in medicine and engineering are classical examples of this line of thinking, as we will see in the following section.

It is much more difficult to develop expert systems for problems that have a synthetic character. Planning is an example, although work is being done in that direction. The most often used approach to representing the domain knowledge (facts and heuristics) needed for an expert system is the production of rules. These are usually referred to as situation-action rules of an if-then set of directives.

The chaining of if-then directives forms a line of reasoning. The rules are actuated by patterns in the global database. Depending on whether the strategy is working forward toward a solution or backward from a hypothesis, processing patterns match either the *if* or the *then* side of the rule. The rule interpreter uses a control structure, often encoded as *metarules*, to find the enabled rule and to decide which rule to apply.

Basic control strategies are top-down (or goal-driven), bottom-up (or data-driven), and a combination of the two. In a combination strategy a convergence process is used to join the top-down and bottom-up lines of reasoning at some intermediate point, which yields the solution. There is, however, no ideal solution for all cases. Data-driven approaches can have the disadvantage of generating many hypotheses not directly related to the problem under consideration. Goal-driven approaches have the disadvantage of perhaps becoming fixed on an initial set of hypotheses and then being difficult to shift in focus when the data available does not support them. However, knowledge representations for facts and relations are not always easy to implement. Certain kinds of knowledge, particularly those without immediate if-then consequences, can be quite difficult to organize efficiently in that sense.

Systems interactivity must also follow a well-defined methodology. Users must describe problems in a strictly defined formal language. The system must respond in the same way and also justify its advice. Stylized and limited explanations of the reasons behind a system's decisions or conclusions must be given.

In terms of development effort, this means that the expert systems developers must have the ability to maintain consistency and resolve conflicts between overlapping items in the knowledgebank. Though several experts may contribute to a project, one must maintain absolute control to ensure quality and responsiveness. The experts building the Esystem may themselves be the greatest contributors to the system's store of knowhow and embedded rules. A prerequisite for the design and maintenance of expert systems is an expert—a point that is often overlooked.

Esystems are unique precisely because they draw conclusions from a store of knowledge. That is why they are said to be knowledge-based. In their logic, they apply rules used by human experts when they make decisions in their field of expertise.

Knowledge is encoded in a symbolic form. Conclusions are drawn through logical or plausible inference rather than by calculation. Subsequently, the expert system displays on request its line of reasoning in a natural-language form. This quality is called *transparency*, as contrasted to the black box approach of an algorithmic program.

Another important characteristic is that expert systems are not locked into any specific decision path. They can choose among alternative paths in their search for conclusions. They weigh facts, scrutinize assumptions, and make choices appropriate to the problems presented to them. Making an expert system is an exercise in the codification of science. To emulate human thinking, a machine intelligence must be constructed. It must be flexible and expandable. These are hallmarks of expert systems.

The set of rules and the methodology making up the knowledgebank can be expanded by

- The addition of new rules
- Corrections to the knowledgebank which are immediately assimilated

This is how an expert system continues to build up its knowledge by adding new information incrementally. The example also identifies what we mean when we say that the Esystem can learn.

Not all expert systems, however, are rule-based. Rule-based systems are most attractive when much of the knowledge in the field comes from experimental associations. When causal information is available, other representations may be more pertinent. An example is networks that link nodes which represent causal relations.

Rule-based systems usually work by:

- Applying rules
- Noting the results
- Implementing new rules based on the changed situation

They can also proceed by directed logical inference, either starting with the initial evidence in a situation and working toward a solution or beginning with hypotheses about possible solutions. In the latter case they will be working backwards to find existing evidence or deduction that supports the stated hypothesis.

Finally, in terms of organization and structure, an expert system is modular: Facts and other knowledge about a particular domain can be separated from the inference procedure (control structure). An expert system differs from more conventional computer programs in several important respects. In a conventional computer program, knowledge pertinent to the problem and methods for using this knowledge are intertwined. Therefore, it is difficult to change the program. In an expert system there is usually a clear separation of

1. General knowledge about the problem, the *knowledgebank*
2. Information about the current problem, the *input data*
3. Methods, *the inference engine* for applying the general knowledge to the problem

With this modularity the program can be changed by simple modification of the knowledgebank. That is particularly true of the rule-based system, which can be altered by the addition or subtraction of rules to or from its knowledgebank.

DENDRAL, MYCIN, AND OTHER ESYSTEMS

The problem-solving approach we have been describing is nicely reflected in the Esystem goals. The solutions which are followed, many with significant success, are best exemplified in the earlier projects: Dendral, Mycin, and Internist are the best examples in the medical profession; Prospector and R1 are among the better known in engineering.

Dendral was built at Stanford University, starting in 1965, by Edward A. Feigenbaum and Joshua Lederberg. Its object was to generate plausible structural representations of organic molecules from mass spectograph data. This approach called for deriving constraints from the data, generating candidate structures, predicting mass spectograms for candidates, and comparing the results with data. Dendral was a rule-based system chaining forward from the data and illustrating the problem-solving approach with expert systems:

- Plan
- Generate
- Test

It has been used for consultancy by organic chemists for more than 15 years, and it is recognized as an expert in mass-spectral analysis.

Dendral was not originally formulated as a knowledge-based aggregate. The *knowledgebank* approach resulted from the failure of conventional computer programming methods in solving the formidable goal the researchers set out to reach: aiding organic chemists in determining the molecular structure of compounds. This is important because it helps demonstrate how open-ended researchers can turn the obstacles they encounter into an ultimate advantage. Dendral led to another program, MetaDendral, which actually discovers new rules about the behavior of fragmented molecules.

Mycin is an Esystem developed in the mid-1970s at Stanford University (by Edward Shortliffe) to help physicians select antibiotics for patients with severe infections. On a number of occasions Mycin has performed at or near the level of expert medical doctors.

The knowledge of infectious diseases is represented in the form of rules. By early 1983 Mycin contained 500 rules dealing with diagnosis and treatment of:

- Bacteria in the blood
- Infection in the cerebrospinal fluid

In the knowledgebank, the rules are expressed in a form that simplifies computer interpretation. An interface is provided to translate them into English for human examination. Furthermore, patient data is stored in the database in the form of attribute-object-value triples. Knowledgebank (rules, methodology) and database complement one another: Mycin must obtain specific knowledge about a given patient.

Mycin works in two phases:

- Diagnostics
- Therapy

In the former, the goal is to apply the rules in the knowledgebank to determine the identity of all suspicious microorganisms. If there is no information in the database about the patient's infection, or if what is known is uncertain, the Esystem has two options. One option is an interactive dialog seeking to obtain knowledge from the user. If obtained, the information is added to the store of knowhow. As an alternative, the Esystem tries to infer the answer from other data about the case.

As an inference system, Mycin reasons backwards from goals to data. Other inference strategies have been used in other domains. For example, in a data-driven strategy the user initially enters all of the information about the problem into the dynamic database. The rules are then applied to *reason forward* from the data to the conclusions.

A new level of complexity is introduced when inference steps are less than certain. Most expert systems that can tolerate uncertainty employ a probability-like measure to weigh and balance conflicting evidence. They may assign probabilities to conclusions and use a form to update those probabilities as information is obtained.

Internist-1 is an Esystem designed for diagnosis in internal medicine. The knowledgebank was built by running difficult cases found in medical journals. These represent some 50 different diagnostic problems. To use Internist-1, a physician enters patient data. As each manifestation is made available to it, the Esystem retrieves the diseases associated with it:

- Each hypothesis is scored.
- Frequencies associated with the manifestation are used.

Retained disease hypotheses are ranked by score. Internist-1 partitions the top hypotheses into groups of competitors. When a diagnosis is chosen, the program recycles to explain the remaining manifestations.

Prospector is a consultation system for mineral exploration. It is designed for problems in regional resource evaluation, ore deposit identification, and drilling site selection. Its knowledgebank is organized around models of different types of ore deposits. In the domain of this Esystem, the usual problems of validation are complicated by the relatively small number of well-known ore deposits of any given type and by the long time between the initial discovery of a deposit and its final characterization. However, Prospector's assessments have repeatedly agreed closely with those of the geological consultants.

Also, in tests involving a prospect undergoing exploration, the program accurately identified the location and extent of ore-grade mineralization. Being based on casual rather than experimental information, Prospector is a networking, rather than rule-based, model. The interconnected nodes represent parts of the physical system in reference. In response to Prospector's questions the user draws contours and fault lines on a digitizing tablet. The result is displayed on Prospector's screen. The Esystem then displays the areas that have the highest probability of containing ore.

Developed by John McDermott at Carnegie Mellon University in the late 1970s, R1 (like XSel) is an Esystem to configure VAX computers. It determines the physical layout and interconnection of computer components and also adds support components missing from an order.

R1 saves engineering time by providing technicians who assemble the systems with information that is much more detailed than the traditional hand-generated specifications. Of over 3000 orders processed in a given 3-month period, over 85 percent of the configurations were flawless, and most of the rest were usable with minor corrections. Errors occurred mainly because R1 lacked information on recently introduced products. While the Esystem may have an embedded capability for learning, the updating of the database is always an important operation.

The implementation of engineering models may lead toward an *intelligent factory* using expert system techniques to ensure that all the machines are working at a high level of efficiency and within acceptable availability levels. The expert system monitors the scheduling of machine tasks to minimize downtime and configure the factory so that work flows efficiently through the plant. The Esystem also monitors breakdowns and presents management with the best alternatives in terms of production and quality assurance. These are developments well within current technology.

HUMAN AND ARTIFICIAL INTELLIGENCE

World knowledge is the information we acquire through formal education and day-to-day experience. This knowledge ranges from the perception and remembrance of facts to crystallized intelligence and fluid intelligence. *Crystallized intelligence* is our ability to use an accumulated body of general information to make judgments and solve problems. It comes into play in understanding and dealing with problems for which there are no clear answers but only better and worse options. *Fluid intelligence* is the ability involved in seeing and using abstract relations and patterns.

The growth of crystallized intelligence can continue well into the eighties for people who remain logically and physically active. Key factors include:

- *Staying involved*, as contrasted to withdrawing from life
- *Being mentally active* and continuing intellectual interests, which increase intelligence through old age
- *Having a flexible personality*

People most able to tolerate ambiguity and enjoy new experiences maintain their mental alertness best through old age.

The next most important issue is *organizing knowledge management*. In businesses that deal mostly with information and knowhow, management has to cope with a new phenomenon. A rapid divergence develops between:

- Power based on position
- Power based on knowledge

This occurs because the base of knowledge that constitutes the foundation of the business changes every day. If the organization sticks to old-fashioned position power to make all of its decisions, the decisions will be made by people unfamiliar with current technology. In general, the faster the change in the knowhow on which the business depends the greater the divergence between knowledge and position power, which brings up the subject of knowledge acquisition for personal and intellectual survival.

Knowledge acquisition is the key problem with Esystems as well. The best way found so far is the construction of systems able to learn from their environment and the job they are doing. This permits them to apply the knowhow they have obtained and, in some cases, to modify it. The knowledge an expert system employs should be made visible to its users so that they can view and even modify the knowledgebank. This is known as transparency. In arriving at a recommendation, the system should maintain an audit trail of the steps and the pieces of knowledge used. Audit trails also provide explanations for recommendations and thereby help users develop confidence in an expert system.

These mechanisms for user feedback allow the knowledgebank to continue to grow long after the knowledge engineer has left. This growth is helped by the fact the knowledgebank includes theorems, heuristics, algorithms, rules of thumb, assumptions, probabilities, and causal laws. To manage such diverse forms of knowledge, a wide variety of knowledge representation and inference schemes has been developed.

- *A knowledge representation scheme is a way to codify knowledge.*
- *An inference scheme is a way to use knowledge to arrive at new knowledge.*

Spaces can be searched either in a forward direction by starting at the initial state and applying the operators to find a path to a goal state or in a backward direction by starting with the goal state and applying the inverses of the operators to find a path to the initial state. Which is the more appropriate way depends both on the problem and on the nature of the space. More particularly, it depends on the data describing the current problem state and on the antecedent *if* part of the operator.

Hence, a forward search is often said to be *data-driven* (or antecedent-driven). In a backward search, applying an inverse operator corresponds to finding all states that would allow the original operator to produce the desired state. It also means setting up these states as subsidiary goals to be reached from the initial state. A backward search is *goal-driven*. By another technique, called *graph-searching*, several paths are explored simultaneously and current states are kept track of. Some paths may be explored faster than others, depending on the procedure and the problem.

Steady updating of knowhow is fundamental because many problem-solving systems are based on the formulation of problem solving as a search procedure. The description of a desired solution is a goal; the set of possible steps leading from initial conditions to possible solutions is the space to be searched.

Problem solving is carried out by searching for sequences that lead to solutions that satisfy a goal. Search is at the heart of a reasoning system, and failure to organize it properly can result in problem solving that is inefficient or unreliable. The simplest approach is to search a solution space exhaustively. This is, however, appropriate only if the space of possible solutions is quite small or if a powerful pruning mechanism is available for quickly eliminating most of the space from consideration.

Each rule in a knowledgebank represents the knowhow behind a single decision. Organizing the rules to work in synergism on different problems is an important task in knowledge engineering. A reasonably simple strategy is to have an interpreter scan the rules to find one whose antecedents match assertions in machine memory. Rules can be organized into networks that determine when they get applied, as when certain data is changed or certain goals are indicated.

In both human and artificial intelligence, *a knowledgebank is a set of stored rules.* Knowledge typically is represented in one of several formal ways:

- If-then logical rules
- Frames or scripts
- Algorithmic formulas

Humans and intelligent machines also need *context data*: the information built up by the system about each particular situation in which a problem arises. The third vital component is the *inference engine*, typically a computer program that provides the strategies to draw inferences and produce solutions to problems.

In both natural and artificial intelligence systems, inference engines are tailored to accommodate knowledge representation and include facilities for dialogs. They draw inferences about a situation as it is being presented and present the logical reasoning behind the solution being generated.

With Esystems, the now-evolving knowledgebanks will be significantly larger than any previously attempted or presented in a database mapping. Typically, they will consist of *several thousand rules*, and they will steadily expand. Research will concentrate not only on the fundamental expert systems but also on speed, vision, and natural-language understanding, as well as new computer architectures. The rules in the knowledgebank will both lead toward decisions and be able to document the choices being made.

There are, however, different challenges to overcome; rule extraction is one bottleneck, and what to do with those rules is yet another. The crux of the Esystem design problems is making models out of perceptions. Expert system design suffers from the same troubles that plague conventional system design efforts. Inexact programs are designed because people are inexact when they try to explain what they do and need. Expert systems designers have an invaluable tool for managing the inexact nature of the work. The challenges are, however, many, and for this reason only 30 percent at the high end of the Fortune 500 companies are at the Esystems crossroads.

INTERACTING WITH THE ESYSTEM

Expert systems software may make computers very easy to use. Some companies are working on programs that will eventually be able to remember an individual's habits in using the computer. The first applications, starting in the 1985–1986 time frame, are typically very rudimentary pattern-recognition techniques in tutorial programs that teach novices how to operate software. The Esystem will adjust the level of tutorial difficulty by determining the proficiency of the user running the program.

These developments will ease communications, but the interaction with the Esystem is a problem to be faced immediately. In this, we must distinguish between designer communications, teach the system more rules, and tune the system—and commodity offerings. With *designer communications*, the main problem is the acquisition of knowhow. The best approach is the design of:

- Self-teaching, self-learning systems
- Computer induction of programs from data
- Other forms of reasoning, including concept formation

Mastery of world-class skill can require the acquisition, storage, and manipulation of more than 30,000 patterns. *Inverse functions* can allow very large question and answer tables to be built. *Inductive inference* will call for fast patterns from examples, with algorithms able to compact the tables into pattern-based decision rules. Being automated, the Esystem amplifies and/or modifies the acquired knowledge: methodology and rules.

The precondition is the availability of a machine-executable formal language accepting *concept expressions* and rejecting other inputs as ill-formed. An Esystem language must be:

1. Pattern matching
2. List processing
3. Object-oriented
4. Recursive
5. In accordance with logical inheritance mechanisms

APL, ADA, Pascal, Basic, and, even more, Fortran and Cobol, impose an inordinate handling load while contributing nothing to the object problem. The currently favored AI languages are:

- *Common Lisp*, as developed through accords finally reached in academia to establish a common and modernized Lisp background.
- *Prolog.* Assures logical inference, pattern-matching, declarative approaches.
- *InterLisp.* Notations, structured text and data, data and program homogeneity, pattern matching, recursive, list-processing generalization, dynamic memory allocation.
- *Prolog and Lisp* with Algoloids.

Machine characteristics should include bit-mapping, window presentation, mouse or other pointing device, good size central and auxiliary memory, and symbolic manipulation. Among the problems to be met are efficient programming, rule description, effective cross-correlation, and the ability to obtain significant results in analysis of phenomena and their presentation. Eventually, knowledge manufacturing will rest on *concept chips*, which are equivalent to multilevel circuits.

Commodity offerings include EMycin, AL/X, Expert, Microexpert, Sage, and Reveal. They typically feature:

1. Strategies for incremental rule acquisition

2. Tools for rule acquisition

3. Rule syntax

4. Test and debugging tools

5. Agile consultation facility

EMycin (Essential Mycin, an underpinning of Mycin) has general applicability and helps build other Esystems. Sacon, Puff, and Litho are examples of Esystems built on EMycin capabilities. However, although EMycin has a general knowledge structure, it is not suitable for all applications. Different theories of knowledge representation constitute the basis of the languages such as Age, KRL, KL-One, RLL, OPS-5, Units, FRL, and Omega.

A Mycin Esystem example helps explain how the system operates. The first and most important part is that of *deduction rules for the knowledgebank*. Rules being admitted are of the form:

```
IF  <hypothesis>  THEN  <action>
```

The *hypothesis* is a logical combination (AND operator) of the type function, object, attribute, value. The *action* is expressed in a chain: object, attribute, value, and certainty. Mycin defines 24 *functions*, same, unknown, definite, ... ; 80 *attributes*, identify, site, sensitive, ... ; 11 *objects*, organism, culture, drug, ... ; and over 300 rules.

The *knowledge of the universe* is expressed in a chain of attribute, object, value, certainty: site, culture, blood. Knowledge engineering translates the concepts in a human expert into machine reasoning. Knowledge systems must also be endowed with the *interpretation of the rules*. Rules are called in a scheme which first produces in-depth research in an and/or tree. Given a goal, the search results in a precomputed list of the rules whose conclusion takes the user toward the objective.

First a valid minimum of rules (a subgroup) is taken. The premises of the rules are valued, and an assurance is obtained for each clause. Conclusion reflects the algorithm:

```
<value of premise> * <certainty factor of conclusion>
```

If deduction is not possible or there are doubts of the validity, a new subgroup of rules is taken. The process is repeated until all clauses are valued by using the necessary rules.

The *query/answer system* manages, in a natural language, the dialog with the user. The research for the natural language is done through *keywords* and the use of *templates* associated with each function. The *explaining of reasoning* calls for a search of the rules used on preceding occasions (to answer how and why questions). It requires a research of specific tools for the present occasion, as well as a demonstration of the rules used.

The *acquisition of new knowledge* rests on the development of new inductive/deductive rules, the updating of existing rules, rigorous control of new and updated rules, and steady evaluation of system consistency. For acquisition of new knowledge (at current state of the art) we employ classical components (rules and methodology) by combining them in an expert manner.

For instance, with data from an electroencephalogram, the Esystem will create a correlation of four channels, confront them, compare them to "normal" behavior, make a cross-correlation, consult tables, find out if system functions are within ranges, provide evidence of fine fluctuations, flash out exceptions, act as watchdog of primary and associated conditions, and provide diagnostics.

14

LAYERS OF KNOWHOW: FROM DECISION SUPPORT TO EXPERT SYSTEMS

Decades ago, Alan Turing debated the virtues of infallibility and intelligence as machine attributes. He wrote:

> It is easy for us to regard [a human mathematician's] blunders as not counting and give him another chance, but the machine would probably be allowed no mercy. In other words then, if a machine is expected to be infallible, it cannot also be intelligent.

Could even an intelligent machine produce a sonnet the equal of Shakespeare's? Turing answered in 1949 that this question was "perhaps a little bit unfair because a sonnet written by a machine would be better appreciated by another machine." Expert systems make this difference. They are appreciated by humans.

But expert systems are not the first software products to come to our assistance in solving problems. A rigorous mathematical methodology was the basis of the analytical concepts applied in naval operations by the British Admiralty in World War I. The results obtained were instrumental in launching operations research (OR) on an appreciable scale by the American forces in World War II.

Operations research was much more successful in military activities than in management practice, although some tools, like George Danzig's linear programming, proved quite helpful as aids to decision making. That happened in the early to mid-1950s. The 1960s were rather sterile in OR in business (except for PERT), and in the 1970s emphasis shifted to management information systems (MIS).

By the late 1970s, a consciousness that what managers truly need is decision support to help them make intelligent choices among several alternatives started to develop. A decision support system (DSS) is different from a management information system. Unlike the latter, it allows managers to select and manipulate information in ways that help them make better, more informed choices in allocation of resources.

The ability to simulate business situations is a characteristic that clearly distinguishes DSS from MIS. To be of use to the decision maker, the model must be able to represent the real situation both in a realistic manner and in a logical format. It must, that is, visualize the multiple dimensions of the business.

Typically, decision support systems are computer-based. A basic characteristic of a DSS is an interactive analytical capability that permits managers to model their problems as completely and accurately as possible. In turn, this provides the basis for testing the impact of different scenarios.

The way we have treated them in the preceding two chapters, Esystems go well beyond the DSS. However, as we will see in this chapter, valid and practical approaches to expert systems are usually built on DSS knowhow. This is the subject to which the first section addresses itself.

A DECISION SUPPORT INFRASTRUCTURE

We spoke of the role of decision support systems in business and industry, and the discussion suggested that the systems should provide management with the equivalent of a flight simulator. Through DSS, different solutions can be pretested in the safety of the computer before trying them out in the real world.

Although early applications were mainframe-based, models that are currently available on microcomputers have the memory and computational power needed to satisfy the requirements of reasonable size DSSs. This book has treated several examples starting with spreadsheet packages. At the same time, a new class of software evolved from financial modeling languages for mainframes. Such languages are used interactively as a shared resource.

A realistic multidimensional financial modeling language permits easy consolidation

• In multiple hierarchies

• Across several dimensions

A convenient feature of such a modeling language is the availability of a variety of built-in communications, presentation, and computation functions. Commonly used algorithmic approaches should be available along with heuristic solutions. But most critical is the ability of the language to integrate different views and findings into one aggregate function.

The dynamic modeling of a business system has two parts. The first is function modeling: identifying and describing functions, their supporting communication paths, and their storage requirements. The second is logic modeling. It focuses on the rules of behavior of the business functions. We could in this sense distinguish three layers of support corresponding to the three main management levels in any organization:

1. The lower layer is covered by the 30 years of accumulating routines of classical data processing. In its current status, it is typically served by mainframes, concentrators, and nonintelligent terminals.
2. The middle layer is proper to office automation. Projects should focus on linking both to the upper and to the lower layer but should not be impeded by either one of the layers.
3. The upper layer is addressed to top management. It is the area best suited for decision support systems and expert systems.

The middle and upper layers are best served by communicating, multifunction personal computers. But attention! Winners do not automate what they do today, whether through paper or classical DP. Losers do so, and end up making the same mistakes faster.

Here is precisely where computer and communications professionals have their business opportunity. The product is for the consumer, but they, the specialists, should have the knowhow to bring forward the new imaginative areas of implementation. Theory, practice, methodology, and tools must be presented to the end user in a coherent way to provide new insights into decision support. To some people with knowhow and the drive to achieve results, new thoughts are thinkable and new solutions are possible.

One of the features that distinguishes the better DSS implementation is data management. Because of poor practices in the past, a number of products have no data manager whatsoever, which means the user has to worry about keeping track of an ever-increasing profusion of information elements.

In contrast, a friendly DSS software package should have a database manager so the user can move between modules in a fully transparent way. No user should have to worry about database manipulation. A good data manager will also allow the user to secure data in a dependable manner, including a workstation-to-mainframe connection.

The role of the computer professional in this connection is fairly evident. The most significant contribution will be in *information modeling*: identifying, describing, and structuring the information required to operate the DSS. These processes determine what types of objects exist and what facts are known about them. Facilities must be provided to collect, store, edit, and validate the descriptors of the information elements involved. First the specialist must define the types of the relations that exist among entities; then measurements of the entities must be provided and used to distinguish one entity from another.

Charles Bachman emphasizes the need for *logic modeling*, dealing with the rules that control the behavior of each function. Logic modeling rules are based on the fact that each of the business system actions and events described in a function model is deterministic in its behavior. There is a function planned for every possible event, and there is a description of the actions that make up the function. The computer expert must be able to establish the proper relations, connections, structures, and metaphors.

Metaphors describe what the computer does as opposed to what people do. Different DSS packages and Esystems imply (as well as apply) diverse metaphors. The TK! Solver, for instance, is a different metaphor than the usual spreadsheet such as Multiplan, yet, both are used on the same types of problems. The expert in computers and communications should go beyond the commodity software offering within the user's reach. As Bachman aptly suggests, the expert should be able to work on a comprehensive business-modeling methodology including information, function, and logic modeling.

In the same way, the specialist should be able to develop and maintain a comprehensive interface between the system and its users that permits operation in a forms mode, a graphics mode, and a business description language readable over large segments of operations. The specialist should design agile access to automated files of business models by a number of simultaneous users while supplying the requisite amount of security and integrity.

Another key function is to permit the creation of multiple versions of a business model to reflect changes over time. In fact, a valid DSS implementation should handle time conversions automatically: consolidate days, decompose semesters into months, but also translate values in terms of time.

To perform such functions in an able manner, the new breed of systems professional must not only possess great knowhow but also update it steadily. There is a significant difference between the level of knowhow demanded of Cobol programmers and that required of specialists in 4GLs, DSSs, and expert systems (Figure 14.1).

The system should be able to compute various lead-lag relations between all kinds of time periods and manage complex, multiple conversions. New versions can be under construction while older ones are in production. Any newer version should be able to include elements of the older versions without the need to recalculate their content.

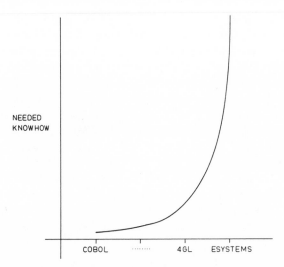

Figure 14.1 Levels of knowhow demanded of Cobol, 4GL, and Esystems programmers.

Furthermore, the DSS should support the use of both national language and corporate language keywords for key concepts of business modeling. It should also be able to handle an extension of business modeling concepts in the direction a particular user might find important. This means the facility of experimentation and evolution in function of the users' requests.

EMPHASIZING THE ANALYTIC ABILITY

One of the most vital features of decision support and expert systems is analytic ability. Once the decision maker has successfully created a financial or business model, how easily can different scenarios be tested? This interactive model interrogation represents the acid test of a DSS.

At the decision support level, specific capabilities that should be investigated include what-if, sensitivity analysis, goal seeking, and risk analysis. Most of the better DSS packages provide these basic interrogation features, but not many are truly interactive and responsive in multidimensional interrogation. This is an expert systems characteristic.

Let's consider a real-life example of what-if concerning price control through spreadsheets. In early 1984, the government of a major country established price controls for the local pharmaceutical industry. They were of the cost-plus type. This changed the price structure of a company's 450 products. A first spreadsheet evaluation helped establish the products to which management should give most attention during negotiations with the government. A second spreadsheet evaluation identified the margins on which the company should insist for its top five income earners. These two evaluations presented full documentation under the new price structure. Management bet on them and the company won a settlement that made profits 12 percent higher than before the price controls were enacted.

Another firm used spreadsheet-level DSS for labor settlements. Through SuperCalc, management evaluated what would happen as a result of demands posed by labor. A total of 22 alternatives concerning a labor force of 5000 were worked out within 2 weeks. The settlement which was reached would have been impossible (within the time frame) without decision support tools. This will become all the more true as management decision requirements increase in complexity. Here is the case of a firm requiring a six-dimensional model able to handle

- Product lines
- Market drives
- Customer types
- Profit margins
- Competitive pressures
- Several different locations

A good multidimensional DSS product should answer these types of questions after one or two straightforward commands in plain English. To develop an expert system able to handle a multidimensional environment interactively, Bloomingdale's, at the time of writing, was working with a group of knowledge engineers from Columbia University. The project's goal was to build an expert system to replace much of the buyer's job. In the initial phase, Bloomingdale's did not picture the system as selecting new items or negotiating a deal with a supplier, but management thought it might be able to do almost everything else.

Intelligent models able to provide support to decision making (and decision makers) should definitely be able to handle databases in new ways. They should relate to the emerging type of text and database structures which increasingly contain qualitative information as well as quantitative data. The new databases are composed of:

1. Hard numbers subject to objective verification
2. Softer, future-oriented numbers and comments

The latter are most important in meeting strategic planning objectives and for reporting on performance.

Soft numbers and hard numbers deeply interest the end user, but the computer professional has a broad field of study and implementation which should be transparent to the user. That's the issue of *structure* for text, data, graphs, and icons. It includes:

- **Data Models.**   These models provide the user with a framework and with formalisms.
- **Data Languages.**   Query, manipulation, and presentation languages simplify the man-information communication.
- **Data Independence.**   This is an attribute to be guaranteed in regard to applications, logical and physical media, and general portability.

Agile DSS and expert system implementations must be able to manage the very large knowledgebases we will need in the future. *Dataflow* concepts can be employed. In a dataflow machine, the processing units do not have to look for data in memory. They address themselves to whatever calculation is necessary when a data packet arrives. Each operation executes automatically once it has sufficient data.

The process can be represented by data value tokens passing along operation nodes. Graphs can readily be combined by joining their input/output nodes. Only actual data values, not memory addresses, are passed around the nodes. In this way, calculations cannot interfere with each other by changing the data value in a shared memory and thereby creating interlocks or side effects. A dataflow architecture features no central control, which allows instructions to execute automatically when all necessary data is available.

Graphics terminals can be used to construct dataflow paths to be executed directly as programs by the computers. Dataflow is one of the architectural approaches to very rapid handling of text, data, and images—both processing and structures. A valid graphics module should generate standard plots and charting, as well as the more complex icons. The user should have full format control over plot size, titles, labels, annotations, scaling, zooming, shading, and color.

It is, indeed, useful to be able to generate multiple graphs per page and to preview and modify each graph on softcopy. Compatibility with a wide variety of printers and plotters is a helpful feature, and so is the production of presentation quality slides and interactive infopages.

Good reporting and display features facilitate the manager's task of evaluating results and disseminating them to others. Hence, an important consideration is the relative ease with which users can develop report formats to suit their exact needs. Whether graphical or tabular, report formats should be easy to view and modify. There should be available standard reporting format options from which users can select instead of having to develop all formats from scratch, each time reinventing the wheel.

As outlined in Chapter 1, computer professionals should pay significant attention to communication linkages. The existence of many fairly large commercial databases underscores this argument. The same is valid of distributed data processing and microcomputers. A vital feature of an effective DSS and expert system is communication capability.

A capital question is this: Does the package support multiple communication linkages to other databases? Is the micro version fully integrated with the mainframe software, thereby permitting easy uploading and downloading of text, data, graphs, and models? Already a critical issue, the *host attachment* will become even more so in the years to come.

A highly related argument centers on the command language facility. This is no longer a simple matter of developing operations. The system's shell should be able to:

- Write messages to the user
- Accept responses from the user
- Validate the responses
- Provide appropriate warning and error messages
- Execute various command sequences depending on the specific responses received

The range of functions to be supported indicates that command language capability lets the experienced user design an interactive application system for a specific set of problems, which can then be employed by others with no knowledge of the intelligent system itself.

But while many sophisticated applications should be seen through, the easier ones must not be forgotten. An example is menus. The main menu must be available at all times. Only appropriate options should be offered, and they must be ordered by frequently occurring sequences.

Option groups should be labeled, and a hierarchical routing structure to the infopages should be developed.*

DEVELOPING EXPERT SYSTEMS OVER DSS

Sophisticated expert systems are scientifically intriguing. By providing more than one order of magnitude greater intelligence than DSS, they enable us to explore areas of human capability in which we have enormous interest, including areas that are relevant to coping with uncertainty. As the preceding two chapters demonstrate, artificial intelligence has, over the years, led to a growing range of results. Those results, in turn, have led the professional community to make promises, many of which have turned out to be more difficult to fulfill than was anticipated.

Serious effort and most commendable results characterize the projects which initially set their sights relatively low, building on acquired experience rather than trying to take one giant step forward. This led to the three-layered structure shown in Figure 14.2:

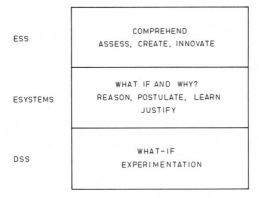

Figure 14.2 The three-layered structure from decision support to expert systems and artificial intelligence.

1. At the bottom is DSS: what-if experimentation.
2. The next higher layer is Esystems: what if and why.
3. The top layer is expert support systems (ESS), able to comprehend, assess, create, innovate.

---

*See also D. N. Chorafas, "Interactive Message Services," McGraw-Hill, New York, 1984.

The Esystems layer is where everybody works at the present time: machine intelligence able to reason, postulate, learn, justify its advice, and relate interactively with the user. ESS is far away in terms of realization, maybe as far away as the mid- to late 1990s. If and when ESS does come around, intelligent machines will embody not only expert knowledge but also common sense and practical reasoning. What distinguishes commonsense reasoning, however, is the ability to draw on an enormous background of experience in the most unpredictable ways.*

We don't yet have the technology to do that sort of thing with computers. Hence, let's concentrate on the background notion behind expert systems as they stand now and will for the next 5 to 10 years. This background notion rests on a simple fact: We increasingly have to apply more expertise to solve problems intelligently. From this comes the postulate that, if properly used, computers and communications can support this evolving need.

Beginning with fundamentals, an Esystem design and development project is based on the premise that the intellectual capability of computer devices is such that computers can reason, postulate, and learn, but *not* necessarily comprehend. Over the more than 30 years of their usage, computers were not handled in a way to:

- Provide evidence
- Calculate uncertainty
- Reach conclusions

Yet, now we have ways to do just those things. We can establish usable knowledgebanks and develop tools which permit computers to emulate human intellect.

In spite of their cleverness, such systems don't need to be large. But they do make a lot of difference to the end user: *It is much easier to interact and converse with an intelligent system* than with a dumb one. Conversation with an intelligent system has this characteristic: It is eventually arriving at some sort of assessment taking place through questions and answers on both sides. The key is "some sort of assessment." Depending on it, Esystems can be of many types that broadly fall into two main classes:

1. *Inductive*, that is, developing their own rules and methods as they find appropriate and going along with acquired experience. Typically, their environments are not clear or change frequently.

---

*Common sense, a proverb says, is the most broadly distributed quality. That's why each of us has so little.

2. *Deductive.* For them, the rules are assigned in advance by the developer. The environment to which they apply is fairly stable in characteristic rules.

Both classes have roughly the physical structure represented in Figure 14.3. The components include hardware for symbolic processing. Esystems are symbolic machines rather than traditional DP-type computers. As a matter of fact, such hardware only now comes to the marketplace at reasonably low cost. Parallel processing machines of fifth-generation type will feature the possibility of thinking along several lines of reasoning at the same time. But there can also be simpler engines possessing artificial intelligence (AI) characteristics.

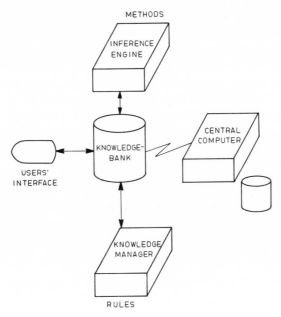

Figure 14.3 Typical structure of an expert system: from local resources to central computer support.

For both the more complex and the simpler solutions an extraordinary range of knowledge and experience is most relevant. The more complex solutions are necessary because we never know what we will need or when we will need it. Nor do we usually even notice that we are using this background knowledge.

Simpler solutions must focus on one well-defined subject, rather than be polyvalent. That is true of PC- and chip-based intelligent engines.

That's why in Chapter 1 it was suggested that at the workstation level Esystems will be highly specialized.

Today, artificial intelligence machines specially tailored to process AI languages are expensive. They range in price from $20,000 to more than $100,000. The economics are changing, however. Texas Instruments, for example, is working under a Department of Defense contract to shrink virtually the entire machine onto a single chip by 1986. In late 1984, NCR introduced a chip specially designed for processing and analyzing images. One application is allowing robots to see. (The chip, developed with Martin Marietta, can do many calculations in parallel, whereas conventional circuits do one task at a time and are rapidly overwhelmed by the number of calculations needed to analyze images.)

Still, the development of a meaningful artificial intelligence chip will require putting at least 10 million logic elements (gates) onto a single piece of silicon. It is, however, expected that by the year 2000 we will have 1 billion gates on a chip. The Department of Defense wants to place AI processors in weapons such as tanks, which would be able to maneuver by themselves, and missiles, which would be able to pick out their own targets. But the largest market for artificial intelligence chips will be industrial and financial: from robotics to investment advisors.

As the range of applications multiplies, we will need a stable methodology to cope with the demand for Esystems. Here is where the best of computer professionals should be applying themselves. As a suggestion, the logical parts of an expert system could involve four components:

1. *Shell:* This includes a general structure, knowledge manager, and user interface.

2. *Base:* Essentially, the knowledgebank and its rules.

3. *Languages:* For instance, Prolog, Lisp, EMycin, Rosie.

4. *Environment:* It consists of pieces which can be put together like an Erector set.

The logical components of this toolkit can be assembled to meet needs. The role played by the logical part is that of making expertise more widely available. It assists experts through an integrated picture, monitors activities too complex for the human brain, and makes a higher level of performance feasible.

IMPLEMENTING EXPERT SYSTEMS

We said that a layered approach characterizes decision support systems and expert systems. Both kinds of systems use facts, rules, and reasoning methods. But DSSs mainly focus on facts, have few rules, and have only one method. To reason, postulate, and learn, expert systems need knowledgebanks with hundreds of rules—and they are rich in methodology. The latter will be further strengthened as the expert systems become increasingly more able to provide evidence, calculate uncertainty, reach conclusions, and document the conclusions.

Like the knowhow of the experts whom they aim to assist, the knowledge of Esystems is specialized. The systems are question-answering models applying themselves in topic domains and engaging in dialog with users. While they include presuppositions and assumptions about the user (and by the user), the more sophisticated Esystems try to overcome possible limitations in user knowledge: Does the user know his goals? Does he express himself perfectly? Does he know about the knowledgebase?

To a great extent, Esystems' queries are translations of user goals, including assumptions about what is said and unsaid. They involve complete answers, need relevant facts, and keep open windows to further information and exploration. Expert systems may possess the capacity to reformulate questions and problems, provide themselves with guidance by user goals, modify their queries as more information becomes known, and go on to new goals. They keep traces of solution paths as well as of the explanations and justifications they give. Successful projects to develop Esystems typically:

1. Are small in size

2. Are addressed to well-defined fields

3. Rest on limited domains of knowledge, but with high knowhow applied to them

The time to develop an Esystem can be very contained, provided the proper skill is applied. Table 14.1 presents seven organizational steps with the corresponding time investment for a financial adviser Esystem. The time investment is divided between the system team and the professional expert in this field of interest. It will be appreciated that this investment is fairly contained and the implementation can materialize in a short timetable.

There is nothing comparable to the long time periods which have, for over 30 years, characterized data processing projects. But good results can be achieved only when there is a precise plan of action and a well-defined approach on how to approach the Esystem model conceptually. Figure 14.4 offers an example. This is an intellectual work of excellence to which computer and communications specialists should apply themselves.

Table 14.1 Time Investment for Financial Adviser Expert System

	Two- or three-person system team	One expert in applic. field
1. Establish goals and timetable	5	2
2. Preliminary work on key factors	20	6
3. Analysis of basic aspects using shell	18	2
4. Prototyping and experimentation	70	20
5. Technical design reviews	12	5
6. System evaluation	15	4
7. Manuals and final report	10	1
	150 days	40 days
• Investment	About 7 worker-months	Less than 2 worker-months
• Timetable	2 or 3 calendar months	

It is to the credit of the management of information systems operations that Bankers Trust took the leadership in this direction. The Esystem model for foreign operations at Bankers Trust was built on an existing DSS structure, and introduced to its design were weighting factors the trader can influence within a given range. However, the expert system tracks the performance of the trader in establishing such factors.

For example, in the part developed for foreign exchange trade data entry (built, as mentioned, on the DSS understructure) the technical market conditions include:

	Weight factor
Forex spot rate	X_1
Forex fund rate	X_2
Trading volume	X_3
Market liquidity	X_4

This emulates the responses of the present-day trader as he quantifies his activities. Though the practice may change as experience is gained with Esystems (the latter being eventually able to generate the weight factors by itself, and protect and redefine them) the results Bankers Trust has obtained are commendable.

Computer professionals should appreciate that even the current level of sophistication in decision rules is in itself a demonstration of the

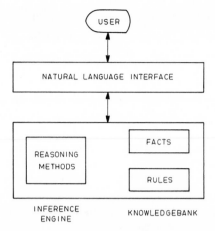

Figure 14.4   A conceptual Esystem model. Reasoning methods, facts, and rules integrate through successive layers.

foundation on which the system is building. Let's look in greater detail into the differences in facts, rules, and reasoning methods between DSS and Esystems. Table 14.2 presents the organization and structure of a decision support system developed for Forex operations. As mentioned, the critical factors are facts, rules, and reasoning methods.

Table 14.2   A Forex DSS Built with a View to Esystems

Facts	Rules	Reasoning methods
Market		
• Currency Forex positions	• P/L calculators	• Spot effect positions
• Contract rates	• Dynamic equilibrium	
• Calculations	between Forex and	
	money markets	
	• Line of credit criteria	
	• Trade criteria	
Internal		
• Profit centers		
• Lines of credit		
• Trading limits		
• Customers and locations		

- The *facts* are divided into internal and external.
- The *rules* are classical decision-tracking criteria.
- The *reasoning methods* (of a DSS) are limited to only one consideration.

Note that the DSS is designed to be sensitive to profit and loss limits, which themselves are a function of trader results: The trader who has had a profit will be willing to take more risk on a day, month, or year basis. Since the year basis is chosen (the system is reset every year), the trader acts conservatively in the early months.

In contrast to the DSS structure, the expert system is richer in reasoning capabilities. As Table 14.3 indicates, not only are the reasoning methods now characterized by four items instead of one but also the list will grow with time and experience.

Quite important, the rules have been redesigned. There is now a two-digit number of rules available to the Esystem, though Table 14.3 presents only three rules as an example. It is not possible to describe all the rules without revealing the structure of the system (which is confidential).

Table 14.3 Esystems for Forex Operations

Facts	Rules	Reasoning methods
Technical information		
• Forex rates	• Stop loss	• Moving average
• Deposit rates	• High/low	• Graphics curvature
• Volume	• Capital limits	• Relativity
• Liquidity		• Support levels
Fundamental information		
• Inflation rate		
• Interest rate		
• Balance of payments		
• Money supply		
• Capital investments		
Psychological factors		
• Expectation: bullish/bearish		
• Sentiment		
• Date		
• Time		

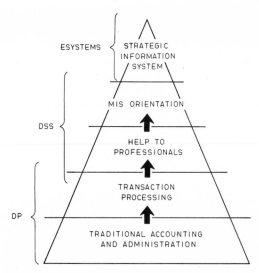

Figure 14.5 A new approach to information systems design: from classical data processing to strategic information systems.

Such developments are, of course, well beyond what decision support systems have ever offered, but neither should we forget the contributions they have made. DSSs have not only produced savings in time but, in this specific area of foreign exchange operations, induced the dealers to:

- Contribute to the building of Esystems
- Do their own fourth-generation-language programming to improve on the established DSS

Furthermore, while the dealer room professionals reap DSS benefits, they are asking for new products. Such new products center on full integration of man and machine intelligence.

Intelligent systems currently under development completely substitute for manual sheets and manual record keeping. In the application described above, foreign exchange trade is handled in a different, more sophisticated manner than with classical computer approaches. This new approach to information systems design is projected in Figure 14.5. The change in focus in computers and communications is most significant; it impacts all professionals in this field. Go ahead we must.

15

SOFTWARE PUBLISHING AND QUALITY ASSURANCE

Because of the evolution which has characterized both software and hardware technology since 1980, we have to change our images of both. We can no longer tolerate a situation in which most or all of the logical and physical components of an information system are provided by the same manufacturer. A unique source policy was followed during the first quarter century of computer implementation and is no longer valid. Not only the software but also the hardware is now being created and marketed through a layered approach. Three strata of hardware can be distinguished:

1. The microprocessor has become a commodity from, for example, Intel and Motorola.
2. The peripheral units, and even some central devices such as fixed hard disks integrated into the CPU, are OEM offerings.
3. The assembly of commercially available components into an aggregate to produce the end system is done by still other companies.

In large measure, this assembly is done by the classical computer manufacturing firms or by newcomers who have been integrated into the computer vendor lot. Even IBM has used, for its PC, products made in Taiwan or Japan or by other companies in the United States. In this sense, machine integration for product offerings has radically changed the way we looked at the manufacture of computers in the past. The impact of the new approach is even more pronounced in the software line, where what were formerly proprietary logical pieces have now become commodities. This is true of:

1. The operating system (Unix, MS-DOS, CP/M)
2. The DBMSs (Ingres, dBase II, and so on)
3. Compilers for programming languages
4. Fourth-generation language offerings
5. Horizontal software (spreadsheets, graphics systems, and so on)
6. Vertical software (applications packages)

Commodity software is brought to the market by software houses and, more recently, by software publishers. The latter are the important new entries in this field. They have developed their own procedures and policies, which we will examine in this chapter.

WHAT IS MEANT BY SOFTWARE PUBLISHING?

Although technology helps solve our problems, it also presents challenges—which means new problems. Looking at this fact from a philosophical viewpoint, we can say: "So much the better. Without problems we are decadent." But from a technical viewpoint we feel compelled to do something about this issue. "Do something" means studying the subject, developing alternatives, evaluating them, reaching for a conclusion, and implementing it.

That is essentially what the companies entering the new broad field of software publishing are trying to do. As Figure 15.1 shows, such companies appeal to four broad marketing strata ranging from commodity operating systems to applications packages. Though the terminology regarding the exact nature, structure, and service offerings of such firms is still unsettled, it will be proper to distinguish between two broad classes:

• Software developers
• Software distributors

The two classes were formerly part of the same software house, but that is not necessarily true now. Into the market has come an impressive range of companies including book publishers and service firms. These are typical examples of software publishers.

If we look very carefully at a list of companies in software publishing, we will see that it includes a broad range of firms coming into the market from diverse and often unrelated fields. This notion is fundamental

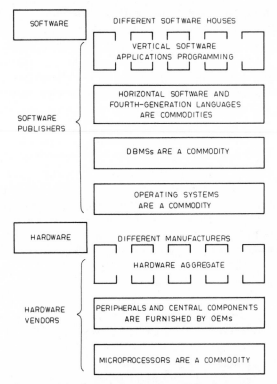

Figure 15.1 Strata of software and hardware that are of concern to software publishers.

because it redefines the issue of the logical products to be offered in the operating environment of computers and communications. There are several types of software publishers:

1. Independent software houses
2. Book publishers
3. Hardware vendors
4. Software distributors

All these firms engage in marketing to the end user. They sell disks through the mail or through retail outlets: computer stores, software-only shops, bookstores, and even mass merchandisers.

Another major way to sell software is by downloading. The particular significance of high-speed downloading underscores the potential of teledistributors. In teledistribution there are both advantages and market barriers.

As for contractual rights, the software developer grants a license to the software publisher—a transferable but not necessarily exclusive right—to distribute the licensed programs. In turn, upon payment of the appropriate fees, the software publisher grants the client a personal, nontransferable, and nonexclusive right to use the software.

A distributor who is also an authorized copier may make copies of customer software, select a name to identify it, sometimes provide modification, and generally furnish the programs to customers and other distributors. A software publisher becomes an authorized copier only if the written agreement with the software developer includes provisions authorizing that action. A software publisher may have his license revoked by the developer if he fails to fulfill his contractual obligations. Usually not less than a 2-months notice is given to this effect.

The client, the object of a distributor–end user accord, will employ the license for his own internal business purposes and/or for furnishing timesharing services to his own customers. This leads to the notion of the source CPU and the object CPU. Each CPU identified by a user licensing agreement becomes a *source CPU*. Licensees may at any time notify, in writing, the software publisher of the machine designation by location, type, and serial number of the primary object and any replacing source CPU, additional CPU that is to become object CPU, or object CPU that is to be changed to source CPU.

Typically, any such designation becomes effective on the software publisher's written accord, dependent on receipt of the appropriate fee. Agreements often involve a single backup CPU to be used as a substitute source or object CPU, without notice to the software publisher, at any time the original machine is malfunctioning, out of order, or undergoing repair.

At the user level, agreements include a termination clause activated if the licensee fails to fulfill one or more of his obligations toward the software publisher. The licensee then sees himself obliged to return to the software publisher all documentation, which renders unusable all licensed programs placed in any storage device.

A steady relation between the user and the software publisher—as well as between the latter and the software developer—is necessary because the products sold by these firms are dynamic and changing in nature. For instance, given the high quality of horizontal software, as well as the functionality of available fourth-generation languages, the problem of finding ready packages in the market becomes much less important than it used to be.

Very high level languages now make it wiser to code the application interactively on the computer rather than buy it in a packaged form. This defines the market drive and, through it, the types of products and services such companies will be selling during the next few years. Typical best-selling items in software publishing include:

- Spreadsheets
- Database management systems
- Financial software
- Word processing
- Communications software

In other words, if we look at the problem of making or buying software from a cost-effectiveness standpoint, the life cycle of a product offering is conditioned by professional practices and drives.

Since in what concerns systems analysis and programming the basic frame of reference has been changed by the wave of fourth-generation languages, both the prevailing considerations and the profit-and-loss aspect have been turned around. This impacts on the market, which takes a new orientation, and it alters the product offerings of the software firms.

Successful commodity software products have been created in three ways:

1. Commissioned by a computer manufacturer, as in the case of MS-DOS
2. On a venture capital basis, for instance, Lotus 1-2-3
3. As a "special" which has then been generalized, for example, Unix

In 1979, the commercial and industrial applications represented only 3 percent of the total usage of the Unix operating system. At that time, employment within the Bell system stood at 55 percent. Four years later, in 1983, the numbers were reversed. The commercial and industrial usage of Unix stood at an impressive 93 percent, while the percent employment in AT&T installations was reduced to 4 percent. As a successful product, Unix was cloned. Xenix and Venix are examples. A similar proliferation of spreadsheets occurred.

Successful software and hardware marketing are closely interrelated. The strength of the PC lies not only in its cost-effective hardware but also—if not primarily—in the many software products available for it. Many systems have been built by using a relational database, and, as stated, applications programs can be developed through a combination of:

- A database language
- A spreadsheet package
- Some code written, for instance, in C or Pascal

The latter should only be the exception; but by supplementing the very high language facilities, it provides a powerful mix.

This is the market to which software publishers address themselves. But a new product is not launched on a simple goodwill basis. It requires the proper infrastructure, as we will see in the following sections.

STANDARDS FOR SOFTWARE DEVELOPMENT

A distinction should be made at the outset between international standards for software and international standards needed to structure a methodology of software development. The former do not exist; the latter are a basic necessity. Since international software standards, if there were any, might have provided a good reference point for international standards in software publishing, we would be well advised to first take a look at what might be taking shape. There are two levels:

1. Recommended practices, which are advisedly followed
2. Standards per se, whose implementation should be policed

The first level amounts to something more than a methodology to be followed by all units engaged in the design and development of a given software product. An example is given in Figure 15.2. Recommended practices, together with a concrete methodology, represent an important step in the growth of software engineering as a profession. They help establish basic procedures to guide the profession in the years to come. They should specify the type of documentation and the minimum amount to be produced, as well as the kind and extent of design reviews that should be held during the development of software programs—by level or class of critical characteristics.

Technical characteristics are critical if, in case of failure, the system running on such software would endanger people or cause large financial losses. Along this line of reasoning, the four basic documents required by the IEEE developing standard are:

1. Software requirements specification (SRS)
2. Software design description (SDD)
3. Software verification plan (SVP)
4. Software verification report (SVR)

The IEEE recommended standard calls for seven reviews, four of which are addressed to the required documents: software requirements

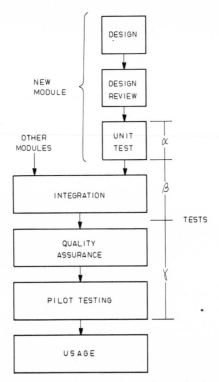

Figure 15.2 An example of software development including alpha, beta, and gamma tests.

review (SRR), preliminary design review (PDR), critical design review (CDR), and software verification review (SVR).

Although the quality assurance standard proposed by IEEE provides only the basic definitions for the subject documents and reviews, it does delineate a minimum set of tasks that should be performed during the development of critical software to provide reasonable assurance that the final product will operate as intended. At the same time, the practice followed by companies heavily involved in software development suggests three phases:

• Definition

• Design

• Manufacturing and testing

and also five types of tests, in a close approximation to hardware development practices:

- Test by emulation
- Alpha test
- Beta test
- Gamma test
- Production test

Let's recall that, for software, the first engineering model is system analysis and design. The basic idea provided the background for the effort which was to follow. In Figure 15.3:

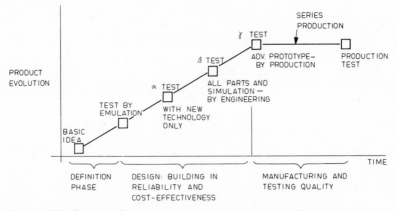

Figure 15.3 Software development sequence as a function of program progress (in time) and product evolution.

Alpha test checks if the coding follows design rules.

Beta test is the first real test of module and system.

Gamma test is the final acceptance test. It is often done at the customer site, even if it has been performed in-house with real applications.

The alpha test is a unit test; beta is an integration test. Together they define a range of activities which has a kernel and add-on features. The latter may vary from one project to another, but the kernel is fairly stable. It includes factual and documented tests related to the following issues:

1. Definition of nomenclature, with all global names
2. Establishment of the data structures

3. Functional description of all routines (processing, databasing, communications)

4. Linkage to the predominant basic software environment

Particular attention should be given to specific tasks to be executed and subtasking concepts. That is true also of:

- Task generators (like Fork in Unix)
- Basic I/O system
- Message traffic
- Message structure as compared to file structure
- File access and file management mechanism
- Performance characteristics and overhead

Open and close routines, kill commands, the use of pipes, and electronic mail to be supported among users—as well as linguistic primitives—have to be clearly defined from the original design phase. The parsing mechanism must be evaluated as to its support for the following facilities among others:

- Scanner
- Interpreter
- Error handler
- Code generator
- File identifier
- Formatter

Arrays, strings, and links must be featured; the syntax and semantics should be solid; and the necessary interpretive routines should be fully provided.

The beta test is a fairly complex engineering job involving the 10 different areas of interest identified in Figure 15.4. In turn, each of these areas is exploded into a number of issues.

The gamma test includes:

1. General functional testing, including software product capability

2. System stress testing with the aim of hitting limits and overlimits, for example, file undersize, file termination, and HW maximum-minimum configuration

3. Error simulation and recovery, including power drops, transients, processes, users, and their interaction.

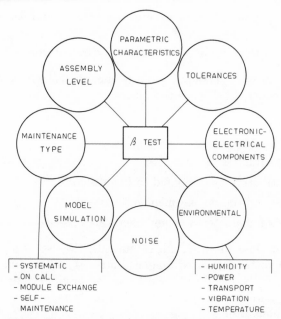

Figure 15.4 A constellation of key issues relative to the beta test.

The gamma test centers on production-related problems rather than design problems. Given the highly interrelated issues of hardware and software, model simulation should include hardware, firmware, and software aspects. This is made more necessary by the tendency to cast software routines in silicon. The first major candidate is operating systems: with Intel 8086, CP/M is in software; with 80186, CP/M will be in hardware; with 80286, MS-DOS may be in hardware. However, a more important reason for the integration of SW/HW design procedures and tests is user visibility.

Through a personal workstation supported by a PC, the user processes data, prepares information individually, controls deadlines, writes texts, draws diagrams, and communicates with DP systems. Whichever requests the user has on the personal computer, the software is at the heart of the problem. It therefore needs to be adequately designed and tested.

When the user is in charge of the application:

• The system and its accompanying procedures must be foolproof.

• All procedures and documentation must be clear and well written.

• The user must be trained on how to use the workstation, including software, hardware, communications protocols, and information elements.

The software designers must realize they are creating a product for any number of users unknown to them. If the procedures are poor or the documentation is unreadable, the system will fail and the hitherto unknown users will become known through their complaints. It is, therefore, a sound policy that everything be precisely defined and be as simple as possible. The end user is responsible for system input, interactive output, connections, backups, and processing.

The challenge is in designing a system that allows good-quality performance. This is more important than efficiency. The criterion is correct, uninterrupted handling of the projected procedures. This requirement imposes greater control and better planning. Good-quality performance calls for participation by all contributing components to assure the project is in an acceptable level of definition—prior to design. The specifications should define error management and the diagnostic system.

Software design goals, for example, no more than 1 error per 10,000 source lines, must be established. Similarly, at the earliest design level, test preparation and planning for quality-control purposes should be worked out. Compatibility testing must stress conformance with standards, languages, system family (upward and downward), competitive products, different hardware versions, and so on.

A good policy is to use structured walkthroughs on the code. Testing can be improved by placing counters, checking the branches in the software, and reading the counters to know if everything has been tested. Benchmarking and regression testing are also valuable strategies stressing:

- Access speed
- Compile time
- Throughput
- Certain critical execution times
- Access to disk (specifying unit number, sector, and so on)
- The interaction of OS routines with horizontal and vertical software

To make measurement meaningful, it is wise to keep testing small bytes at the execution level. User-oriented testing will also involve supporting the user's viewpoint in software implementation. In contrast, testing specifically done for the computer expert will search among other things for deficiencies associated with system calls.

The problem of establishing definitions for most of the software engineering terms in general use must be addressed for both populations. It is most important to establish a basic vocabulary of software engineering and thereby decrease confusion and facilitate precise communication.

QUALITY, RELIABILITY, AND TESTING PROCEDURES

As our dependence on software increased, reliability became a key feature. This responsibility must be assumed by professional software engineers who specify, design, test, implement, and deliver software-based services. Their attitude must reflect recommended standards of professional practices and norms of professionality.

The authority and responsibility of those in charge of the design, production, testing, and inspection of software should be clearly stated. The programs must facilitate determination of the effects of quality deficiencies and quality costs. Facilities and standards necessary for the creation of the required quality should be effectively managed. A valid program should include control procedures leading to the effective execution of responsibilities.

To those ends the IEEE Standard for Test Documentation defines the content and format of eight documents that cover the entire testing process from initial planning to final report: Test Plan, Test Design Specification, Test Procedure Specification, Test Item Transmittal Report, Test Log, Test Incident Report, and Test Summary Report. Their relations to each other and to overall testing procedures are fairly well established by the IEEE Standard 829-1983.

A sister document, the IEEE Standard for Software Configuration Management Plans (Standard 828-1983) provides requirements for configuration identification, control, status accounting, reporting, audits, and reviews. With this recommended standard as a basis, a company's software quality program should set forth requirements to be satisfied through precise statements of work.

The software developers should be responsible for compliance with all provisions of rules and bylaws and for furnishing specified SW services which meet all the quality requirements. If any inconsistency exists, corrective action should be provided. For that reason, the software quality program must be planned and used in a way that supports software reliability effectively. Personnel performing quality functions must have:

- Sufficient, well-defined responsibility
- Authority to take action
- Organizational freedom to identify and evaluate quality problems and initiate or provide solutions

Management must regularly review the status and adequacy of the software quality program and identify the collective requirements and specifications. It and its top experts must also provide guidance for implementing standards that have been completed, such as:

- Software configuration management
- Design documentation
- Software testing

It is to the advantage of the individual company if the internal software quality standards provide recommendations that reflect the current state of national and international recommendations for software design, even if it is known that they will continue to evolve. Both technical and financial considerations are behind this advice. Figure 15.5 contrasts reliability and maintenance costs for new and old software products. Though for a new product there is somewhat lower reliability at the beginning of its life, this rapidly changes as the product matures.

Baby failures, maturity, and wear-out failures are a process we know well from hardware experience. We should keep the experience well in mind, because it tends to repeat itself with the software. When we look

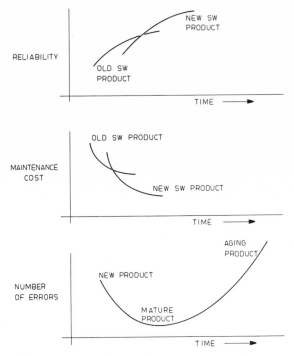

Figure 15.5 Reliability and maintenance costs for new and old software products.

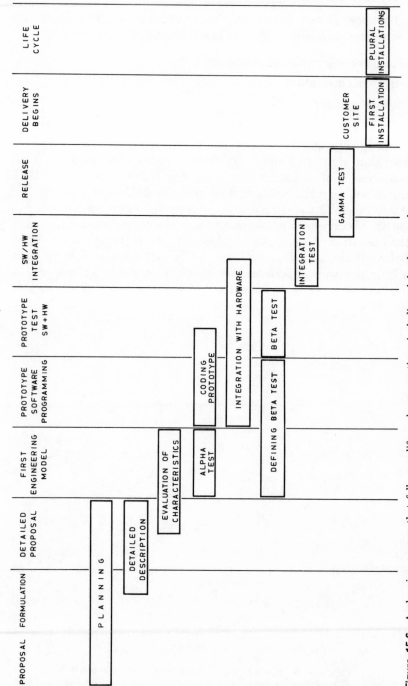

Figure 15.6 A planning process that follows a life cycle perspective—including alpha, beta, and gamma tests.

248

into the hardware aspects of a system, in-field product quality criteria include:

• Mean time between service calls (MTBSC)
• Mean time between failures (MTBF)
• Mean time to repair (MTTR)
• Cost of yearly maintenance
• Life cycle cost

MTBF is important for the vendor; MTBSC is the critical criterion for the user. Essentially, the latter unit of measurement is reflected in system performance. As far as MTBSC is concerned, a computer manufacturer found that the failure rate absorbed in the field is due to the following reasons on a percent basis:

• Design, 56 percent
• Production, 19 percent
• Field engineering, 15 percent
• End user, 10 percent

Since the emphasis on software reliability is relatively recent, there is less experience in collecting meaningful statistics. Therefore, the first step should be one of establishing the right methodology. Figure 15.6 suggests a planning process which includes the alpha, beta, and gamma tests we have outlined. Though the time scales in the figure are relative, it will be appreciated that it normally takes a long time to run the beta test. Therein lies the interest in acceleration through diagnostic and forecasting methods. This, too, is a matter of methodology.

The tests to which we refer are also meaningful in controlling the performance of the software development effort. For instance, the alpha factor helps set the quality of the design team. Among valid and documented procedural steps is one to require, from the earliest practical phase of software performance, that complete design reviews based on requirements be carried out to identify possible weaknesses. Design reviews should disclose soft spots and provide for subsequent inspection techniques.

Although these issues may sound more appropriate for software developers than for software publishers, in the distribution sense of the term, they are in reality highly relevant to three populations of people involved with software:

• Designers

- Distributors
- Users

All three have a vested interest in software quality, and they must protect it through the proper methodology and tools. Among the latter is online diagnostics, as we will see in the following section.

Software must be designed defensively. The designer must assume that the worst can and will happen:

- Invalid data will be presented to the system.
- Unforeseen usage will occur.
- Modifications will have to be made.

Programs must be designed and implemented in a modular fashion—modular by end use, as programs are viewed by users. When a failure occurs in software residing in the hardware, it must be possible to replace only the component that failed.

Commodity software must also be properly documented and be precise in terms of supported functionality. Frequently, users find that supplier-developed programs do not support the claims made for them and that they give meaningless error responses. The bugs have not been located and corrected soon enough to preclude wasting many precious hours trying to solve problems others have already solved.

These are matters of concern to the software publisher as they are to the clientele. As an increasingly important population of noncomputer professionals purchases and runs its own hardware, quality and reliability will become key issues in being and keeping competitive.

Although built-in user-friendly features are increasingly in demand, testing procedures for software, to assure the quality of the end product, have not yet attracted the attention they deserve. This issue is destined to become highly important and capable of deciding the success or failure of a software product.

DIAGNOSTICS AND MAINTENANCE POLICY

Contrary to logic and good practice, software is rarely designed for convenient repair. Worst of all is documentation. Without adequate documentation, the user can hardly understand how the facility works. Because documentation is not an independent end item, but must at all times reflect an exact correspondence with or representation of a software product, it must be changed whenever the corresponding facility is changed.

In the preceding section we saw the great importance of documentation. Ideally, it should be computer-based and communicated memory-to-memory for visual presentation or hardcopy, as the prevailing requirements indicate. Good documentation can be of great help in software diagnostics.

Also emphasized has been the wisdom of building software reliability from the drafting board. The objective must be to make software at least as reliable as hardware and place much emphasis on designing for prevention of failure rather than for repair.

- Software is always subject to long repair time, which has a severe impact on a user's operation.
- But since software does not deteriorate in use as hardware does, there should be no need for preventive maintenance if it is delivered in reliable working condition.

That is why it has so often been said that good initial system design, implementation, and testing are of paramount importance.

Tests and diagnostics, however, are more valuable when they match the manufacturer's policy. That is true of telediagnostics also. With the exception of computer manufacturers, few software publishers currently provide such service. Yet, it will be a critical issue in the years to come as installations multiply and some software products are distributed in hundreds of thousands of copies (MS-DOS, VisiCalc, and so on).

Like any other service, diagnostics requires the proper infrastructure. Telediagnostics is the nearest thing to a self-service approach which can be implemented through software design oriented to its usage and better diagnostic tools. A diagnostic plan is important. Statistics and error messages are meaningful if they are used in the right manner. To discover a problem, there should be a rational way to synthesize symptoms and employ sound techniques.

Most personal computer users have neither the time nor the experience to do diagnostics themselves, so they should ask the help of a diagnostic center. This may be provided by the user company, an independent service, or the software publisher. Like hardware maintenance, which has gone through successive evolutionary stages, software maintenance changes over time. At present, however, there is no better example for a new maintenance policy than the level which we have reached with hardware, the maintenance of which is more mature.

Most vendors are now establishing a maintenance policy which includes six key approaches.

1. *A remote diagnostics* capability provided as an online service. The quality database thereby created helps in items 2, 3, and 4.

2. *Onsite maintenance* by the manufacturer's own personnel, to be done only when absolutely necessary.

3. *Self-diagnostics*, which enable the user to test the machine components at the WS, components with built-in diagnostics that can recognize they have failed and notify the user.

4. *Self-maintenance*, the customer is trained to do his own maintenance program. A spares inventory is at the site, with customer replaceable units dispatched from one of the field logistics locations of the vendor as needed.

5. *Fixed time/usage replacement.* The component self-destructs at a known point, or in any case is replaced. The use of discardable, customer-replaceable components also calls for more simplified and modular construction.

6. If the replaced unit can be repaired, the customer-assisted maintenance program provides for *mail-in*. The defective unit is mailed back to the vendor and a new unit is returned to the customer.

In the general case, the customer has the option of purchasing spare units with which malfunctioning units can be replaced at the cost of only a few minutes of system interruption. A major midwestern American bank which used this approach for its large park of PCs estimates that it will eventually save an impressive $1 million per year in maintenance fees.

In other words, with improved and simplified diagnostic facilities, plus some training in the use of tools, the user should be able to determine whether a malfunction can be repaired without resorting to supplier help. This is not yet a widening practice with software, but it can be nicely implemented with very high level languages such as spreadsheets and database programming systems.

As an example of hardware policies which may soon find their way into software, the vendor of two recently announced systems—a super-micro (Tower) and a family of PCs (Decision Mate V)—has established a coherent maintenance policy and diagnostics with the objective of greater reliability and serviceability. With Tower, this is based on the following levels of diagnostics:

1. Level 0 aims to determine the basic integrity of a part.

This is implemented in ROM code. The processor-memory-control (PMC) monitor diagnoses memory, disk control, tape control, serial I/O, and so on.

2. Level 1 consists of out-of-service, free-standing tests.

The tests don't run concurrently with Unix (the operating system of this computer), since they are last-resort diagnostics. They are menu-driven like level 2 (as explained below), but they do destructive tests in terms of stored data. The objective is to:

- Get out of SW/HW errors Unix might support
- Investigate periodic errors
- Run nonforgiving types of testing (without trying to recover)
- Run night-long tough tests on the HW system only

Even the I/O card has a level 1 test procedure.

3. Level 2 runs concurrently with Unix.

This is a powerful test feature. All I/O drivers include a concurrent, software-implemented diagnostics capability. This is the in-service type. In-service maintenance and diagnostics include:

- Communications maintenance
- File system maintenance
- System error log
- Display system release
- Help

The system provides for:

- Starting a diagnostic session
- Generating a system device test
- Flashing results to user
- Canceling displayed results
- Canceling commands given for diagnostics
- Returning to menu

There are option screens for the end user, and they are all of the yes/no decision type. What's more, the user can self-maintain the system, provided he or she takes the vendor's maintenance course.

4. Level 3 maintains statistical tallies and handles communications level diagnostics. These, like level 2, run concurrently with Unix.

For disk reformatting and recovery, there is a maintenance system, a version of Unix, running from floppy. It is very useful if the system will not boot. This maintenance solution runs on two diskettes: one contains Unix; the other contains the file system. The latter features a disk file check to be exercised on the hard disk, and it also supports interactive recovery. In fact, it is advisable never to reformat the disk without the maintenance system. The same software permits the user to check floppies for error. It can run on levels 0 to 3 and operates from DM V when signing from DM V into the Tower.

For DM V, the diagnostics work on three steps, of which steps 2 and 3 are for maintenance technicians and step 1 is for the end user.

1. On power-on, it tests the microprocessor(s), graphics processor, all memory modules (64-Kbyte and additional memory), printer, and disk drive interface (but not the hard disk).

2. Using the special maintenance cartridge, it implements more exhaustive diagnostics.

Test 1 makes sure that each memory location is accessible. The cartridge (which occupies one of the slots) assures the content and also checks the disk drive; it then displays specific control characters. Finally:

3. A specific Winchester-type test controls the hard disk, which is an optional attachment to the machine.

The direction in which the vendor works for future releases should be to assure that the unit will become easier to diagnose and repair. To achieve that, however, the vendor will need to spend a lot of time and money on R&D. There is, of course a trade-off with hardware. As the PC becomes less costly, smaller, and lighter, it becomes easier to take the PC back to the vendor and get another machine than to repair it. A similar statement can be made of software maintenance if we employ the facilities offered by fourth-generation languages.

Now let's integrate what has been written into a coherent service strategy. It is to the advantage of both vendors and users to:

1. Diagnose the fault remotely

2. Provide for a service specialist for corrective action

This is just as valid for software as for hardware. The corrective action can be on a self-service basis, but user training is required to achieve this end.

Fundamental to a sound and effective SW/HW maintenance policy is the ability to keep a maintenance database. Unix can do that; it periodically unloads its contents onto a database backup, either on tape or on floppy. This is one of the important activities to integrate into the

OS functionality: supporting queries capability and providing statistics on information retained in the maintenance database.

System maintenance for HW and SW should also integrate a variety of logs: signing in, changing dates, running tests, and so on. The more sophisticated the applications we put on the system, the greater should be our concern about maintenance. That is true at all levels of implementation. We have to think in terms of *systems integration*. One of the major uses of personal computers will be to retrieve and download data from corporate mainframes for analysis and interactive presentation. Both end-user-oriented reporting functions and quality assurance hould be served through this facility.

16

CASE STUDIES ON BUILDING UP NEW IMAGES

Virtually all computers have a memory, CPU, input/output devices, a programming language, and applications software. Whether the available facilities are used well or badly depends on the people who make them work. Automation or no automation, the human resources are always the most important.

Fourth-generation languages (4GLs) are powerful programming systems. The people who use them will decide whether they are employed in an excellent manner, just well, or poorly or even give disastrous results. Whatever their names or levels of sophistication may be, 4GLs are designed to enable users of all backgrounds to perform a wide range of information management tasks with computers. They can get to work without having to learn details that computer specialists have kept close to their chests for three decades.

The user of a 4GL can range from a seasoned system analyst to the company's president who never took a computer course other than two or three direct hands-on experiences with the PC and a fourth-generation language. But whether a novice or a mature computer person, the user who approaches a job with new concepts and new images will be far better off than one who does not.

In short, what do we wish to get out of the information system? We wish to get the most for the job we have in hand—and for the job we expect tomorrow. Eating (even information) whets the appetite. As

Figure 16.1 suggests, technology can help both in producing a service and in delivering it. That's the role of the information system. But are we ready to exploit it as we should?

Data is ready when we are. To help gauge how ready the user is—and also to offer some guidance—I have written the following four case studies. Let me add some advice: Read them when relaxed. There is no criticism between the lines, unless one mirrors oneself in them.

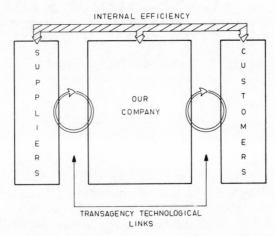

Figure 16.1 Technology can help both in producing a service and in delivering it.

First Case Study: Questions on Distributed Systems

The 10 rules for information systems planning outlined in Table 16.1 come from experience. This experience, however, may be different from yours. For each rule, comment on:

1. How it fits your personal experience.

2. How you react to it in terms of guidelines for

   • *Personal computing*

   • *Distributed databases*

   • *A communications-intensive environment*

Document your answers.

Table 16.1 Distributed Information Systems Planning

Rule 1: We deal not with one network, but with four networks
- DB
- DC
- DP
- EUF

Rule 2: Two frames of reference must be observed in each computer and/or network:
- Logical
- Physical

Examples from video presentation are the pel and pixel. Network examples are the physical structures and their layered logical organization.

Rule 3: A message is a file in the database (pipe), and every file must be designed as a message.
New languages incorporate pipe management commands and mailboxes.

Rule 4: Use local storage for local operations. The traffic in the network should be kept at the necessary minimum.

Rule 5: Programs should by preference be stored at the microfile of the WS. Programs are more local than data. Programs and data should be treated as corporate resources.

Rule 6: Microfiles and local databases should be updated in realtime. Consistency with central databases should be assured in 24-hour intervals.

Rule 7: Data entry should be done *only once*, and the data should be used many times.

Rule 8: Computers should *not* be programmed. First get the software, then the hardware.

Rule 9: Systems planning should stress:
- Portability (machine independence)
- Restart/recovery (and journaling)
- High availability
- Online auditing
- Security/protection

Rule 10: Keep the computers and communications systems simple, small, and for a "stupid" user. The better is the enemy of the good.

SECOND CASE STUDY: SOLUTIONS IN HW, SW, AND SYSTEM FUNCTIONALITY

Figure 16.2 presents four possibilities regarding hardware connections and software-supported functionality. Identify:

1. The quarter-space that is more representative of your operations

2. The OS and DBMS under which your DP/DB/DC operations run (one or more)

3. How you propose to streamline your system

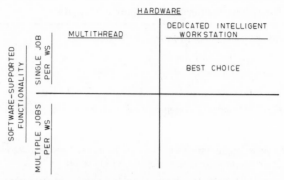

Figure 16.2 Quarter spaces identified by hardware connectivity and software-supported functionality.

4. Which of the four solutions you consider best for
   • Streamlining your operations
   • Projecting into the future

THIRD CASE STUDY: GALASSISMS

The manager of a data processing operation (physically young but logically aged) reacted negatively to introducing personal computers to his operations.

• Read the text carefully.
• Evaluate his reactions.
• Reflect on how his reactions apply to your case.
• Comment on them.

Brief Introduction

While no system is foolproof, fools would try anything to delay or even destroy the beneficial impact of change. Misunderstanding of one's professional and personal interests plays a great role in this regrettable policy. As Dolos gave his name to acts of treason, Ephialtes to nightmares, Lenin to the institutionalized state supermarket, and Stalin to the ossified bureaucracy, so a data processing manager became famous for his *galassisms*. They consist of ill-conceived excuses to avoid effort, delay, and change and trick management into a self-destructive obsolescence.

Just because they are ill-conceived, they render a great disservice to their creator and to all those who make trivialities their standbearer. But they also offer a good service to those who read them, understand them, and avoid them. It would have been a poor choice to spend precious time on galassisms if it weren't for the fact that they are often-heard excuses. By remaining unanswered, they risk taking on a false weight. The best way to face excuses and obstructionism is to deflate them: Ridicule has always been a great weapon.

Case Study

Let's start with the facts. The now infamous "technical arguments" which we will cover were developed in a conference which took place with top management. They contrasted the "advantages" of a mini-computer solution to the "disadvantages" of personal computers. Their author presented six reasons why, in his judgment, the minicomputer "is superior to the micro." All this took place in late 1982, a dozen years after the mini had been accepted in the business environment and a few years after it had passed its peak.

Carefully examined, the "reasons" we will be considering tell a completely different story, and they turn out to be crushingly negative to the minicomputer and highly favorable to the micro. But let's look at them one by one:

1. *Languages:* The minis—this argument goes—support COBOL. The micros don't; they work with Basic and Pascal.

2. *File Management:* The minis have DBMS. The micros are at the file management level.

3. *Connection to Host:* The mini-to-mainframe (this argument goes) can run at high speed, say, 9.6 kBPS. PC-to-host usually works at a lower capacity, for instance, 300 baud.

4. *Workstations:* With the minicomputers, the argument says, the currently available terminals can be retained. With PCs and local area networks (LANs), all the WSs must be new.

5. *Vendors:* Whether we talk of LANs or PCs, the suppliers are new companies. This brings the installed base away from the now "classical" sources of hardware and software.

6. *Technical Maintenance:* The best *technical maintenance* is in the hands of the mainframers and the terminal manufacturers.

Need for Response

These arguments run, of course, much deeper than may be apparent at first sight:

- Either we develop, test, and implement new and better approaches for doing business or we will be condemned to live in the past.
- Either we move ahead with the new technologies or we stay put till we lose both our market position and our professionality.

Grave mistakes have always severe consequences: Are we going to stay on the wrong road until we are extinct?

What's *your* reaction? State your opinion quite clearly.

FOURTH CASE STUDY: TIMETABLES FOR IMPLEMENTING PCS AND LANS

Introduction

A leading bank which implemented intelligent workstations (WSs)—based on personal computers (PCs) and interconnected through local area networks (LANs)—presents an excellent case study on how timetables can be accelerated with the new technologies.

The implementation, to which reference is made in the first case study, took place in 1980–1981. The second case study centers on 1984. The four years difference is visible in terms of tools and approaches.

You are asked to:

- Select a typical application in your environment which reflects characteristics of this case study.
- Think about PC/LAN and fourth-generation language implementation.
- Project an implementation timetable and document your projection.

Your proposal should be made in writing.

From Stand-Alone PC to Local Networks

Sorting out the principles to apply with the new solution to information processing, management made a major decision about PCs. It went like this: "Don't look to personal computers and local area networks to save money, but to obtain a better service. In the end, though, you will also save money." Accordingly, the system design was oriented to give the managers and professionals something new: A better, more efficient Forex operation, not a number-cruncher intended to "reduce" personnel.

To help implement this idea, management first thought of nonintelligent terminals at the workstation hooked to a PDP-11. This machine was to front-end another PDP-11 that for years had done Forex accounting, and the solution had gone as far as ordering the mini. Then the personal computer approach, together with local area networking, came under study. As a result, the design was radically changed.

The impact of the change was significant. Rather than run after the computer people to do a faster and more polished job, users and management sought ways to improve the departmental functions at the level at which the transactions are done. At the same time, the small group of systems experts who worked together with the end users earned the users' respect by the results which had been achieved. Results are the best credentials. Said one specialist:

> When end users see the systems analysts doing a solid job, they come around. Professionals appreciate professionalism. If an analyst's credentials are established, the outcome is frank and candid conversations which lead to valid solutions.

Indeed, the timetable has been fast and effective, as successive versions have been released:

- Version 0 was available in June 1980 on an Apple II computer, and it was self-made.

The programs were written by one of the Forex operators and adopted by another, but the application did not spread throughout the organization. The professionals were not yet accustomed to the PC. The object of these PC-based programs was to automate the work classically done by the foreign exchange operator on paper. This included both record keeping and calculating.

The limitation of the stand-alone solution became apparent with practice. As experience accumulated, the wisdom of interrogating the correspondent online, looking up margins by currency, and updating the database in realtime was evident.

- Version 1 became available in March and April 1981.

This is essentially a version 0, plus, since it consisted of the same programs polished up by an information scientist working alone for less than 2 months. Version 1 was an interactive solution but without networking capabilities. The personal computers worked stand-alone until September 1980.

By September 1980, a small group of information scientists was instituted: one chief and three programmer-analysts. It is precisely this group which, in order to increase the available computer power, thought of implementing an online star-type solution with a PDP-11, and the bank went so far as to order the machine. But a more careful look at user needs altered the perspective. The *real* problem was not computer power, but a user-friendly solution through intelligent, communicating workstations.

Project management became aware of the LAN capabilities, and for the next 2 months the specialists worked on the possibility of implementing a LAN with Apple computers. The Nestar/Zynar Cluster/One network was selected.

- Version 2 involved the migration from stand-alone personal computers to networking.

The proper benchmarks were established. The feasibility of the online application was demonstrated during December 1980, and the first LAN installation was made. This first try involved 25 Apple II computers. The problem became one of dimensioning the application within the intense operating environment of a Forex activity.

Putting a microcomputer on every desk, in every facet of the work, would have required 86 PCs. Having established precise goals and a budget, the project team started working on financial approval for the other 61 personal computers which were needed.

Implementation Following Management Approval

In April 1981, management approval was given. The implementation which followed this approval brought the available power to 1.3 microcomputers per dealer. Including a graphics tablet and a printed circuit board (PCB) interface, it meant nearly five microprocessors for each workstation.

By August 1981, the results obtained from the first PC and local area network were such as to suggest the establishment of four interconnected LANs. As a cognizant executive remarked, "We first saw whether the system would work and only then decided to buy it."

Equipment was ordered, and it was timed to arrive in three lots so that the machines in each lot would be installed and operating before the next lot was received. The last lot reached the bank in December 1981.

As the equipment was phased in, the treasury department, of which Forex is a part, added more dealers online on the local area network and introduced lots of changes. Each version capitalized on the preceding one. Since Apple computers on Cluster/One can work with different OS releases and different programming languages (Basic, Pascal), no applications software was thrown away as usually happens with the mainframe and the mini. Instead, each successive version built on the preceding one.

This had an evident effect on costs and productivity. The basic applications software required only 6 worker-months of effort. The rest of the work has been fine tuning as the dealers' ideas have developed, experience has accumulated, and the operation has improved.

To appreciate the impact of this operation, let's look back for a moment to the beginning of the pilot LAN operation. After a week of management and clerical training the implementation took place in mid-September, with six workstations being installed at the desk level. The PC was mounted under the desk. The numeric keypad, video, and printer were installed at desktop. Space was at a premium. With version 2, the data being collected was coded so the full Apple keyboard was not needed. All the data was entered through the keypad.

Statistics were carefully kept on failures and their background reasons—power line surges, mechanical shock, or static electricity. The power line surges were tracked down to the electric staplers used at many of the desks. Line isolators between the floor outlet and the computer were replaced to eliminate the surge problem. Static electricity has been more difficult to eliminate. The static buildup occurred because of the wall-to-wall carpeting in the office. It was first decided to regularly coat the work area with a spray that cuts down on static electricity (which builds up as people move around). A more lasting solution was to install antistatic mats in the work area to eliminate static buildup.

System-wise, to minimize the impact of these failures, the data collected at the workstations is written out to the file server of the LAN every 10 to 15 min. The original plan called for doing so at 2-hour intervals. To handle the increased disk activity without degrading system performance, a 16.5-Mbyte hard disk was installed to replace the floppy disk system. A couple of years later the file server was again updated.

Network communications run at 240 kBPS (kilobits per second). Experience has shown that this speed is more than adequate to serve the supported stations with their applications software.

The determining factor in system throughput has been the speed of the disk system and the processor attending it. Workstation response time is determined by the speed of the applications program it is running and by the amount of I/O to do. With version 2, the maximum time for consistent image after a transaction is well under 30 sec. The average response time is approximately 3 sec.

Management identified the following advantages in this implementation:

1. The information has been developed together with the dealers as ideas and wishes clarified.

2. The bank has been committed to capital investments only after the demonstration of successful results, not before.

In contrast, major financial commitments prior to having a clear picture are commonplace with mainframes and often occur with minicomputers.

3. With accumulated experience and system fine tuning, newer versions were instituted.

Version 3 supported graphics tablets and two videos per workstation.

4. In no case was there a need to spend time finding excuses "after the fact"—or concocting the most unthinkable reasons for failures.

By being projected from the dealers, the system worked well from the beginning. Rather than spend time on frictions and failures, the analysts' knowhow was invested in advancing the application to the benefit of everyone concerned with the project.

Advantages as Seen by Management

Here is how a senior bank executive responded to the design and implementation of this PC and LAN solution:

1. Cobol is not supported—and that's why personal computers are so interesting.

People trained on Cobol don't make good microdesigners and microusers—nor are they fit to handle the resources current technology makes available.

2. No DBMS? Well that's an advantage. The closer we are to the information the better.

Security should be handled at the applications level. This will also improve efficiency: 60 to 70 percent of a mainframe's power is typically used moving data around the different supports.

3. The cost is just right. It would have been justified through quality improvements even if there were no productivity results.

A PC costs less than a nonintelligent terminal. If, for instance, a 4341 small mainframe is chosen, then to the cost of the terminals should be added the share of the SW/HW cost of the resource. Considering the LAN and its servers—and distributing the cost among its components—the bank established the price of the end user WS at about $5000. This includes interfaces, backups, and shared resources. The cost would have been double or more to do the same job with a mini, and the communicating intelligent WS is more flexible and more reliable.

4. Lower initial costs make faster write-off and renovation feasible.

Cost-effectiveness has still another aspect. If the investment is low—as this case study proves—we can afford to write it off faster. This, too, has a price: It is an advantage which we should enter in our table of "for" and "against" a particular solution.

5. With intelligent WSs, the people developing the application get a much better understanding of *what* is being done and are quicker to see *how* to do it.

The contained size of the equipment permits the development of a better understanding of user needs, applications perspective, software, hardware, and the system aggregate as a whole.

But to gain benefits, our whole way of thinking must radically change to embrace the new realities. The mainframe syndrome strangles its supporters. Efficiency no longer depends on deriving the last bits of processing power from big mainframes.

In the 1950s, 1960s, and even much of the 1970s, people gathered in computer centers—hospital-like environments with air conditioning and observation galleries—to discuss the sex of angels. Learned papers on how to salvage another 2 percent of processing power dominated computer conferences for 20 years.

Now such concepts are irrelevant. In the 1980s, the cost of the CPU is no longer the dominant concern. Instead, disks, printers, and terminals generally cost more than the entire central processor.

6. Intelligent WSs are giving cost-effectiveness a new direction.

As the prices of the components drop, *the time that users spend on the systems becomes more important.* We need rapid access to information, the possibility of reviewing alternatives online, and the ability to make decisions quickly. Personal computers are dedicated to providing this environment. They are ready for work when we want to use them.

Our computer and communications networks must respond to our needs and schedules and do so in a timely and accurate manner. A workstation is typically dedicated to one person or task. Only the common database and transport facility are shared with other people.

Programmer Productivity with a Fourth-Generation Language Application

A credit insurance application in a banking environment was first programmed for DP. For many years, it had been handled manually, and more recently with word processing support. The most important data processing aspects involved 15 functions. These have been programmed as follows:

- Six through standard Ingres statements
- Three in Equel (30 percent Ingres, 70 percent C)
- Four in report by form language (RBF) with one file in the relational database
- Two in RBF (involving more than one file)

This application manages eight principal files, eight different videoforms, and six hardcopy outputs.

The total effort in fourth-generation language involved 18 worker-days (80 percent of a worker-month) by a former machine operator with no programming experience. The total programming work was done with 90 Ingres statements and a limited number of C language instructions. Had this work been done in Cobol, it would have taken:

1. 14,000 statements for outputs only (14 types, at about 1000 statements per output). This corresponds to 14 worker-months.

2. Another (estimated) 7000 statements for table and file management. This represents further 7 worker-months. Mature programmers produce on the average 1000 to 1200 fully documented and tested Cobol statements per worker-month. Usually 1 month of system analysis gives 2 to 2.2 months of code. Hence, a corresponding effort must be added for SA at the level of:

3. 10 more worker-months of system analysis.

Comparing the three measures in terms of labor employed, the productivity ratio in favor of fourth-generation programming stands at:

1. 17.5 : 1
2. 26.2 : 1
3. 38.7 : 1

These ratios will be higher if we account for the fact that in the 18 days the programmer gained his first experience. The ratios would also significantly increase if costs were taken into account: Mature programmers cost much more than novices; systems analysts are paid a multiple of what programmers get.

System Analysis Capabilities with a
Fourth-Generation Language

Banks which have programmed the automatic routing of commercial and financial paper with Cobol or PL/1 typically require 2 years of work by a group of three or four persons. With part-time assistants, this investment exceeds 8 worker-years of computer professionals' time. Four main subsystems are involved in this application:

1. The buildup of the automatic-routing database (The collection of the information elements is not included in the above estimate.) The database itself includes four sections: locality (province and postal area code), corresponding bank, branch office, and limited topology (street address) around the branch office.
2. Programs for the steady updating of the database
3. The automatic-routing subsystem (basically, batch-oriented)
4. Interactive programs for the handling of exceptions and rejects

The writing of programs able to handle the routing correspondence related to regions, banks, and branch offices amounts to roughly 80 percent of the work. Topology matches make up the other 20 percent.

In the majority of cases the client specifies bank and branch office. Therefore, the match must be precise. This accounts for the relative weights in terms of effort. Programs available for the automatic routing of commercial and financial paper average 40,000 to 50,000 Cobol statements—without accounting for file management routines and other utilities. Evidently, system analysis time is added to the time required for the lines of code.

Ingres has been used as a fourth-generation language to do this work starting from scratch. The prototype relative to 80 percent of the required work (as explained) was accomplished by an experienced programmer-analyst in 4 hours, working interactively with the machine.

Using the facilities included in Ingres and its query subsets, the programmer/analyst only needed to do:

- Two read routines
- One infopage format
- A couple of calculation routines
- Calls to the databasing macros

An estimated 90 percent of the work was done in Equel and 10 percent in C.

Use of the fourth-generation language gained not only faster development but also full freedom from the rigidity of classical approaches. Prototyping did away with the writing of huge specifications, helped improve product quality, and for the first time in this environment gave real-life feedback on the results obtained.

CONCLUSION

Neanderthals were not idiots. Their brains were as large as, if not larger than, those of today's people. They buried their dead and for about 80,000 years thrived in Europe and Asia. Neanderthals differed from their successors in two known respects: *body shape and tools*:

- They were stockier and stronger, though upright and dexterous.
- They used simple, all-purpose stone tools.

Those who came after them used ever more sophisticated and specialized implements of bone and stone, then of copper, iron, and plastics—and eventually computers.

As people learned to work with their tools, the finished products bore little resemblance to the raw material. Design replaced adaptation. This brought undoubted advantages. Replacing the stabbing spear with the throwing spear increased the range at which animals could be killed, reduced the risk of injury, and eliminated the need for large numbers of cooperating hunters. These advantages freed more hands for added-value jobs: art, building, writing.

It has been suggested that climate, particularly the worsening weather, accentuated these changes. In warmer climates, people use general-purpose tools; each Eskimo tool, by contrast, is very carefully designed for one or two jobs. The Eskimo must use his long winter evenings to make implements that can be very efficient when summer comes. But why did the Neanderthals not innovate? A leading hypothesis is that the single most important obstacle was intellectual. To make specialized tools in the winter for use next summer requires forward planning. It also calls for abstract thought.

The nature of added value changes with ages, but there is always an added value to the processes which have become widespread and, therefore, commonplace. Is our world able to exploit this concept, use forward planning, apply abstract thought and imagination—or is it destined to fade like the Neanderthals?

ACRONYMS AND ABBREVIATIONS

ADF	Advanced Development Facility
AI	artificial intelligence
AP	application program
AS	application system
BDOS	basic disk operating system
BIOS	basic input/output system
BPW	bits per word
CAD	computer-aided design
CAM	computer-aided manufacturing
CCP	console command power
CCITT	International Telegraph and Telephone Consultative Committee
CEPT	Committee of European Post and Telecommunication (after which the 1983 Videotex standard was named)
CPU	central processing unit
DB/DC	database and data communications
DBMS	database management system
DEC	Digital Equipment Corporation
DIA/DCA	document interchange architecture and document content architecture
DP	data processing
DP/MIS	data processing and management information system
DRCS	dynamically redefinable character set

DSS	decision support system
EDP	electronic data processing
Email	electronic mail
ESS	expert support system
Esystem	expert system
4GL	fourth-generation language
5GL	fifth-generation language
Gbyte	gigabyte (1 billion bytes)
HLL	high-level language
HW	hardware
IE	information element
IOCS	input/output control system
IS	information system
Isoft	integrated software
ISO/OSI	International Standard Organization/Open System Interconnection
KB	knowledgebank
kBPS	kilo bits per second
Kbyte	1024 bytes
KIP	knowledge information processing
kIPS	kilo instructions per second
LAN	local area network
Mbyte	megabyte (1 million bytes)
MIPS	million instructions per second
MIS	management information system
ML	machine language
MTBF	mean time between failures
MTTR	mean time to repair
NA PLPS	North American Presentation Level Protocol Syntax
NL	natural language
OA	office automation
OR	operations research
OS	operating system
PBX	private branch exchange
PC	personal computer
PCB	printed-circuit board
PDI	picture description instruction
pel	logical picture element
pixel	physical picture element
QMF	query management function

SA + P	system analysis and programming
SBS	small-business system
SNA	system network architecture
SQL	structured query language
SSS	solid-state software
SUT	software usability test
SW	software
TPA	transient program area
UDI	Universal Development Interface
VDI	Virtual Description Level Interface
VHLL	very high level language
VLSI	very large scale integration
WP	word processing
WS	workstation

INDEX

About the Author

Dr. Dimitris Chorafas has been involved in the computer field since 1953 in various capacities, including programmer, analyst, designer, project manager—and for the last 25 years consultant to the presidents of major corporations. His projects have ranged from top-level company reorganization to information systems architecture, computer design, and strategic software aspects. Since 1961 he has been an international corporate consultant. That status, combined with his being a university professor, has taken him to 60 different countries. Over the last decade, he has specialized in real time operations, mini- and microcomputers, the reduction of overall expenditures, electronic banking, office automation, management productivity, and the optimization of DP usage, both equipment and personnel. Dr. Chorafas has written numerous technical articles, is the author of fifty-three books, and has been published in 16 countries.